The Political Heart of Criminal Procedure

ESSAYS ON THEMES OF WILLIAM J. STUNTZ

Edited by

Michael Klarman
Harvard Law School

David Skeel
University of Pennsylvania Law School

Carol Steiker
Harvard Law School

CAMBRIDGE
UNIVERSITY PRESS

CAMBRIDGE UNIVERSITY PRESS
Cambridge, New York, Melbourne, Madrid, Cape Town,
Singapore, São Paulo, Delhi, Tokyo, Mexico City

Cambridge University Press
32 Avenue of the Americas, New York, NY 10013-2473, USA

www.cambridge.org
Information on this title: www.cambridge.org/9781107019416

We are grateful to Lauren Chitwood Schauf for her help and insight at every stage of this project, and to Anna Crowe and Juhyun Park for carefully reviewing the manuscript.

First published 2012

Printed in the United States of America

A catalog record for this publication is available from the British Library.

Library of Congress Cataloging in Publication data

The political heart of criminal procedure : essays on themes of William J. Stuntz /
[edited by] Michael Klarman, David Skeel, Carol Steiker.
p. cm.
Includes bibliographical references and index.
ISBN 978-1-107-01941-6 (hardback)
1. Stuntz, William J. 2. Criminal procedure – United States. 3. Criminal justice, Administration of – United States. 4. Criminal law – United States. I. Klarman, Michael J. II. Skeel, David A., 1961– III. Steiker, Carol S. (Carol Susan)
KF9619.A2P68 2012
345.73′05–dc23 2011038540

ISBN 978-1-107-01941-6 Hardback

Contents

Contributor List

Anne M. Coughlin Lewis F. Powell, Jr., Professor of Law and Joel B. Piassick Research Professor, University of Virginia School of Law.

Joseph L. Hoffmann Harry Pratter Professor, Indiana University Maurer School of Law.

Dan M. Kahan Elizabeth K. Dollard Professor, Yale Law School.

Orin Kerr Professor, George Washington University Law School.

Michael Klarman Kirkland & Ellis Professor of Law, Harvard Law School.

Andrew D. Leipold Edwin M. Adams Professor, University of Illinois College of Law.

Richard H. McAdams Bernard D. Meltzer Professor, University of Chicago Law School.

Tracey L. Meares Deputy Dean and Walton Hale Hamilton Professor of Law, Yale Law School.

Erin Murphy Professor of Law, New York University School of Law.

Daniel Richman Paul J. Kellner Professor of Law, Columbia Law School.

Louis Michael Seidman Carmack Waterhouse Professor of Constitutional Law, Georgetown University Law Center.

David Skeel S. Samuel Arsht Professor of Corporate Law, University of Pennsylvania Law School.

David Alan Sklansky Yosef Osheawich Professor of Law, University of California, Berkeley.

Carol Steiker Henry J. Friendly Professor of Law, Harvard Law School.

Bill Stuntz Former Henry J. Friendly Professor of Law, Harvard Law School.

Introduction: Appreciating Bill Stuntz

Michael Klarman, David Skeel, and Carol Steiker

In the fall of 2009, we started planning a conference at Harvard Law School to celebrate the life and scholarly achievements of Bill Stuntz. Had it been up to Bill, this celebration never would have happened. "I feel uncomfortable about this," he emailed one of us. "It all seems to me undeserved – I'm not at that level – and I would think no one would be interested in writing for or publishing it."

Although characteristically modest, Bill was obviously wrong about his stature within the legal academy, where he is widely esteemed as the preeminent criminal procedure scholar of his generation. "Of course I'll be there," one leading scholar replied to our invitation. Every other invitee likewise accepted – quickly and enthusiastically, even when attendance required rearranging prior commitments.

Bill had another concern about the conference – one that the three of us shared. When conference planning began, Bill was already well into his second year of a Stage 4 cancer diagnosis; the prognosis was bleak. Neither he nor we wanted a funereal conference, with dark suits, long faces, and mournful tributes. Yes, we wanted space for fond recollections from mentors, colleagues, students, and friends,[1] but the heart of the conference that we envisioned would consist of scholarly explorations of Bill's work, its influence, and its relevance to modern criminal justice. We asked leaders in the field to contribute written essays, and the work they submitted turned out to be even more remarkable than we had imagined.

[1] See "A Celebration in Honor of William J. Stuntz," Harvard Law School, March 26–27, 2010, Web cast of fourth session, available at http://www.law.harvard.edu/faculty/wstuntz/.

We present these essays here as our collective tribute to our extraordinary colleague and friend, the late Bill Stuntz.

Stuntz began his teaching career at the University of Virginia School of Law in the fall of 1986, just two years after graduating from that same institution. Bill's initial overture to the law school had been, shall we say, inauspicious: His student application was rejected. Undeterred, he and his wife Ruth moved to Charlottesville anyway, and Stuntz worked for a year as a clerk at a local inn. Having established state residency, Stuntz reapplied and was admitted. Three years later, he graduated first in his class with numerous prizes, and went on to prestigious clerkships, first in Philadelphia with U.S. District Court Judge Louis Pollak, former dean of the Yale and University of Pennsylvania law schools, and then with Supreme Court Justice Lewis Powell.

When Bill returned to Virginia as an assistant professor in 1986, his new colleagues wondered what subject he would choose as his specialty. Robert Scott – one of Stuntz's law school mentors and later his dean – lobbied hard for Bill to follow his footsteps into commercial law, a field with a distinguished history that was entering a particularly vibrant phase owing to the advent of the law-and-economics movement. Had he chosen this path, there is no doubt that Stuntz would have quickly become a star.

Instead, much to Scott's chagrin, Stuntz chose to cast his lot with criminal procedure, a field that many considered moribund. The Warren Court had revolutionized the law of criminal procedure in the 1960s, with decisions such as *Mapp v. Ohio* (1961), (applying to the states the exclusionary rule for illegally seized evidence); *Gideon v. Wainwright* (1963); (requiring states to provide free counsel to indigent defendants in all serious criminal cases); and *Miranda v. Arizona* (1966); (interpreting the Fifth Amendment to require police to provide the famous warnings to criminal suspects in their custody and to respect any invocation of the right to remain silent). Criminal procedure scholars had helped lead and shape that revolution.

However, public backlash against rising crime rates and President Nixon's reconstitution of the Supreme Court had brought the criminal procedure revolution to a crashing halt around 1970. Over the next two decades, scholarship in the field languished as law reviews published endless liberal lamentations over the latest Burger Court retrenchment. The time seemed unpropitious for a talented young scholar to launch a career in this field. Ron Allen, later Bill's coauthor on a leading criminal procedure casebook, remembers telling Stuntz that becoming a criminal procedure scholar was sure to "kill brain cells."

Nobody would make such a claim about criminal procedure – or, more generally, criminal justice – scholarship today. The field has been dramatically reinvigorated and transformed – in large part owing to the work, and the influence, of William J. Stuntz.

Stuntz made his scholarly debut with *Self-Incrimination and Excuse*,[2] an article that explored the poor fit between Fifth Amendment case law and privacy and autonomy – the values that were said to animate self-incrimination doctrine. For example, the Supreme Court had held that, despite the impairment of privacy and autonomy, law enforcement officials were permitted to require criminal defendants to provide blood samples and to identify themselves at the scene of an accident. Stuntz offered a novel alternative account of the privilege against self-incrimination by analogizing it to criminal law's doctrine of excuse: Just as the criminal justice system partially excuses defendants for behavior committed under duress – not because that behavior is right but because it is understandable – so does it recognize that defendants put to the choice of lying, being jailed for contempt for refusing to testify, or incriminating themselves by telling the truth are unlikely to play the part of heroes. Stuntz argued that this excuse-based understanding of the privilege made sense of many otherwise inexplicable aspects of the doctrine such as waiver, use immunity, and required production of documents.

In his second major article, *Waiving Rights in Criminal Procedure*,[3] Stuntz examined the seeming tension between the broad array of robust rights protected by the Supreme Court under the Fourth, Fifth, and Sixth Amendments and the apparent ease with which the Court permitted those rights to be waived through defendants' ignorance and even police deception. Stuntz rejected the conventional explanation that the Warren Court's successors were simply undermining rights of which they disapproved through lenient waiver rules. Instead, he sought to reconcile the tension by noting that criminal procedure rights often protect the interests of people other than the rights holder. For example, Fourth Amendment protections against unreasonable searches and seizures are designed to safeguard the rights of innocent people, but when the protections are enforced by the exclusion of relevant evidence, criminals are rewarded. Stuntz argued that waiver doctrine reduced these windfall

[2] 88 COLUM. L. REV. 1227 (1988).

[3] 75 VA. L. REV. 761 (1989).

benefits by permitting waivers of rights when third-party beneficiaries could be independently protected.

In another early article, Stuntz dissected the Fourth Amendment's warrant requirement.[4] On its face, that requirement is puzzling: Legal standards are generally enforced post hoc for the obvious reason that ex ante reviews, most of which will subsequently prove to have been unnecessary, are expensive. Stuntz rejected the usual explanations for the warrant requirement – for example, he noted that although magistrates can provide "neutral" oversight, so can post hoc reviewing judges – and he offered three alternative accounts. First, in a system using monetary damages to redress illegal searches and seizures, a warrant requirement provides police officers with a safe harbor in order to avoid the overdeterrence of socially useful searches – a special problem given the difficulties of accurately valuing the intangible harms caused by illegal searches. Second, in a system that uses the exclusionary rule to enforce the Fourth Amendment, post hoc reviews of probable cause determinations inevitably bias the outcome because the judge knows that the police search uncovered evidence of criminal behavior. Forcing the police to demonstrate probable cause before the search avoids that bias. Finally, post hoc review encourages police perjury because details gleaned from the search can be used to buttress the case that probable cause existed ex ante. Stuntz suggested that disagreements among the Justices over the scope of the warrant requirement can be understood to turn on which concern – decision-maker bias or police perjury – is predominant.

In a 1992 article,[5] Stuntz cast new light on a controversial line of decisions that relaxed usual Fourth Amendment standards for searches conducted by government officials unrelated to the gathering of evidence for criminal prosecutions. For example, school principals searching students' lockers and belongings, government hospital administrators searching physicians' office files, and probation officers searching the homes of their charges are all freed from the usual warrant and probable cause requirements. Many academic commentators criticized these decisions, and the Court itself offered no coherent explanation for them. In his usual counterintuitive fashion, Stuntz explained how these rulings actually *benefited* the class of persons whose rights were seemingly infringed. Because these

[4] *Warrants and Fourth Amendment Remedies*, 77 VA. L. REV. 881 (1991).

[5] *Implicit Bargains, Government Power, and the Fourth Amendment*, 44 STAN. L. REV. 553 (1992).

administrative officials exercise broad control over the lives of the people whom they wish to search, restricting search authority might well lead the administrators to resort to even more intrusive measures. A principal who is not permitted to search lockers can simply eliminate them. Legislators denied the option of authorizing searches of probationers might abolish probation.

This early work displays many of the virtues that Stuntz aficionados would later come to celebrate. Although these articles are doctrinal and therefore, in some sense, conventional, they uncover novel patterns in familiar material, connect seemingly diverse fields, and evaluate legal doctrines at least partially on the basis of the incentives they create and the consequences they produce. In addition, for someone who never practiced criminal law – or any other sort of law, for that matter – Stuntz's scholarship (and his teaching) were remarkably well grounded in the practical realities of day-to-day police work.

In the second phase of his scholarly career, Stuntz broadened his focus from discrete doctrinal issues to a systemic study of the complex, interacting mechanisms of criminal justice. His scholarship became more normative and less descriptive. Instead of simply explaining existing doctrine, he argued for a fundamental reorientation of large swaths of the law of criminal procedure. His work was strikingly nonideological and unpredictable. At one moment, he could sound like a Reagan conservative lambasting the Warren Court; at the next, he sounded like a Great Society liberal castigating race and wealth discrimination. Although his perspective was idiosyncratic and eclectic, it was united by a single, overarching theme: a powerful condemnation of the stark racial and class inequalities that mark the criminal justice system and of the political pathologies that produce these inequalities. His entry points into these critiques were the intersection between criminal procedure and criminal justice and a fresh study of the historical forces that shaped modern criminal procedure doctrines. Like all of Bill's work, his scholarship during this "middle phase" is written with verve and passion. Unlike most legal scholars, though, Bill wrote in a conversational tone that was clear, remarkably free of jargon, and – astonishing but true – entertaining to read.

This phase of Stuntz's work began with companion articles published in 1995, in which he used historical analysis to explain why contemporary criminal procedure doctrine was mistakenly focused on informational privacy rather than on other values such as personal autonomy.

In *The Substantive Origins of Criminal Procedure*,[6] Stuntz pointed out that landmark eighteenth-century British self-incrimination and search cases were concerned with curbing the government's ability to prosecute religious heretics and political dissenters, not run-of-the-mill criminals such as murderers and rapists. Procedural doctrines were used to accomplish the substantive ends of protecting free speech and free exercise of religion in an era and a society that lacked any analogue to the Bill of Right's First Amendment. During the *Lochner* era, in the late nineteenth and early twentieth centuries, criminal procedure doctrines were again put to substantive use – as a tool to protect businesses such as railroads from government regulation. When *Lochner* was finally repudiated, this substantive orientation of criminal procedure was collateral damage. It was replaced by the modern obsession with informational privacy. Stuntz argued that this obsession made little sense and that criminal procedure doctrine ought to be reoriented toward the goal of preventing police violence.

Stuntz further developed these points in *Privacy's Problem and the Law of Criminal Procedure*.[7] Here, Stuntz noted two oddities regarding privacy protection. First, in the criminal context police officers are often severely constrained in their ability to invade personal privacy. For example, they must have probable cause before they can require a car driver to open a glove compartment or a pedestrian to disclose the contents of a paper bag he or she is carrying. Yet, outside the criminal context, government officials routinely require individuals to disclose very private information – for example, on tax forms, where they are required to reveal their bank records and the objects of their charity. Second, although our criminal procedure regime forbids a police officer from, say, turning over a stereo to see its serial number when investigating bullets being fired through the ceiling of an apartment, it has almost nothing to say about the amount of coercion the officer can use against people while conducting that investigation. Criminal procedure would do well, Stuntz argued, to pay greater attention to what he regarded as the more serious problem of police coercion and violence.

In one of his most important articles, *The Uneasy Relationship Between Criminal Procedure and Criminal Justice*, published in 1997,[8]

[6] *The Substantive Origins of Criminal Procedure*, 105 YALE L. J. 393 (1995).

[7] *Privacy's Problem and the Law of Criminal Procedure*, 93 MICH. L. REV. 1016 (1995).

[8] *The Uneasy Relationship Between Criminal Procedure and Criminal Justice*, 107 YALE L. J. 1 (1997).

Stuntz showed how the criminal procedure revolution of the 1960s arguably redounded to the detriment of its intended beneficiaries: criminal defendants – especially innocent ones. Criminal justice is a system with interrelated parts: Court decisions expanding the constitutional rights of criminal defendants may lead other institutional actors to respond in perverse and unexpected ways. For example, legislatures responded to the explosion in criminal procedure protections by ratcheting up punishments and expanding the scope of criminal liability. These changes, in turn, allowed prosecutors to pressure more defendants into accepting guilty pleas. Legislatures also reduced funding for overburdened public defenders, thereby providing powerful new incentives for them to pursue plea bargains. When defense counsel did not immediately plead their clients guilty, the system in effect encouraged them to raise procedural issues, which could be pursued cheaply, rather than issues of guilt or innocence, which involved costly investigation and trials. The result was a decline in resources available for defendants who were factually innocent and an exacerbation of class disparities between affluent defendants who could afford to hire lawyers and poor defendants stuck with underfinanced public defenders. Finally, overcriminalization enhanced the risk of racial discrimination by expanding prosecutorial discretion.

Bill's growing concerns about race and class discrimination are evident in other work from this period. In 1998, Bill explained how the disparate punishments meted out to largely white cocaine users and largely black crack users were likely caused by systemic factors rather than individual racist acts.[9] Street sales of crack in poor urban neighborhoods are cheaper to investigate than are private sales of powder cocaine in upscale suburban neighborhoods. In addition, urban drug crime has more devastating effects on local communities, partly because it is more likely to be violent and partly because these communities often are already teetering near the edge of collapse. Thus, it is rational for police and prosecutors pursuing drug trafficking to target open-air drug markets in poor, predominantly minority neighborhoods (much as they targeted prostitution and alcohol in an earlier era). Still, Stuntz worried that a system widely perceived to be racially biased could not maintain legitimacy in the minds of those who disproportionately bore its costs. Stuntz therefore argued for reducing the sentencing disparity between the use of crack and powder cocaine, using investigative techniques that targeted the collateral effects of drug

[9] *Race, Class, and Drugs*, 98 COLUM. L. REV. 1795 (1998).

markets rather than the buyers and sellers themselves, and allocating more law enforcement resources to upscale drug markets.

In 1999 and 2000, Stuntz explored how Fourth and Fifth Amendment case law benefits the wealthy at the expense of the poor.[10] The Supreme Court's Fourth Amendment doctrine affords far greater protection for wealthy suspects living in nice homes, working in private offices, and driving their own cars than it does for poorer suspects who use public transportation and hang out on the streets. By raising the costs to the police of searching more affluent suspects, Fourth Amendment doctrine inevitably shifted law enforcement attention to the poor. Thus, Stuntz argued, Fourth Amendment law was "in no small measure responsible for the drug war's enormous racial tilt."[11]

Stuntz argued that the *Miranda* doctrine was similarly perverse. It provided a zone of protection for well-informed defendants – usually either the wealthy or criminal recidivists – "while unsophisticated suspects have very nearly no protection at all."[12] Because prosecutorial resources are scarce, any doctrine making it more expensive to prosecute one group – those who invoke their *Miranda* rights – makes it comparatively cheaper to prosecute another – those who waive them. Rather than inviting well-counseled suspects to avoid questioning, Stuntz urged the Court to limit coercive police interrogation practices.

These important scholarly contributions came in the midst of major changes in Stuntz's personal and professional life. In 1999, Bill wrenched his back while changing a flat tire, exacerbating a childhood injury and leaving him in excruciating pain for the remainder of his life. In 2000, he relocated with his family from Virginia to Harvard and transferred his baseball loyalties from the Baltimore Orioles to the Boston Red Sox. Bill quickly became an institutional leader at Harvard, as he had been at Virginia, serving regularly on appointments committees, mentoring junior faculty, and earning the admiration and affection of his colleagues. Then, in early 2008, he was diagnosed with cancer, which after multiple rounds of chemotherapy and several surgeries, eventually led to his death in March of 2011.

While these upheavals were going on in his personal life, Bill's criminal justice scholarship took on a still broader focus. During the last decade

[10] *The Distribution of Fourth Amendment Privacy*, 67 GEO. WASH. L. REV. 1265 (1999); *Miranda's Mistake*, 99 MICH. L. REV. 975 (2000).

[11] 67 GEO. WASH. L. REV. at 1285.

[12] 99 MICH. L. REV. at 977.

of his life, he turned his attention to the political economy of the criminal justice system and the pathological politics that produced it. His work also acquired a more empirical focus. Bill became an avid consumer of crime data and criminological research. (Anyone who dropped by Bill's office during this time would have been struck not only by the extraordinary state of disarray, which was typical of Bill, but also by the vast collection of volumes of the Department of Justice's *Sourcebook on Criminal Justice* and the FBI's *Uniform Crime Reports*.) Bill also began to apply his keen analytical insights to entirely new fields. He wrote about law and Christianity, politics, war and terrorism, the pain that characterized his daily life, and the cancer that ultimately ended it.

In a now classic 2001 article,[13] Stuntz explained the phenomenon of overcriminalization as a product of institutional incentives rather than ideology or politics. Federal and state legislators have strong incentives to expand criminal liability. On the one hand, expansion deflects blame for the harm caused by the newly criminalized activities. On the other hand, when blameless defendants are caught in the expanding net of criminal liability, legislators can blame overzealous prosecutors for abusing their discretion. One might suppose that, for just this reason, prosecutors would resist this expansion, but in fact they too argue for it because it eases their task of proving cases and inducing guilty pleas. Few interest groups oppose this united front. After all, no one wants to be accused of lobbying for criminals.

The result of this web of institutional incentives is a "pathological" system of bloated criminal liability and vast prosecutorial discretion. Judges, whose institutional and cultural incentives might incline them more to safeguard the interests of criminal defendants, have few effective tools with which to counteract legislative overcriminalization, and they are increasingly excluded from the criminal adjudication process by plea bargains and legislative constraints on sentencing. These trends, in turn, lead to sporadic enforcement of criminal law, which undermines its credibility. Instead of trials designed to separate the innocent from the guilty, the system is dominated by plea bargaining, which sweeps up the innocent and guilty alike. This system is also too predisposed to criminalize widely practiced but officially condemned vice, because police and prosecutors can target enforcement toward a small, politically powerless segment of the offending population. The best strategy for fixing this system, Stuntz argued, was to empower judges to place constitutional

[13] *The Pathological Politics of Criminal Law*, 100 MICH. L. REV. 505 (2001).

limits on legislative overcriminalization, through some combination of fair-notice requirements, desuetude constraints, and restoration of judicial discretion over sentencing.

In a related article, published a few years later, Stuntz analogized the criminal justice system to a funnel.[14] At the broad end are the many citizens who find themselves in contact with the police. As the funnel narrows, one finds the smaller number of suspects who get charged, and then finally the even smaller number who go to prison. Stuntz argued that the Supreme Court had mistakenly focused on the broad end of the funnel. When police conduct harms a large number of people, they can form political coalitions to protect themselves and are thus less in need of judicial solicitude. Worse yet, by taking these issues out of politics, the Court pushed legislatures to devote greater resources to those spheres that they were permitted to govern. The upshot was that legislatures, determined to circumvent the Court's procedural rulings, focused on the narrow end of the funnel by expanding the scope of the substantive criminal law and authorizing more prison construction. Finally, the constitutional law of policing encouraged more law enforcement against poor defendants, while the constitutional law of trial procedure widened the gap between the plight of poor and wealthy criminal defendants.

Stuntz called for a radical overhaul in the constitutional law of criminal justice – reform that he believed was possible, albeit not very likely. Courts had a useful role to play, but less in defining the procedures for criminal investigation and adjudication than in ensuring equality of treatment and constraining the discretion of police and prosecutors. The constitutional law of policing, Stuntz argued, should focus less on protecting privacy and more on constraining violence, discrimination, and corruption. The constitutional law of criminal adjudication should focus more on adequately funding defense counsel, mandating consistent enforcement of criminal prohibitions, and ensuring that only the guilty get punished. Courts should insist on consistent punishments for similar crimes and be alert to racial disparities in sentencing. They should constrain prosecutors from inducing plea bargains through threats of excessive punishment.

Stuntz increasingly used contemporary issues of broad interest and great importance to shed light on criminal procedure. Invoking the O. J. Simpson murder trial and Kenneth Starr's investigation of President Bill

[14] William J. Stuntz, *The Political Constitution of Criminal Justice*, 119 HARV. L. REV. 781 (2006).

Clinton as illustrations, he explained the folly of applying the same Fourth Amendment standards regardless of the severity of the alleged criminal behavior.[15] In the Simpson trial, the usual standard proved senselessly strict, forcing the prosecutors to concoct a dubious story about concern for Simpson's safety to secure admission of the bloody glove they discovered on his doorstep. Conversely, in the Clinton case, the courts should have imposed a higher standard of proof before issuing subpoenas to investigate the relatively trivial offense of lying to cover up sexual activity.

Similarly, in an essay written in the wake of the 2001 terrorist attacks, Stuntz argued for a more flexible interpretation of the Fourth Amendment to deal with the new threat from terrorism.[16] For example, police ought to be able to search terrorist suspects on a lower threshold of suspicion, but with greater scrutiny of the nature of such interactions, especially with an eye for ferreting out coercion and violence. Likewise, Stuntz argued for greater law enforcement power to gather private information but with greater constraints placed on its public disclosure outside of criminal trials.

In his last decade, Stuntz also began writing more about law and the Christian faith that was central to his life. Although Christianity is a radical faith, Stuntz insisted in a 2003 article on Christian legal theory,[17] its radical implications may have more to do with how law is practiced – that it might entail treating all work as "an offering to God" – than with the law's content. Stuntz then outlined three possible implications for Christian thinking about the law itself. A radically Christian approach to the Bible's pervasive concern for justice for the poor might call Christian lawyers to somehow enter into their poor clients' distress. Stuntz was more critical of a second possibility, legal moralism, noting the dangers of undertaking moral crusades to criminalize vice or enshrine in law one's positions on culture war issues such as abortion and gay rights. Stuntz thought that such efforts were often self-defeating, both because they tended to generate political backlash and because the selective enforcement of vice laws sometimes undermined the very norms that they were intended to bolster.[18] Third, he called for humility – an

[15] *O.J. Simpson, Bill Clinton, and the Transsubstantive Fourth Amendment*, 114 HARV. L. REV. 842 (2001).

[16] *Local Policing After the Terror*, 111 YALE L. J. 2137 (2002).

[17] *Christian Legal Theory*, 116 HARV. L. REV. 707 (2003).

[18] See also *Self-Defeating Crimes*, 86 VA. L. REV. 1871 (2000).

awareness of the fallibility of human intellect, which ought to make one humble in one's convictions and chary in the use of law to solve complicated problems.[19]

Over the last decade of his career, Bill wrote increasingly for popular as well as scholarly audiences. He explained how President George W. Bush's appointments to the Supreme Court were like those of Harry S. Truman.[20] He explored the virtues of "soft policing" while cautioning that its methods often entailed greater invasions of individual privacy than traditional policing.[21] He called for increased federal funding of local law enforcement.[22] He supported the surge in Iraq, analogizing it to Ulysses S. Grant's summer-long siege of Robert E. Lee's army in Virginia in 1864, and he rejected the application of economic concepts, such as the fallacy of sunk costs, to war.[23] Bill believed that terrorism should be fought militarily rather than through criminal prosecutions.[24] In 2004 he rightly predicted that President George W. Bush would defeat challenger John Kerry and that Tom Daschle would become the first Senate majority leader in fifty years to lose his job.[25] He explained why people of faith should worry about public displays of religiosity both because of the risk that they might be perceived as exclusionary and because religion might become contaminated by the public sphere.[26] In a 2004 essay singled out by David Brooks in the *New York Times* as one of the finest essays of the year, Bill tried to bridge the gap between the academic left and the Christian right, exploring the possibility of finding common ground on issues such as abortion and aid to the poor.[27] He thought that Christians could teach academics about humility and that academics could teach Christians about the love of argument.[28] (Of course, he taught all of us

[19] See also *Christianity and the (Modest) Rule of Law*, 8 U. PENN. J. CONST. L. 809 (2006).

[20] "The Truman Show," *The New Republic* (2005).

[21] "Lessons from London: Why More Eavesdropping is Better than Less," *The New Republic* (2006).

[22] "No Cop Left Behind," *Boston Review* (2005).

[23] Iraq articles, *The Weekly Standard* (2006); "1864 Redux?," *TCS Daily* (2004).

[24] "Terrorism and the Mob," *TCS Daily* (2004).

[25] "Daschle May Lose," *TCS Daily* (2004); "Why Truman Defeats Dewey," *TCS Daily* (2004).

[26] "Turning Faith into Elevator Music," *TCS Daily* (2005).

[27] "Academic Left and Christian Right," *TCS Daily* (2005).

[28] "Faculty Clubs and Church Pews," *TCS Daily*; widely distributed thereafter (2004).

about both.) He wrote about the gift of his faith and of the special gifts that God gave to those who suffered.[29]

Bill also wrote with grace and insight about his physical pain and about the cancer that ultimately killed him. His pain, Bill explained, felt like "an alarm clock taped to one ear, with the volume turned up."[30] He was tired, always tired – "very, very tired."[31] He noted the agony for cancer patients of "living in between" – the chemo treatment, the remission, the cancer's return.[32] Nobody could tell how long that "between time" would last – "My doctors don't know, and God isn't talking."[33] How ought one to make plans when one doesn't know "how long it will be till the sand runs out?"[34]

Bill posted blog entries both as therapy for himself and "as a window into the world" of suffering for others; it was an "ugly world" but one that was home to so many people.[35] He noted how living with chronic pain and illness was like living "life in the closet" – "a secret world, a world my friends and loved ones cannot know – and, I pray, one they never will know."[36] Secrets seem shameful; sufferers worry that some failing of theirs, some character flaw, had left them to "inhabit this strange and terrible unseen place."[37] Bill hoped to open the closet door so that others could see inside.

Bill thought it possible to draw meaning from a life characterized by "weariness and pain [that] are everywhere."[38] He did not deny the ugliness of the pain that clung to him "like a stain that cannot be cleansed," but he rejoiced in the fact that God was not repulsed by the ugliness but instead "wrapped His arms around it" and sought to cleanse it.[39] Bill found humor in his drug treatment – for example, from a drug labeled "5-FU."[40] He came to appreciate the beauty of living in the moment, when one no longer assumes one will be around for the college graduation of one's children or the birth of one's grandchildren. Experiencing the beauty of the Charles River from his hospital bed brought a smile to his face. Though cancer and its treatment "are nasty businesses" – he would not pretend otherwise – he also found in them "benefits unimagined,"

[29] "Three Gifts for Hard Times," *Christianity Today* (2009).
[30] *Less than the Least* blog, Nov. 20, 2008.
[31] Feb. 28, 2008.
[32] Aug. 3, 2008.
[33] Aug. 3, 2008.
[34] Aug. 3, 2008.
[35] Feb. 28, 2008.
[36] Nov. 20, 2008.
[37] Nov. 20, 2008.
[38] Feb. 28, 2008.
[39] March 2, 2008.
[40] Nov. 20, 2008.

especially the love and kindness of his friends and family.[41] Though cancer was "a supremely ugly disease," he found its treatment sometimes "a kind of beauty," as when he watched nurses and doctors in the cancer unit treat a teenage victim with kindness and compassion.[42]

Managing the pain and the side effects of the cancer drugs required nearly all of the mental concentration that Bill could summon. Characteristically, he worried that between the pain, nausea, and fatigue, he could no longer teach or write effectively. Just three months before he died, though, Bill finished both his book manuscript and his last semester of teaching.

In the fall of 2011, Harvard University Press published Bill's last scholarly work, *The Collapse of American Criminal Justice*. This book is a fitting capstone to his career and brings together many of the themes that preoccupied his scholarly life. Thankfully, Bill lived long enough to complete his magnum opus; tragically, he did not survive to enjoy the plaudits that it has received. We think that it is one of the best books ever written about the law.

In the book, Stuntz traces the history of the American criminal justice system in search of explanations for our current conundrum – a massive incarceration rate, strongly correlated with race. We have reached a place, he claimed, where our system more closely resembles that of the Soviet gulag than of the rest of the Western world with which America is ordinarily compared. How could this have happened?

For Stuntz, our current morass called to mind Jefferson's famous metaphor for the dilemma faced by antebellum slave holders, who held the "wolf by the ears": How could they emancipate millions of blacks from slavery without igniting deadly violence against their former masters? Modern-day Americans, Stuntz believed, saw themselves facing a similar quandary: How could they end mass incarceration without liberating hundreds of thousands of prisoners whose return to the streets would likely restore the horrific crime rates of the 1970s and 1980s? Stuntz argued that much as southern slave owners misconceived the consequences of emancipation, so too, many Americans today misunderstand the relationship between mass incarceration and crime rates.

The book centers on Stuntz's observations regarding the peculiar relationship between crime rates and incarceration rates over the past fifty years. In the 1950s and 1960s, the United States experienced enormous

[41] Sept. 19, 2008. [42] June 28, 2010.

increases in the rate of violent crime – in some cities, murder rates increased more than tenfold – while incarceration rates in some states simultaneously declined by as much as 30 to 40 percent. Over the following few decades, incarceration rates increased exponentially – in some states, by as much as seven-fold or eightfold – while crime rates first continued to rise and then began to fall, albeit very slowly. American prisons and jails that housed fewer than 200,000 inmates during the early years of Nixon's presidency held more than 1.5 million at the beginning of Obama's. Of male black Americans who fail to graduate from high school, 70 percent will be incarcerated during their lifetimes. Such mass incarceration not only decimates minority communities but also undermines the legitimacy of the criminal justice system in the minds of those who are so disproportionately victimized by it.

Stuntz blamed much of this predicament on the Warren Court's ill-timed criminal procedure revolution. By erecting procedural impediments to the punishment of violent crime in the midst of growing public panic about a crime epidemic, the Court ensured a political backlash, which nationalized the crime issue, launched a tsunami of retributivism in criminal punishment, and inspired legislatures to respond in ways that produced assembly-line justice, which poorly sorts the innocent from the guilty.

Always the hopeful reformer, Stuntz offered recommendations for escaping our current predicament. First, he urged a return to the sort of localized, relatively nonpunitive criminal justice system that characterized northern cities in the late nineteenth century. This was a system in which the same ethnic minorities that constituted the bulk of the criminal population also made the relevant decisions – in local politics, as local police officers and prosecutors, and as jurors – that determined how many of their ethnic compatriots to incarcerate. Today, by contrast, many of the decisions that send young black and Latino men to jail in extraordinary numbers are made by government officials relatively unaccountable to local politics – national and state legislators, unelected federal prosecutors, and state's attorneys elected at the county level (which often mix more powerful white suburbs with disempowered minority urban cores). Stuntz also advocated returning to a regime in which judges have discretion to interpret criminal statutes to do justice and in which juries, rendered largely irrelevant by plea bargaining, can use their power to nullify unfair prosecutions. The constitutional law of criminal justice, Stuntz urged, should focus less on procedural protections that benefit mostly the guilty and more on substantive constraints that curb overcriminalization, curtail racially disparate punishments, and require that criminal statutes be enforced consistently or not at all. Invoking social science studies that show that more policing is a better way to fight crime than more incarceration, Stuntz applauded experiments in community policing, which can effectively deter crime, while enhancing the legitimacy of law enforcement in the neighborhoods that it targets.

The Collapse of American Criminal Justice is breathtaking in its historical scope and its analytical insight. Stuntz treats his readers to an account of the contrasting procedural/substantive styles of the American Bill of Rights and the French Declaration of Rights, and he traces the historical roots of the Bill of Rights' criminal procedure guarantees to substantive concerns about political and religious persecution in Great Britain during the seventeenth and eighteenth centuries. Stuntz explores the contrasting criminal justice systems of the Jim Crow South and the urban, immigrant-dominated cities of the Northeast. He explains the growing involvement of the federal government in the suppression of vice – lotteries, prostitution, the opium trade – in the early twentieth century, and he notes the ways in which Prohibition's enforcement in the 1920s was much more defensible than our modern War on Drugs. He offers an account of how mid-twentieth-century politicians such as Thomas Dewey, Estes Kefauver, and Robert Kennedy became expert practitioners of the symbolic politics of crime and of how the political backlash generated by the Warren Court's criminal procedure revolution led liberal Democrats and conservative Republicans into bidding wars to demonstrate their relative toughness on crime. Readers will come away from *The Collapse of American Criminal Justice* not only with a richer understanding of our mass incarceration society and its history but also with a sense of awe at the author's learning, breadth of understanding, creative capacity, and moral vision.

Stuntzian perspectives have transformed our understanding of the criminal justice system. Today almost everyone working in the field appreciates the interrelationship between criminal law and criminal procedure. Although debate about the Warren Court's criminal procedure revolution continues, few modern observers would deny that it produced unintended and, sometimes, perverse consequences. Whether or not they embrace Stuntz's conclusions, most modern scholars agree that criminal justice should be understood as a complex system with interrelated parts and a distinctive political economy. It is hard to believe that none of these propositions had been established before Bill turned his attention to criminal justice.

The contributors to this volume are diverse in nearly every respect except one: Each is a leading scholar of criminal justice who has been influenced by Bill Stuntz and his scholarship. The disparate ways in which they have been influenced is itself a testament to the scope and richness of Bill's academic contributions.

This book is divided into three major parts, which represent three principal strands in Stuntz's work. The chapters in Part I address the political economy of substantive criminal law. Part II considers issues arising in the context of police investigations. The principal concern in Part III is the role of discretion and emotion in criminal justice. In a brief concluding chapter, Stuntz himself suggests possible avenues for future scholarship.

PART I: THE POLITICAL ECONOMY OF SUBSTANTIVE CRIMINAL LAW

This part begins with the chapter "The Political Economy of Capital Punishment," written by Joe Hoffmann, whose friendship with Stuntz spans a quarter century from the time when Hoffmann was clerking for Chief Justice William Rehnquist at the same time that Stuntz was clerking for Justice Lewis Powell. Here, Hoffmann describes the new path toward death penalty abolition recently taken in Illinois. "Virtual abolition" (or "I've fallen and I can't get up" abolition) occurs when the death penalty temporarily gets off track for some reason, and a particular type of political dysfunctionality prevents it from regaining its footing. Based on his own experience testifying before the Illinois legislature in 2005, Hoffmann recounts the fate of a bill that would have required, as a condition for imposing capital punishment, that the fact finder certify "no doubt" – as opposed to simply "proof beyond a reasonable doubt" – of the defendant's factual guilt. This bill was defeated by an unusual coalition of capital punishment supporters, who viewed it as a disingenuous effort to abolish the death penalty, and capital punishment opponents, who feared that it would legitimize the death penalty. Virtual abolition happened in Illinois largely because no individual actor – judge, governor, or legislator – had to take the politically risky step of endorsing abolition.

More than twenty-five years ago, Richard McAdams, the author of Chapter 2, inherited not only Bill Stuntz's desk at the *Virginia Law Review* but also the decaying leftover pizza slices still inhabiting it. In "Bill Stuntz and the Principal–Agent Problem in American Criminal Law," McAdams credits Stuntz with pioneering the analysis of criminal law in terms of agency costs. Corporate law scholars are familiar with the problems that arise when ownership and control of a business firm are separated, but few scholars before Stuntz thought about criminal law in such terms, even though agency problems are arguably even more prevalent in this sphere. Avoiding confusing jargon, Stuntz explained how multiple agents – legislators, prosecutors, police, judges, jurors, defense lawyers – interact to produce the complex system of criminal justice that we know today. McAdams explains how agency problems underlie many of the pathologies that Stuntz identifies in the system: legislative overcriminalization, unequal enforcement of vice crimes, and the explosion of plea bargaining.

In "Overcriminalization for Lack of Better Options," Danny Richman, who also first met Stuntz during a Supreme Court clerkship in 1985–1986, explores a previously unexplored facet of the overcriminalization phenomenon: the "demand side." Richman directs our attention to the interest groups that lobby for the use of criminal law to regulate issues that might have been better addressed by civil law. These interest groups are attracted to the criminal law because criminal prosecutors tend to be better funded than other administrative officials and because criminal enforcement has greater cache. He also notes how opponents of regulation have often embraced criminalization as a means of avoiding the creation of new regulatory apparatuses. Although there is no simple solution to these incentives to overcriminalize, Richman calls for an increased focus on noncriminal institutions and sanctions as tools of regulation.

In "Stealing Bill Stuntz," David Sklansky, yet another colleague of Bill's from his Supreme Court clerkship days,[43] imagines Stuntz as our new Charles Dickens. Just as all political camps sought to claim Dickens as an ally, so, too, has Stuntz been embraced by everyone from Burkean conservatives to radical critical race theorists. Sklansky attributes Stuntz's

[43] Some have wondered why such a large percentage of the leading scholars in Criminal Justice today started their careers as Supreme Court law clerks in 1985–1986. Perhaps Bill Stuntz's influence rubbed off from an early age?

broad appeal to three themes that pervade his scholarship. First, criminal justice is a complex system with interrelated parts. This theme reveals Stuntz's scholarly commitment to understanding the real world in all its complexity, and it induced a certain humility in his scholarship, though not a fatalistic paralysis. Second, the criminal justice system has its own distinctive political economy. This theme relates to Stuntz's pragmatism and puts him at odds with other theoretical approaches, such as originalism and expressivism, which are less focused on devising rules that promote social welfare. Third, Stuntz's scholarship evinces concern with improving the lot of the least advantaged participants in the system, especially racial minorities. This commitment led Stuntz to focus on the need for greater empathy, which, he thought, would be promoted by more local democracy. From Stuntz's work and life, Sklansky draws two broad lessons. First, much as Stuntz himself bridged the divide between religious and secular communities, people of diverse views should be able to reason about divisive issues of criminal justice in respectful and constructive ways. Second, even though Stuntz himself thought that criminal law's pathologies resulted from the impersonal mechanics of public-choice theory, his career demonstrates the importance of personal leadership, idealism, and decency.

PART II: POLICE INVESTIGATION

The chapters in Part II focus on issues arising from police investigation. In "The Accidental Feminist," Anne Coughlin, Bill's co-clerk in Justice Powell's chambers in 1985–1986, analogizes police interrogation to seduction and rape, thereby combining insights drawn from both criminal law and criminal procedure in good Stuntzian fashion. The laws of both rape and confession emphasize the importance of distinguishing consent from coercion; both tolerate fraud but not violence; both involve activity usually conducted in private; both are usually zero-sum games; and both often involve strangers using power against their victims. Coughlin provocatively asks why the law of criminal interrogation treats men, who dominate the pool of criminal suspects, as if they were women, who dominate the pool of rape victims.

In "The Distribution of Dignity and the Fourth Amendment," Tracey Meares explores the constitutional regulation of police searches and seizures. Meares's earlier work in this area, which drew on Stuntzian concerns regarding distributional justice, argued that courts should evaluate search-and-seizure tactics on the basis of whether the community adopting them had internalized the relevant costs. In this chapter, Meares emphasizes "evenhandness" and investigates how that concept relates to the Fourth Amendment requirement of individualized suspicion. In her view, randomized procedures conducted without reasonable suspicion, such as sobriety checkpoints, are praiseworthy, both because they avoid racial profiling and because they encourage encounters that respect the dignity of those who are targeted.

In "Why Courts Should Not Quantify Probable Cause," Orin Kerr rejects the notion that courts should attempt to quantify the meaning of the Fourth Amendment's probable-cause requirement. Kerr observes that affidavits filed by police officers in support of search warrants generally fail to inform the magistrate about investigative techniques that have been tried but failed to produce incriminating evidence and about those that were not tried at all. Kerr worries that quantitative standards, because they implicate powerful cognitive biases, would divert judges from attending to this omitted information and thus generate less accurate results than standards that simply encourage judges to rely on their intuitive "situation sense."

In "DNA and the Fifth Amendment," Erin Murphy explores whether the privilege against self-incrimination should forbid law enforcement agencies from mandating the collection of DNA samples from convicted criminals or, more broadly, from all criminal suspects. So far, critics of mandatory DNA testing have been discouraged from utilizing Fifth Amendment arguments against it because of the Supreme Court's decision in *Schmerber v. California* (1966), which rejected a Fifth Amendment challenge to compelling a suspect to provide a blood sample. Murphy suggests that *Schmerber* may have been undermined by the court's recent expansion of Fifth Amendment rights in the context of compelled production of documents – an expansion accurately forecast by Stuntz himself in his first law review article. Murphy thinks that the new approach to documents throws into doubt the use of compulsion without some sort of individualized suspicion, yet she admits to being troubled by two arguments that are themselves Stuntzian in origin. First, mandatory DNA samples do not expose suspects to the "cruel trilemma" of perjury, self-incrimination, or contempt. Second, Murphy worries that if police and prosecutors are prevented from coercively obtaining DNA samples, they will resort to alternative means of securing them, such as offering criminal defendants lighter sentences in exchange for a DNA sample. Nonetheless, she concludes on Stuntzian distributional grounds that the Fifth

Amendment case against coercively obtaining DNA samples from criminal suspects deserves another look.

PART III: EMOTION, DISCRETION, AND THE JUDICIAL ROLE

The chapters in the book's final part focus on two related concepts that are sometimes thought to be in tension with the rule of law – emotion and discretion. Bill thought that both were important, and his later work, especially on the distributional consequences of our criminal justice system, spelled out why.

In Chapter 9, "Two Conceptions of Two Conceptions of Emotion in Criminal Law," Dan Kahan identifies and analyzes two different conceptions of emotion in criminal law: a *mechanistic* one that conceives of emotions as thoughtless, nonvolitional forces, and an *evaluative* one that understands them as thought-pervaded moral assessments. Kahan accepts this distinction but rejects the prevalent view of the evaluative conception as implicating a decision maker's self-conscious moral evaluation. Rather, Kahan sees evaluation as emanating from cultural frameworks that unconsciously shape the intensity of emotions and other facts that generally fall within the mechanistic conception of emotion. For Kahan, this insight explains why decision makers believe they are assessing emotions mechanistically when, in fact, they are morally evaluating them.

Andrew Leipold, one of Bill's successors both at the *Virginia Law Review* and in Justice Powell's chambers, is the author of "Patrolling the Fenceline: How the Court Only Sometimes Cares About Preserving its Role in Criminal Cases." Leipold explores the extent to which the recent Supreme Court has been consistent in preserving a robust role for judges and juries in criminal cases. In three important lines of cases, the Court has aggressively protected this authority from prosecutorial overreaching. It has restored some of judges' traditional power over sentencing, asserted judicial control over terrorism cases, and ensured that courtroom testimony is subject to adequate cross-examination. However, two other recent decisions seem to depart from this pattern. In *United States v. Ruiz*, the Court refused to overturn a plea bargain in which the prosecutor's office had failed to turn over exculpatory evidence in its files (so-called Brady material), which it would have been obliged to disclose had the case gone to trial. In *United States v. Cotton*, the Court ruled that the government's failure to allege the elements of a crime in an indictment did not automatically deprive the federal courts of jurisdiction over the case. In these cases, Leipold argues, the Court failed to explain its deference to executive branch conduct of criminal prosecutions. The court's unwillingness to closely superintend the plea bargaining process is especially troubling, Leipold notes, because plea bargaining is, as Stuntz himself observed, "not some adjunct to the criminal justice system; it *is* the criminal justice system."

In "Three Puzzles in the Work of Bill Stuntz," Mike Seidman explores a series of puzzles regarding the way Stuntz exercised his own authorial discretion throughout his professional career. First, given Stuntz's call for Christians to "come out of the closet" and openly bring their Christian perspective to bear on legal problems, why did Stuntz almost never refer to his own deep Christian beliefs in his criminal justice writings? Second, how can someone be as humble as Stuntz yet simultaneously be so certain of the exclusive truth of Christianity? Third, how can an "atheist/agonistic Jew" such as Seidman, with very different political leanings than Stuntz, feel such a "profound connection" to the man and his work? Stuntz's personal humility may solve the first puzzle: A humble Christian might well be reluctant to parade his religious views in public scholarship. The answer to the other puzzles, Seidman argues, lies in the inevitability of unconstrained choice in what Seidman thinks is a "meaningless universe": Stuntz chooses to embrace Christianity, Seidman, agnosticism and communitarianism. Nonetheless, neither can avoid making choices grounded less in reason than in faith.

In "The Mercy Seat: Discretion, Justice, and Mercy in the American Criminal Justice System," Carol Steiker explores the role that the concept of mercy might play in promoting reform of the criminal justice system. Steiker, one of Bill's colleagues at Harvard and his successor as the Henry J. Friendly Professor of Law, describes how the religious concept of God's mercy might give rise to a human counterpart in criminal justice. Like Seidman, Steiker notes Stuntz's avoidance of religious imagery in his own work, but she explains how Stuntz's thoughts on both criminal justice and Christianity might contribute to the development of a human-scale conception of mercy. Steiker observes that conventional wisdom has deemed discretion within the criminal justice system an evil to be rooted out. One of Stuntz's signal contributions, she argues, has been to show that discretion-cabining reforms have often made the system *more* arbitrary and discriminatory. Counterintuitively, the solution to too much discretion may actually be more discretion, of a type best described as mercy. Stuntz's work, Steiker concludes, sheds valuable light on how one might reconcile a revival of discretionary mercy with rule-of-law justice.

EPILOGUE

The volume concludes with Bill Stuntz's own words. In "Three Underrated Explanations for the Punitive Turn," he suggests promising avenues for future criminal justice scholarship. First, Stuntz urges further study and reform of the relationship between state and local governments in criminal justice: Because prison is essentially a "free" good to local law enforcement (because it is paid for at the state rather than local level), local prosecutors have tended to vastly overuse it. Second, he urges further study of the divergence between the choices made by local police and by local prosecutors: In recent decades, police arrest rates have tended to rise and fall with changing crime rates, but prosecutions and prison sentences have fluctuated far less predictably. Finally, Stuntz argues that criminal law reformers have focused too much on technical codification and too little on ensuring that only people with culpable mental states get punished. Stuntz notes that none of the three developments he criticizes were ideologically motivated or intended to produce the mass incarceration that they did. For this reason, he is characteristically hopeful that a nonideological solution to our mass incarceration problem can be found.

Bill Stuntz transformed the field of criminal justice scholarship over the past quarter century. He bridged the gap between criminal law and criminal procedure; he taught us to think about criminal justice as a system with interconnected parts and a distinctive political economy; he shed light on current conundrums through the use of history; he illuminated the unintended and often deleterious consequences of the Warren Court's revolution in criminal procedure; and he proposed possible escape routes from our current predicament of mass incarceration, which destroys lives, devastates minority urban communities, and delegitimizes the legal system that produces it.

But Bill Stuntz did not merely enlighten us with his brilliant scholarship. He was also our colleague, our friend, our trusted advisor, and our inspiration.

Bill was a fabulous classroom law teacher. From his first days at Virginia, students adored him. He was a master of the material; he was comfortable at the podium; he was brilliant; he was funny; he was excited by and appreciative of student contributions; and he engaged and stretched their minds. Bill was also extraordinarily accessible to students: He never set office hours because he was always in the office and was happy to talk with students whenever they dropped by, and for as long as they wished.

Bill was also the best colleague and friend we could imagine having. He was curious, knowledgeable, generous with his time, fun to talk to, and the consummate team player. He read our scholarship with a meticulous eye, and his comments were always invaluable: detailed, incisive, constructive, encouraging. He performed this service not only for us, but for an entire generation of criminal procedure (and other) scholars across the country. Stuntz was the Bill Russell of legal academia: He helped make all of his teammates – as well as his "competitors" – the best that they could be.

Bill was an extraordinary institutional citizen. He served on appointments committees at Virginia and Harvard more than half of his years as a tenured professor, and he was widely esteemed for his discernment and judgment. Countless colleagues, junior and senior, sought out his counsel with regard to their teaching, their scholarship, their professional careers, and their personal lives. Bob Scott, Bill's dean at Virginia, groomed Bill to be his successor as dean – an appointment that would have been greeted with acclamation by the Virginia faculty had Bill been interested in the job, and Elena Kagan, his dean at Harvard, later called him "the dean's pet." A decade after Bill moved to Harvard, a former dean called him the most important person on the faculty.

Bill was also a wonderful friend. He was kind, considerate, sincere, dependable, cheerful, and self-deprecating. (One of the favorite jokes about Bill among his friends and colleagues involves recollections of the many times that he dropped by their offices; shed pearls of wisdom about law, politics, sports, and life; then apologized profusely for taking up so much of their time.) In twenty-five years, we rarely heard Bill say an unkind word about another person, nor can we recall anyone else saying anything unkind about Bill.

Last but not least, Bill taught us the important lesson – especially vital to recall in today's fiercely polarized political culture – that people who do not see eye to eye politically can still respect, admire, and cherish one another. We sometimes – two of us, often – disagreed with Bill about which candidate to support for public office, but political disagreement never got in the way of a deeper sense of connection. Nobody who knew him could ever question Bill's integrity, his good will, and his compassion for the least advantaged in our society. Through his example, he taught us that political disagreements are often about means rather than ends, and that more is to be gained by empathizing with and understanding our political opponents than by demonizing them.

Bill's legacy will live on for decades through his scholarship and in the hearts and minds of thousands of students and scores of colleagues. We believe that he was one of the greatest law professors of his generation, as well as one of the most beloved. It is our privilege and our pleasure to present this volume of essays, testifying to his influence and dedicated to his memory.

PART I

The Political Economy of Substantive Criminal Law

1

The Political Economy of Capital Punishment

Joseph L. Hoffmann

On March 9, 2011, the State of Illinois formally abolished capital punishment. Illinois thus became the sixteenth state without a death penalty, and one of four states – the others being New Mexico, New Jersey, and New York – to join those ranks within the past five years.[1] Governor Pat Quinn, a Democrat, signed Senate Bill 3539, the abolition law sent to him by the Illinois legislature almost two months earlier, and also commuted the death sentences of all fifteen inmates on death row in Illinois.[2]

Abolitionists across the United States and around the world rejoiced, including Sister Helen Prejean and the Reverend Desmond Tutu, both of whom had personally encouraged Governor Quinn to sign the bill.[3] The European Union issued a congratulatory message,[4] and Amnesty International USA's Executive Director, Larry Cox, called it "a landmark day for Illinois and the United States." According to Cox, "No state has tried harder to fix its death penalty system, but after 10 years it became patently clear that it was broken beyond repair."[5]

[1] Tony Mauro, "Illinois Abolishes Death Penalty," March 9, 2011, available online at http://www.law.com/jsp/law/LawArticleFriendly.jsp?id=1202485449648.

[2] Id.

[3] John Schwartz & Emma G. Fitzsimmons, "Illinois Governor Signs Capital Punishment Ban," *New York Times*, March 9, 2011, available online at http://www.nytimes.com/2011/03/10/us/10illinois.html.

[4] See "Declaration by the High Representative on Behalf of the European Union on the Abolition of the Death Penalty in the State of Illinois, USA," March 11, 2011, available online at http://www.consilium.europa.eu/uedocs/cms_data/docs/pressdata/en/cfsp/119772.pdf.

[5] Amnesty International USA Press Release, "Amnesty International Praises Governor Quinn for Signing Illinois Death Penalty Abolition Bill," March 9, 2011, available online at http://www.amnestyusa.org/document.php?id=ENGUSA20110309001.

In this chapter, I offer a few observations of my own about the recent abolition of the death penalty in Illinois. My chapter reflects one of the many invaluable lessons I learned from Bill Stuntz. Bill taught me, as he did so many others, to pay closer attention to the structural and institutional dimensions – in other words, the political economy – of criminal justice. Here I intend to examine one particular aspect of that political economy that, in my view, has begun to emerge as a new and potentially important phenomenon in the modern evolution of the American death penalty.

Let me tell you a story. It is a true story, although a difficult one to document, because there are relatively few public records of the relevant events. However, I was both a witness to and tangentially involved in the events, so I am hopeful that my testimony will be accepted as evidence that these events really did occur.

In early 2005, Illinois State Representative and House Minority Leader Tom Cross introduced a bill, H.R. 2704,[6] to reform one small part of

[6] 2005 Bill Text IL H.B. 2704, Illinois 94th General Assembly, February 22, 2005. In its original form, which was later amended, the bill started with the following legislative findings:

> Legislative findings. The General Assembly hereby finds and declares that a fundamental difference exists between the death penalty and any other penalty that may be imposed upon a defendant. The death penalty contains an element of finality that cannot be attributed to any other penalty that may be constitutionally imposed upon a defendant. The General Assembly finds and declares that this difference, based upon this element of finality, reaches down into the procedures used to sentence a convicted defendant. The court may provide, by itself or through a jury, a standard of scrutiny to the disposition of a defendant convicted of first degree murder and subject to a potential sentence of death that reflects the finality of the penalty. The General Assembly finds and declares that nothing in the Criminal Code of 1961 or in this Act amending the Criminal Code of 1961 shall provide that the test of residual doubt, as applied to a potential death sentence that could be imposed upon a person convicted of first degree murder and subject to a potential sentence of death, can be applied to any other sentencing process carried out under the laws of the State of Illinois. The General Assembly finds and declares that the test of residual doubt, as applied to a potential death sentence that could be imposed upon a person convicted of first degree murder and subject to a potential sentence of death, must be applied to the procedure of death penalty sentencing only, and this test must not be applied to any other sentencing process carried out under the laws of the State of Illinois.

The bill then made the following addition to the Illinois death penalty statute:

> Residual Doubt – Jury Determination
>
> The court shall instruct the jury that if the jury determines that the evidence was sufficient beyond a reasonable doubt to sustain the verdict of guilty for first degree

Illinois's death penalty law. The bill consisted of a proposal to impose a new, and higher, burden of proof of guilt during the sentencing phase of a capital trial. Under the bill, no death sentence could be imposed unless the jury, at the sentencing phase of the trial, found unanimously that there was "no doubt" about the defendant's guilt. In a bench trial, the same finding would have to be made by the trial judge. However, if such a finding could not be made by the fact finder, then the defendant would have to receive a life sentence.

Representative Cross believed that this was a small but significant reform that would help to reduce the risk that the death penalty would ever again be applied in Illinois to a person whose factual guilt was in doubt: "Just because I'm for the death penalty doesn't mean we should sentence people that are innocent to Death Row."[7] Cross successfully enlisted the support of not only some of his moderate Republican colleagues but also several more liberal Democrats. In February 2005, the Chicago Tribune described the bill as a "bipartisan plan."[8]

At a March 10, 2005, hearing in the Illinois House Judiciary Committee, a number of witnesses testified for and against the bill. I testified in favor, having previously supported a similar proposal as the Co-Reporter for Massachusetts Governor Mitt Romney's Council on Capital Punishment.[9] One of the arguments I made in favor of the no-doubt bill was that jurors often feel lingering or "residual" doubt about a defendant's guilt – doubt that is insufficient to prevent a conviction, but that nevertheless makes jurors feel that a death sentence is inappropriate. Empirical research, including the Capital Jury Project, confirms the frequent occurrence of such residual doubt,[10] but it is not always clear what can, or should, be done about it. In one Illinois death penalty trial, during jury deliberations, the jurors sent a note to the trial judge asking whether they were allowed to consider residual doubt as a possible mitigating

> murder but does not foreclose all doubt respecting the defendant's guilt, the jury may not determine that death is the appropriate sentence and the court shall sentence the defendant to a term of natural life imprisonment.

The bill also imposed the same no-doubt standard upon the judge, if the sentencing hearing were conducted without a jury.

7 Ray Long, "A Bid to End Execution Doubts; Bipartisan Plan Would Raise Standard of Guilt," *Chicago Tribune*, February 26, 2005, Sec. C, at p. 1.

8 Id.

9 See infra at notes 32–38.

10 See William J. Bowers et al., *Foreclosed Impartiality in Capital Sentencing: Jurors' Predispositions, Guilt-Trial Experience, and Premature Decisionmaking*, 83 Cornell L. Rev. 1476 (1998); William J. Bowers, *The Capital Jury Project; Rationale, Design, and Preview of Early Findings*, 70 Ind. L. J. 1043 (1995).

circumstance. The trial judge refused to answer, and the Illinois Supreme Court affirmed, saying that residual doubt was irrelevant to the capital sentencing decision.[11] I testified that residual doubt should always be treated as relevant in a capital case, and that H.R. 2704 was necessary to ensure that it would be treated as such.

I then sat and watched as two leading spokespersons for Illinois prosecutors, the State's Attorneys for Cook County (Chicago) and DuPage County (suburban Chicago), testified. These two prosecutors argued to the committee members that the bill should be rejected because it was a thinly disguised attack on the Illinois death penalty, which would open up a "Pandora's box" because no jury would ever be able to find that there was *no* doubt about a capital defendant's guilt.[12] This was described as an impossibly philosophical inquiry tantamount to counting the number of angels who can dance on the head of a pin. One of the prosecutors specifically labeled the no-doubt bill as an "effective repeal" of capital punishment in Illinois.

The next person to testify was the official designee of the Illinois public defenders. This witness testified that the no-doubt bill should be rejected because it was merely a thinly disguised effort to restore legitimacy to the Illinois death penalty and thereby overturn the moratorium on executions that had then been in place in Illinois for five years. The public defender witness specifically stated that a vote for the no-doubt bill was a vote in favor of resuming executions in Illinois.

At the end of the hearing, the bill barely passed out of committee on a tight 9–7 vote. The deciding vote in favor was cast by the committee chair, a Chicago Democrat who stated that he actually opposed the bill but would vote "yes" to expose the futility of seeking a "perfect" death penalty. In his words, "I'm going to vote 'yes' on this bill because I think it does add to the hypocrisy, I really do."[13]

The no-doubt bill then moved on to the full House. Fortunately, the bill received the unequivocal public support of both the Center on Wrongful Convictions at Northwestern University[14] and the *Chicago*

[11] People v. McDonald, 168 Ill. 2d 420; 660 N.E.2d 832; 1995 Ill. LEXIS 190 (Ill. S.Ct. 1995).

[12] Erika Slife, "High Death Penalty Standard Advances," *Chicago Tribune*, March 11, 2005, Metro Sec., at p. 2.

[13] Id.

[14] See 2005 Legis. Bill Hist. IL H.B. 2704, March 10, 2005 (reporting testimony of Rob Warden, Center on Wrongful Convictions, Northwestern Law School, in support of H.R. 2704 before the House Judiciary Committee).

Tribune[15] – two highly respected entities that, in the 1990s, had been central to the discovery and publicizing of thirteen innocent men on death row in Illinois. Those thirteen exoneration cases were what led then-Governor George Ryan first to impose a moratorium on executions in 2000, then to appoint a special blue-ribbon committee to study and propose a slate of extensive reforms to the Illinois death penalty, and finally – on January 11, 2003, Ryan's last day in office – to commute the death sentences of every person on Illinois's death row.[16] The *Chicago Tribune*'s March 16, 2005, editorial about the no-doubt bill made this statement:

> Given the deeply troubling experience in Illinois, it should be easy for supporters and opponents of capital punishment to agree on this: When the state is going to impose the ultimate, irreversible punishment, there should be no doubt that the person paying for the crime is the one who committed it. That's the purpose of Tom Cross' bill, and that's why it should be law.[17]

The day after the *Tribune* editorial ran, the Illinois House of Representatives passed H.R. 2704 by a 66–49 vote.[18] The bill then moved to the Illinois Senate, where the Senate President, Emil Jones of Chicago, a liberal Democrat and death penalty abolitionist, had already declared his support.[19]

I was sufficiently dismayed by the way the bill had been whipsawed in the House Judiciary Committee to write a short op-ed letter, which was published by the *Chicago Tribune* in April 2005. In the letter, entitled "No Doubt, Death Penalty Reform is Difficult," I wrote this:

> One might think that such a reform would be easy to pass. But one would be wrong. The bill is strenuously opposed by both prosecutors (who claim that it would mean the end of the death penalty in Illinois) and abolitionists (who claim that it is part of a right-wing plot to increase the public legitimacy of the death penalty, end the current moratorium and resume

15 Editorial, "Leaving No Doubt," *Chicago Tribune*, March 16, 2005, Sec. C, at p. 22.

16 Jodi Wilgoren, "Citing Issue of Fairness, Governor Clears Out Death Row in Illinois," *New York Times*, Jan. 12, 2003, available online at http://www.nytimes.com/2003/01/12/us/citing-issue-of-fairness-governor-clears-out-death-row-in-illinois.html.

17 Editorial, supra note 15.

18 Christi Parsons & Erika Slife, "Tough Execution Rule Gains; Illinois House OKs Bill to Raise Standard for the Death Penalty," *Chicago Tribune*, March 17, 2005, Sec. C, at p. 4.

19 Id.

> executions in Illinois). Because of this two-pronged assault, the bill barely made it through the Illinois House and now awaits its fate in the Illinois Senate.
>
> Of course, the claims of the prosecutors and the abolitionists can't both be true. In fact, neither claim is true.... It's not a panacea for the death penalty, but it's a step in the right direction.[20]

On May 18, 2005, the Illinois Senate Executive Committee held a public hearing on H.R. 2704. Once again, I testified in favor, making many of the same arguments I had made at the House Judiciary Committee hearing back in March. Professor Andrew Leipold, a coauthor and close personal friend of mine, testified in opposition. Professor Leipold pointed out that having two different standards of proof of guilt – "beyond a reasonable doubt" for the guilt decision and "no doubt" for the capital sentencing decision – was likely to engender jury confusion and could, over time, actually erode the "beyond a reasonable doubt" standard to the detriment of all criminal defendants. This was a perfectly reasonable and carefully reasoned argument, and it illustrated how easily reasonable minds could disagree about the wisdom of the no-doubt proposal.

Unfortunately, the Senate committee hearing did not turn out to be a very welcoming place for such reasoned arguments. Neither my own words nor Professor Leipold's seemed to have any impact at all on the committee members. We both sat in silence as several leading prosecutors and public defenders got up and reprised their testimonies from the March hearing. Once again, we heard the same contradictory claims – one side claiming that the no-doubt bill was really an "abolition" bill, and the other side claiming that it was actually a bill to "restore" the death penalty. Of course, these same claims also had been made privately, during intense lobbying efforts over the preceding several weeks. I could tell from the reactions of the committee members that these arguments had taken their toll. When the prosecutors spoke, many Republican members of the committee, and a few Democrats, nodded their heads in agreement. When the public defenders spoke, many of the other Democrats on the committee seemed to approve. When the final vote was taken, the committee – controlled by Democrats – soundly defeated the bill on a 9–3 vote, ensuring its demise.[21]

[20] Joseph L. Hoffmann, "No Doubt, Death Penalty Reform is Difficult," *Chicago Tribune*, April 23, 2005, Voice of the People, Sec. C, at p. 24.

[21] Ray Long & Rick Pearson, "Death Penalty Bill Killed; Measure Would Have Set Highest Standard for Prosecutors," *Chicago Tribune*, May 19, 2005, Sec. C, at p. 1.

The point of this story is not to argue the merits or demerits of the no-doubt bill; it is to point out that the political rhetoric surrounding the bill was a little bit odd, to say the least. The bill was described, within the very same committee hearing, as both a bill designed to restore the death penalty in Illinois and a bill designed to abolish the death penalty in Illinois. It could not have been both of those things. In the end, though, *both* of these arguments prevailed. Conservative Senate Republicans and Democrats voted against the bill en masse because of the abolitionist charge, and liberal Democrats voted against it en masse because of the restorationist charge. Almost nobody was left in the middle to vote for the bill.

In short, everything turned out exactly as I had pessimistically predicted in my April letter to the *Chicago Tribune*:

> Death penalty proponents, including most prosecutors, resist anything that would make it harder to obtain a death sentence. Death penalty opponents don't really want to reform the system, either, because they would rather see it fail and collapse than be fixed and continue to exist. Finding the middle ground between these two extremes can be almost impossible.[22]

The sad experience of witnessing the demolition of the Illinois no-doubt bill caused me to begin to think a little bit differently than I had before about the political dynamics of death penalty reform. In the past, I had mostly observed situations in which reform proposals were being offered in an effort to modify an operational (or at least a semi-operational) death penalty system. Such reform proposals, more often than not, ended in total failure – because the support of those individuals with legitimate concerns about the unfairness, inequity, or overbreadth of capital punishment was usually completely outweighed by the vocal opposition of prosecutors, victims' advocates, and others who supported the continued broad availability of the death penalty.

A few death penalty reform proposals have managed to succeed, even against the odds, including a 2003 statutory change in Indiana that broadened the opportunity of the Indiana Supreme Court to receive new evidence on behalf of a capital defendant.[23] Another modest success was the so-called Fundamental Justice Amendment, which in 2003 gave the Illinois Supreme Court the legal authority to overturn any death sentence,

[22] Hoffmann, supra note 20.

[23] See Indiana Code 35–50-2–9 (k), available online at http://www.in.gov/legislative/ic/code/title35/ar50/ch2.html. The statute as amended provides the following:

without regard to procedural issues or other barriers to relief, "if the court finds that the death sentence is fundamentally unjust as applied to the particular case."[24] This reform was described by cosponsors Senator John Cullerton and Senator Kirk Dillard as "ground breaking in scope and conception," requiring the court to evaluate the death sentence as "a moral issue, not a legal one, ... based on the facts of the particular case and the moral compass of the decision maker."[25] Another original sponsor of the bill, Senator Peter Roskam, called it a "gut-check standard."[26]

Nonetheless, most death penalty reform efforts – at least if they involve making substantial changes to an existing and functioning death penalty system – cannot survive the polarized and hostile political dynamic that always surrounds the death penalty. I am now in the process of conducting an empirical analysis of state death penalty legislation over the past ten

(k) A person who has been sentenced to death and who has completed state post-conviction review proceedings may file a written petition with the supreme court seeking to present new evidence challenging the person's guilt or the appropriateness of the death sentence if the person serves notice on the attorney general. The supreme court shall determine, with or without a hearing, whether the person has presented previously undiscovered evidence that undermines confidence in the conviction or the death sentence. If necessary, the supreme court may remand the case to the trial court for an evidentiary hearing to consider the new evidence and its effect on the person's conviction and death sentence. The supreme court may not make a determination in the person's favor nor make a decision to remand the case to the trial court for an evidentiary hearing without first providing the attorney general with an opportunity to be heard on the matter.

24 See Illinois Legislative Code, Chapter 38, Paragraph 9–1 (i), 720 ILCS 5/9-1 (i), available online at http://www.ilga.gov/legislation/ilcs/fulltext.asp?DocName=072000050K9–1.

25 See John Cullerton, Kirk Dillard, & Peter G. Baroni, "Capital Punishment Reform in Illinois – A Model for the Nation," Dupage County Bar Assocation Brief, at 10–12 (April 2004), available online at www.ilesq.com/A_Model_for_the_Nation.doc; see also Robert Weisberg, *Apology, Legislation and Mercy*, 82 N.C. L. Rev. 1415, 1438 (2004) (statute "enables appellate judges to grant mercy to otherwise properly sentenced capital defendants because, in the view of the appellate court, the technical and procedural rules by which they were supposed to monitor capital sentencing could not capture the moral concerns that society demands"); Joseph L. Hoffmann, *Protecting the Innocent: The Massachusetts Governor's Council Report*, 95 J. Crim. L. & Criminology 561, 577 n. 83 (2005) (discussing the Fundamental Justice Amendment). Ironically, the Fundamental Justice Amendment has been largely ignored by the Illinois Supreme Court, which – despite the view of the cosponsors that it was a "ground breaking" reform – saw it as merely restating authority that the court already possessed. See People v. Thompson, 222 Ill. 2d 1; 853 N.E.2d 378; 2006 Ill. LEXIS 609 (2006); but see id. at 59 (McMorrow, J., dissenting).

26 See transcript of Illinois Senate, Regular Session, 92nd General Assembly, December 4, 2002, available online at http://www.ilga.gov/senate/transcripts/strans92/ST120402.pdf.

years or so that reveals just how precious little real progress of this kind has been made.

The political circumstances that doom most death penalty reform initiatives are depressing but fairly predictable. One group of usual suspects (those who advocate or lean toward abolition of the death penalty) proposes and supports most of these reform proposals, and a very different group of usual suspects (those who favor the death penalty) opposes almost all of them. The stronger side – usually, in most places, the opposing side – wins.

What I observed in Illinois in 2005, however, was a different kind of situation. In Illinois, the death penalty system had already become broken – at least in terms of actual executions – some five years earlier. A serious crisis of legitimacy had brought the entire "machinery of death"[27] to a grinding halt. It was crystal clear to all that it would take major legislative action – in the form of truly meaningful legislative reforms – to restart that machinery. Even after Governor George Ryan left office in early 2003, incoming Governor Rod Blagojevich – a supporter of capital punishment – felt compelled to continue the execution moratorium.[28] Blago's successor, Governor Pat Quinn, did so as well, explaining at the time that legislative reforms creating "zero tolerance" for error were a clear prerequisite before he would consider lifting the moratorium.[29]

However, legislative action to reform the death penalty, even when it occurs against the backdrop of a broken and dormant death penalty system, turns out to be extremely difficult to accomplish. That's because of the weird political dynamic that emerged in Illinois – where both sides turned sharply against the middle, for diametrically opposite reasons, leaving only a small minority of committed moderates in support of the proposed reform.

This dysfunctional political dynamic, creating strange bedfellows of liberals and conservatives in passionate alliance against the middle, tends to arise mostly in certain kinds of circumstances involving extreme

[27] The quoted language comes from Justice Blackmun's opinion in Callins v. Collins, 510 U.S. 1141, 1145 (1994) (Blackmun, J., dissenting from denial of certiorari); see also infra note 50.

[28] Rick Pearson, "Governor Says Ban to Stay on Death Penalty; but Gambling May Be Expanded," *Chicago Tribune*, April 24, 2003, Sec. C, at p. 1.

[29] NBC Chicago, "Quinn: Keep Moratorium on Death Penalty," August 3, 2009, available online at http://www.nbcchicago.com/news/politics/illinois-quinn-moratorium-death-penalty-52307157.html.

political polarization. We saw something a little bit like it in connection with the so-called Obamacare health insurance legislation in 2010,[30] which nearly foundered because some liberals in Congress threatened to join almost all of the conservatives in opposition to a large and messy compromise bill. The conservatives opposed the bill on principle, even though their involvement in the drafting process might have improved the bill immensely. Some liberals also opposed it because they passionately believed they had the political upper hand and could manage to enact a "better" bill more in line with their own political interests.

In the death penalty context, many abolitionists believe, as a matter of principle as well as a long-term practical strategy, that they should not support any death penalty reforms that might succeed only in legitimating and thereby entrenching the death penalty.[31] Such liberal opposition to death penalty reform becomes especially likely whenever the death penalty is placed in temporary hiatus as a result of a serious legitimacy crisis – precisely because the ultimate abolition victory then begins to seem closer than ever.

On the other side, however, a large proportion of retentionists long ago became deeply suspicious of almost all serious death penalty reform efforts, especially those that would significantly reduce the total number of death sentences and executions. Retentionists tend to see such reforms as mere baby steps in the direction of abolition, especially when (as in the usual scenario) they are being proposed and advocated mostly by persons known to be abolitionists.

In situations such as the one in Illinois, both liberals and conservatives tend to be pushed to their respective corners. This was the extreme and dysfunctional political dynamic that destroyed the Illinois no-doubt bill. It is possible that the bill would have been defeated anyway, but it had no chance at all once the committed and passionate forces on both of the political wings turned their full fire against it.

Looking back, I probably should have recognized the same dysfunctional political dynamic a couple of years earlier, when I served as Co-Reporter for the Massachusetts Governor's Council on Capital

[30] Sheryl Gay Stolberg & Robert Pear, "Obama Signs Health Care Overhaul Bill, With a Flourish," *New York Times*, available online at http://www.nytimes.com/2010/03/24/health/policy/24health.html.

[31] See, e.g., Carol S. Steiker & Jordan M. Steiker, *Should Abolitionists Support Legislative "Reform" of the Death Penalty?*, 63 Ohio St. L. J. 417, 424 (2002) ("[W]e worry that reform may actually lead us away from abolition, toward a future where the death penalty remains a stable and accepted part of our criminal justice system").

Punishment.[32] The council was appointed in 2003 by then-Governor Mitt Romney to fulfill a campaign promise he had made to try to restore the death penalty to the Commonwealth of Massachusetts. The council included prominent prosecutors, defense attorneys, medical experts, and forensic scientists. The council was given a full range of discretion – indeed, the Governor himself personally and strongly encouraged the council – to include any proposals that would help to make the death penalty both fair and foolproof, or at least as fair and foolproof as any human institution can possibly be. Working with the Governor's Council provided me with the rare chance to develop a set of "best practices" for the death penalty.

The council unanimously agreed on ten broad recommendations for a better death penalty. The proposed reforms included the following: (1) a very narrowly defined list of aggravating circumstances that could support a death sentence; (2) the statewide review of any local prosecutor's decision to seek a death sentence; (3) improvements to defense representation in capital cases; (4) changes to decrease the biasing effect of the selection process for death-qualified juries; (5) special jury instructions about the dangers of overreliance on human evidence; (6) a requirement of DNA or similarly "conclusive" scientific evidence supporting the defendant's guilt; (7) a no-doubt standard for proof of guilt at the capital sentencing phase of the trial; (8) independent scientific review of all scientific evidence in a capital case, including the accreditation of crime labs and the certification of forensic scientists; (9) broad authority for trial and appellate courts to set aside unjust death sentences; and (10) a "death penalty review commission" to review all claims of substantive error in capital cases and to study and report on the causes of such errors.[33] The Sunday *New York Times Magazine* – perhaps with tongue in cheek – actually included the Massachusetts death penalty proposal in its special December 2004 issue, "The 4th Annual Year in Ideas."[34]

Although I still cringe every time someone refers to the Massachusetts proposal as an attempt to create the "perfect death penalty," I was very glad that the Massachusetts Governor's Council could agree on a set of

[32] The Council's Final Report is available online at http://www.lawlib.state.ma.us/docs/5-3-04Governorsreportcapitalpunishment.pdf; see also Joseph L. Hoffmann, *Protecting the Innocent*, supra note 25, at p. 561.

[33] See Final Report, Massachusetts Governor's Council on Capital Punishment, supra note 32.

[34] Emily Bazelon, "The Foolproof Death Penalty," 4th Annual Year in Ideas, *New York Times Magazine*, December 12, 2004, at p. 73.

bold recommendations that, if ever adopted either in Massachusetts or elsewhere, would surely go a long way toward addressing and remedying many of the problems that currently plague the administration of capital punishment. However, in the seven years since the Massachusetts Council's report was issued – and during which it was the subject of both a major academic conference and a major law review symposium[35] – *not one* of the reform proposals contained in the report has been adopted by any state with a death penalty. The Illinois no-doubt bill, H.R. 2704, came the closest, but – even in a state such as Illinois, with a patently obvious and desperate need for serious death penalty reform – it still failed.

I should have predicted this outcome from the start. On the day that the Massachusetts report was made public, the death penalty abolitionists predictably came out firing. One such critic opined that the proposal "doesn't hit at enough of the real problems in the system that causes false convictions"; another simply called it "wrong-headed."[36] A little more surprising to me, at the time, was the almost simultaneous negative response from the death penalty retentionists. For example, Kent Scheidegger of the Criminal Justice Legal Foundation argued that the proposed statute was far too narrow in its death-eligibility criteria: "If you're going to define the worst of the worst, I think the kidnapping, rape, and murder of a child has got to be up there."[37] Other advocates of capital punishment likewise turned their guns quickly against the proposal, despite the obvious fact that it might well have created the best opportunity in years to resurrect the death penalty in Massachusetts. That did not seem to matter. Most death penalty advocates seemed to prefer no death penalty at all to one that would be accompanied by such a strong set of safeguards and limitations.

Thanks to the report of the Massachusetts Governor's Council on Capital Punishment, Governor Romney managed to fulfill his promise to develop a bill and send it into the legislative process. The bill failed miserably, however, falling by an almost 2–1 margin in the Massachusetts House.[38]

The Massachusetts debacle should have opened my eyes to the hard reality that neither side of the death penalty debate really wants to see

[35] See Symposium Issue, *The Massachusetts Governor's Council on Capital Punishment*, 80 Ind. L. J. (Winter 2005).

[36] See Scott S. Greenberger, "Panel Offers Death Penalty Plan; State Would Use Standard of 'No Doubt,'" *Boston Globe*, May 3, 2004, Metro Sec., at p. A1.

[37] Id.

[38] Brian C. Mooney, "Facing Hard Realities, Romney Accrued Modest List of Successes," *Boston Globe*, December 16, 2005, Metro Sec., at p. A1.

real and substantial reform of the death penalty. Perhaps I did not come to this realization at the time because the Massachusetts death penalty turned out to be such a nonevent. Nothing came of it, and outside of Massachusetts – perhaps with the exception of the readers of the Sunday *New York Times Magazine* – hardly anyone heard about it. I basically chalked the whole thing up to experience and moved on.

That brings us back to Illinois, where the very same dysfunctional politics of the death penalty ultimately led to an event of worldwide significance – the recent decision to abolish the Illinois death penalty. What lessons, if any, can be drawn from the way that capital punishment in Illinois eventually met its demise?

In recent years, a number of important scholarly analyses have been published that address the future course that abolition of the death penalty in America (and elsewhere in the world) might take. Many of the most impressive of these analyses appear as contributions to a recent book coedited by Professors Charles Ogletree, Jr., and Austin Sarat.[39] Some of the possible paths to abolition discussed therein include (1) classic Furman-type de jure abolition; (2) continued judicial narrowing through the "evolving standards of decency" approach, a la *Atkins v. Virginia*[40] and *Simmons v. South Carolina*[41]; (3) gradual desuetude in a growing number of weakly retentionist states; (4) bold acts of legislative or executive courage, as occurred recently in New Mexico and New Jersey; and (5) smaller acts of subtle resistance or outright defiance by low-level actors that effectively gum up the capital punishment works, eventually perhaps leading to a political decision to abolish.[42]

[39] Charles J. Ogletree, Jr., & Austin Sarat, The Road to Abolition? The Future of Capital Punishment in the United States (New York University Press, 2009); see also David T. Johnson & Franklin E. Zimring, The Next Frontier: National Development, Political Change, and the Death Penalty in Asia (Oxford University Press 2009) (discussing prospects for abolition of the death penalty in Asian countries).

[40] Atkins v. Virginia, 536 U.S. 304 (2002) (rejecting the death penalty for mentally retarded defendants).

[41] Roper v. Simmons, 543 U.S. 551 (2005) (rejecting the death penalty for juvenile defendants).

[42] See Carol S. Steiker & Jordan M. Steiker, "The Beginning of the End?," in Ogletree & Sarat, supra note 39, at p. 97 (discussing judicial abolition, judicial narrowing, and gradual desuetude); Bernard E. Harcourt, "Abolition in the United States by 2050: On Political Capital and Ordinary Acts of Resistance," in Ogletree & Sarat, supra note 39, at p. 72 (discussing acts of political courage as well as acts of small-scale resistance); Michael L. Radelet, "The Executioner's Waning Defenses," in Ogletree & Sarat, supra note 39, at p. 19 (discussing prospects for Furman-style abolition decision by the Supreme Court).

What all of these abolition paths have in common is the requirement that somebody – a judge, a governor, a legislator, a low-level actor, or some combination thereof – must actually make the controversial decision that an active and functioning death penalty must be stopped. Somebody must go on the record and make a visible choice that, even during this era of growing public and judicial skepticism about capital punishment,[43] may nonetheless have serious negative consequences for the chooser, either politically or (if it is a judge rather than a political figure) in terms of the perceived legitimacy of the judiciary.

It seems to me, however, that the recent Illinois experience suggests the possibility of a new and different path to abolition – one that is potentially important because it does not rely on any single actor or set of actors to make the difficult decision to abolish an active death penalty. For lack of a better term, I call this alternative the path of "I've fallen and I can't get up."[44]

Here's how it works: If the death penalty somehow goes off the tracks – even temporarily – for any reason that calls the basic legitimacy of the death penalty system into serious question in the eyes of John Q. Public, then it may prove infeasible to put it back onto the tracks and resume normal operations unless, and until, significant legislative reforms have succeeded in restoring that legitimacy. However, the deep political dysfunctionality that surrounds the death penalty may make it virtually impossible for the legislature to accomplish such significant reforms. At that point, the death penalty ends up in permanent stasis – the machinery has ground to a halt, and it cannot be restarted. The result is a kind of virtual abolition.

That is exactly what happened in Illinois. During the ten years after the moratorium on executions in Illinois was originally declared by Governor George Ryan in 2000, some relatively modest reforms were enacted by the Illinois legislature, but not nearly enough.[45] The most significant of these

43 See, e.g., Baze v. Rees, 553 U.S. 35 (2008) (Stevens, J., concurring in the judgment) (expressing strong personal view that the death penalty is unconstitutional under the Eighth Amendment, due to the costs greatly outweighing the benefits, but nevertheless declining to ignore existing Supreme Court precedent that the death penalty remains constitutional).

44 This well-known phrase was first used in a 1989 series of commercials for LifeCall, a medical and security alarm device. See http://en.wikipedia.org/wiki/I%27ve_fallen_and_I_can%27t_get_up!

45 The reforms that were actually enacted in Illinois – including both reforms specific to the death penalty and those that affected the criminal justice system in general – are listed and described in John Cullerton, Kirk Dillard, & Peter G. Baroni, "Capital Punishment

legislative reforms were those that changed the treatment in court of certain kinds of human evidence – changes that, for the most part, were not explicitly limited to capital cases. Only a small handful of changes were made to the death penalty statute itself in Illinois over those ten years: (1) minor changes, going in both directions, in the scope of the aggravating circumstances that create eligibility for death; (2) a change in the standard for the weighing of aggravating and mitigating circumstances by the jury; (3) a nonbinding suggestion that prosecutors consult on statewide guidelines for seeking the death penalty; (4) the expansion of judicial authority, at both the trial and appellate levels, to overturn death sentences; (5) the creation of a statewide fund to pay for the expenses of capital trials; and (6) the creation of a state-level death penalty study commission.[46] None of the changes managed to convince a series of Illinois governors, or the public in general, that the Illinois capital punishment system could once again be trusted and that executions should therefore be resumed.

Was it possible that some unforeseeable event, such as a particularly heinous capital crime, could have broken this logjam and led to the resumption of executions in Illinois – either with or without further legislative reforms?[47] Of course. That kind of event can always be a game changer, no matter what the underlying political dynamics may be. But in Illinois, that didn't happen.

Reform in Illinois – A Model for the Nation," Dupage County Bar Assocation Brief, at 10–12 (April 2004), available online at www.ilesq.com/A_Model_for_the_Nation.doc.

The authors of this article list nineteen reforms that were adopted in Illinois, all of them during 2003. However, the magnitude of this legislative effort must be measured against the totality of what was originally proposed by Governor George Ryan's Commission on Capital Punishment in 2002. The Commission's Report contained eighty-five separate proposed reforms – the vast majority of which were never even considered by the Illinois legislature. See Report of the Governor's Commission on Capital Punishment, April, 2002, available online at http://www.idoc.state.il.us/ccp/ccp/reports/commission_report/summary_recommendations.pdf; see also Rob Warden, *Illinois Death Penalty Reform: How It Happened, What It Promises*, 95 J. of Crim. L. & Criminology 381, 383 (2005) ("Some of the measures are tepid, some apply only to murder cases, and the efficacy of others will depend on how they are implemented – God, as Mies van der Rohe reminds us, is in the details").

[46] See Cullerton, Dillard, & Baroni, supra note 45.

[47] In Massachusetts, the shocking and brutal murder of ten-year-old Jeffrey Curley, whose body was sexually assaulted and then dumped in a river, nearly prompted the return of capital punishment in that state in 1997; the bill eventually came within one vote of passing. See Adrian Walker & Doris Sue Wong, "No Death Penalty, By One Vote; Momentum for a State Law is Halted as House Member Changes His Mind," *Boston Globe*, November 7, 1997, Metro Sec., at p. A1.

Furthermore, the longer the implementation of the death penalty remained dormant in Illinois, the more the people of Illinois began to question whether it was worth the time, trouble, and tax dollars to keep on sentencing defendants to death. Such questions began to be raised with increasing frequency by Illinois politicians, because even though many of them want to appear "tough on crime" by supporting capital punishment, they usually have an even greater political incentive to do whatever they possibly can to ensure that they do not have to raise taxes on their constituents – especially to support a capital punishment system that is no longer even operational. In Illinois, this ultimately proved to be a lethal three-way combination: (1) perpetual legislative impasse that precluded serious death penalty reform; (2) growing public reluctance to pay for an expensive but nonfunctioning death penalty system; and (3) the slow but gradual realization that life goes on, even without an active death penalty.[48] This was the lethal combination of forces that eventually brought down the Illinois death penalty.

[48] See Franklin E. Zimring, *Plenary Address: Symbol and Substance in the Massachusetts Commission Report*, 80 Ind. L. J. 113, 121–122 (2005):

> All over the modern world, the abolition of capital punishment, that now extends to every developed nation but the United States and Japan, has been a two-stage process. Stage one, which happens long before capital punishment is ever abolished, is that execution ceases to play any significant part in the process of crime control. Then later, sometimes a lot later, we stop the practice. We have policy debates after stage one about state execution. We know we don't need it. But now we can debate whether nonetheless we might still want it. It might make us feel good. But the debate is fatefully altered by the fact that we know we don't need it.
>
> Executions, in my analysis, stopped being anything we needed for crime control in the United States by the middle of the twentieth century, if not before. Since about 1997, virtually everybody acknowledges in one way or another that we don't need executions in the United States. Now we're only debating whether we want them.... Now, what does this have to do with the Massachusetts Blue Ribbon Commission? I'm going to use a Texas expression to describe the Massachusetts Blue Ribbon Commission Report's penalty standard. I think that that report describes a death penalty that is "all hat and no cattle." It prescribes a death penalty that would never in all likelihood produce a single execution. Does that make the report unimportant? No, it doesn't. But it gives the report a different kind of importance. The death penalty in Massachusetts, certainly for Governor Romney, has a great symbolic importance. But it isn't that Governor Romney wants actual executions. Not with this Commission Report! What he needs is a statute on the books. But the long-range actuarial problem with that in political morality and legal theory is that if we really don't wish to take gratuitous risks of fatal mistakes, and if we really know we don't need a death penalty for public safety, why take chances at all? Why play with symbols? What do we have to gain? I do not think that that is a question that the Blue Ribbon Commission was designed to answer, and I'm not arguing that the work of the

The glaring irony here is that the same extremist politics that typically thwarts most efforts at serious reform of the death penalty when the system is fully operational can also make it virtually impossible to enact serious reform of the death penalty, even when such reform becomes absolutely necessary because the system has ceased to operate as a result of a crisis of legitimacy. In other words, the same political forces that usually work to preserve the capital punishment status quo can also, under a different set of circumstances, serve to destroy it.

I make no claim that this alternative path to abolition is preferable to any of the other paths. Indeed, there are many reasons to favor the others, not least of which is the fact that what I have called "virtual abolition" is relatively easier to reverse. I claim only that more attention should be paid to this alternative abolition scenario, because – in at least some real-world situations – it may prove far more feasible than awaiting a bold act of political or judicial courage. In addition, recognizing even the possibility of virtual abolition may help to highlight the true value of certain intermediate strategies. For example, the American Bar Association's ongoing call for a national death penalty moratorium may start to look like a pretty good long-term abolition strategy, once one recognizes the political path by which such a temporary moratorium can lead first to virtual, and eventually to actual, abolition.[49]

Justice Harry Blackmun once famously remarked, "I no longer shall tinker with the machinery of death."[50] The United States Supreme Court as a whole, however, has proved ready, willing, and more than able to tinker with the death penalty repeatedly over the past twenty-five years – notwithstanding the fact that such tinkering may not have done any real good. State legislatures, in contrast, are generally far less likely to tinker with the machinery of death because of the extreme political

Commission in any sense answered that question. But I think the risks they were willing to take to avoid error and the standards that they provided as minima for the invocation of capital punishment have made it quite clear that the penalty that they are legislating for is no longer regarded as a necessity in the control of crime in the state that they were discussing. And since we are all now sure we don't need state executions, sooner, rather than later, they will cease.

49 The ABA's Moratorium Project started in 2001. See http://www.americanbar.org/groups/individual_rights/projects_awards/death_penalty_moratorium_implementation_project.html.

In the words of Frank Zimring, "Inevitably, the right kind of moratorium is just a way of buying abolition of the death penalty on the installment plan." See Franklin E. Zimring, Plenary Address, supra note 48, at 124.

50 Callins v. Collins, 510 U.S. 1141, 1145 (1994) (Blackmun, J., dissenting from denial of certiorari) ("From this day forward, I no longer shall tinker with the machinery of death."); see also supra note 27.

dysfunctionality that surrounds the issue of capital punishment. That inability to act, in certain kinds of situations, can lead to a virtual abolition that may prove to be just about as effective as the real thing. We have now seen this happen in Illinois, and it could also happen elsewhere. In such situations, nobody ever really has to stop the "machinery of death." For want of a decent mechanic, the machinery simply rusts in place.

2

Bill Stuntz and the Principal–Agent Problem in American Criminal Law

Richard H. McAdams

INTRODUCTION

In economics, a principal–agent problem arises when there is a divergence of interest between one person – the principal – and the agent he or she employs (or otherwise relies on) to perform some costly task.[1] Law-and-economics scholars should pay as much attention to the principal–agent problem in criminal law as they do to the problem in corporate law – perhaps more.[2] Although the corporate division of ownership and control creates a substantial agency problem, it seems to pose a *less* substantial problem than the one in criminal law. Among other reasons, corporate agents are hierarchically arranged so that shareholders need only monitor and motivate the top corporate officer, who can then monitor and motivate lower-ranked agents. By contrast, the public's agents in the criminal justice system – legislators, police, prosecutors, juries, chief executives, and prison officials – are not hierarchically arranged; they enjoy separate discretionary domains. Moreover, corporate principals can usually find reliable output measures for what they care about – share price – in daily newspapers, whereas criminal law output data are inherently more complicated, contestable, and remote. Finally, corporations are subject to market competition, which will eliminate organizations that do too poor a job of controlling agency costs. Criminal justice agents are rarely subject to market competition and, by comparison, political competition allows more agency slack.

[1] See, e.g., Eric A. Posner, Coase Lecture: Agency Models in Law and Economics (2000).

[2] The point I am making about criminal law applies to public law more generally: law-and-economics scholars of public law are far less likely to examine pervasive principal–agent problems than are economists of corporate law. We do not have a substantial literature, for example, on how best to structure the pay of military generals, teachers, cabinet officers, bank examiners, or welfare case workers.

Despite these points, the field of law and economics pays not more but less attention to agency costs in criminal law than in corporate law. Agency costs are famously central to the economic analysis of corporate governance and have been since Jensen and Meckling's classic 1976 article on the subject.[3] Canonical statements of the field begin with agency costs and model corporate law as a mechanism for minimizing those costs.[4] By contrast, principal–agent models play at best a peripheral role in the economics of criminal law. Here, the analogue to Jensen and Meckling is Gary Becker's 1968 article on the economics of criminal law; the analogue to agency costs is optimal punishment. Becker first showed how an ideal social planner might achieve optimality by minimizing the sum of crime costs and crime-control costs. Since 1968, law-and-economics scholars have stayed largely on the path of optimal punishment, extending Becker's model in countless directions. Not everything is about optimal punishment, and there is some literature specifically on agency problems among criminal law enforcers, particularly about prosecutors[5] and also the problem of corruption.[6] There are even a few,

[3] See M. C. Jensen & W. H. Meckling, *Theory of the Firm: Managerial Behavior, Agency Costs and Ownership Structure*, 3 J. Fin. Econ. 303 (1976). Ronald Coase's paper on the firm is also an essential starting point. See Ronald H. Coase, *The Nature of the Firm*, 4 Economica 386 (1937). He characterized firms as contractual in nature and the agency theory is then a theory of the problems that arise between the various contracting parties.

[4] See Frank H. Easterbrook & Daniel R. Fischel, The Economic Structure of Corporate Law 14 (1991) ("To understand corporate law you must understand how the balance of advantage among devices for controlling agency costs differs across firms and shifts from time to time"); Robert Daines & Michael Klausner, "Economic Analysis of Corporate Law," in The New Palgrave Dictionary of Economics 257, 257 (Steven Durlauf & Lawrence E. Blume, eds., 2nd ed., 2008), where they state that the "primary 'contract' of interest is that between management and shareholders [which is] conceptualized in terms of the agency-cost model of Jensen and Meckling (1976), with management viewed collectively as agent, and shareholders viewed collectively as principal"; and John Armour, Henry Hansmann, & Reinier Kraakman, "Agency Problems and Legal Strategies," in The Anatomy of Corporate Law: A Comparative and Functional Approach 35 (2d ed., 2009).

[5] See, e.g., Stephanos Bibas, *Prosecutorial Regulation versus Prosecutorial Accountability*, 157 U Pa L Rev 959 (2009); Sanford C. Gordon & Gregory A. Huber, *The Political Economy of Prosecution*, 5 Annual Rev. Law & Soc. Sci. 8.1-8.22 (2009); J. Mark Ramseyer, Eric Rasmusen, & Manu Raghav, *Convictions versus Conviction Rates: The Prosecutor's Choice*, 11 Amer. Law & Econ. Rev. 47 (2009); Anne Morrison Piehl, Edward L. Glaeser, & Daniel P. Kessler, *What Do Prosecutors Maximize? An Analysis of the Federalization of Drug Crimes*, 2 Amer. Law & Econ. Rev. 259 (2000).

[6] See, e.g., Susan Rose-Ackerman, Corruption and Government: Causes, Consequences, and Reform (1999); A. Mitchell Polinsky & Steven Shavell, *Corruption and Optimal Law Enforcement*, 81 J. Public Econ. 1 (2001).

though just a few, papers on the more general agency problem in criminal enforcement.[7] However, compared to optimal punishment, there is no sustained or comprehensive analysis of the agency problem and no conventional model for criminal system agents.[8] For instance, there is a large economic literature on how best to structure the pay of corporate CEOs, but virtually no literature on how best to structure the pay of police or prosecutors.[9]

Thus, in Mitchell Polinsky's and Steven Shavell's recent syntheses of the economics of public law enforcement and criminal law,[10] they focus overwhelmingly on the issue of optimal punishment because that topic continues to dominate the literature. By contrast, their syntheses give scant attention to the principal–agent problem in criminal law. When Polinsky and Shavell do discuss the problem, it is only in the limited context in which the potential criminal is a collective entity such as a corporation that consists of principals and agents. In other words, the discussion includes the agency problem within the potential *targets* of criminal punishment but does not address the agency problem for the *creators* and *enforcers* of criminal law – legislators, police, prosecutors, chief executives, and others. In short, it would be extremely peculiar to imagine an economic scholar of corporate law who did not refer to the principal–agent problem in her or his work, but one could thrive as an economic scholar of criminal law without making any mention of the concept.

One might justify this differential treatment of agency costs by noting that corporate law is contractarian but criminal law is not. The state does not dictate most corporate action; it seeks only to create default rules to

7 See David Friedman, *Why Not Hang Them All: The Virtues of Inefficient Punishment*, 107 J. Pol. Econ. S259 (1999); Keith N. Hylton & Vikramaditya S. Khanna, "Political Economy of Criminal Procedure," in Criminal Law and Economics (N. Garoupa, ed., 2009).

8 To illustrate the difference, on September 28, 2011, I conducted two Westlaw searches on the JLR database. As an estimate of the articles addressing optimal punishment, I retrieved 93 documents by searching: (economic/s criminal) /p ((optimal efficient) /3 (deterrence punishment incapacitation)). As an estimate of the number of articles on the agency problem in criminal law, I retrieved only 17 documents by searching: (economic/s criminal) /p ("principal-agent" "agency costs" "problem of agency").

9 On prosecutors, see Tracey L. Meares, *Rewards for Good Behavior: Influencing Prosecutorial Discretion and Conduct with Financial Incentives*, 64 Fordham L. Rev. 851 (1995).

10 See A. Mitchell Polinsky & Steven Shavell, "Public Enforcement of Law," in Handbook of Law & Economics 139 (A. Mitchell Polinsky & Steven Shavell, eds., 2007); A. Mitchell Polinsky & Steven Shavell, "Public Enforcement of Law," in 5 The New Palgrave Dictionary of Economics 38 (Steven Durlauf & Lawrence E. Blume, eds., 2nd ed., 2008).

enable efficient private organization. The aim of those default rules is to minimize agency costs. By contrast, in criminal law, the state does not seek merely to enable private contracting and to minimize agency costs among law enforcers. Optimal punishment theory aims to explain what ends the mandatory criminal rules seek to maximize.

Nonetheless, even if it made sense for economic scholars to *begin* the analysis of criminal law with the study of optimal punishment, it is not sensible for the field to progress for decades without a shared and sustained inquiry into the problem of criminal law agents. Indeed, the agency lacuna in criminal law and procedure presents a serious problem for those studying optimal punishment: There is no single social planner to implement the policies of optimal punishment; worse, real-world criminal law agents lack the information and incentive to coordinate their overlapping powers to achieve this optimal outcome. As one simple example, consider Becker's famous prescription that optimality requires inversely calibrating the severity of sanctions with the probability of detection. His specific recommendation was to increase severity and decrease the certainty of punishment. Economists appear not to have noticed that the incentives motivating police and prosecutors usually cause them to spend greater effort to investigate crimes carrying heavier penalties. If the legislature raises the sanction for drunk driving or identity theft, that will likely cause the probability of detection for those crimes to rise rather than fall. Thus, there is nothing terribly novel about the claim that police and prosecutors are agents of the public, but there remains too much novelty in exploring the implications of this idea.[11] What we really need to know is how to structure the agency relationships in the criminal justice system so as to minimize agency costs and *then* how to optimize the system subject to the remaining constraints of agency costs.

It should be embarrassing to economists that they lack a detailed and comprehensive account of criminal law agents that is based on a large body of research. The good news is that we have the work of Bill Stuntz. Against the background in which law-and-economics scholars neglect the principal–agent problem in criminal law, Stuntz made the issue central to his analysis of American criminal law and procedure. The irony is that Bill is not, by most accounts including his own, a law-and-economics

[11] I criticize economists in the text, but I should note that retributive theorists are worse on this score, generally giving no attention to the institutional framework of criminal law. Whereas economics has neglected its own agency tools to explore criminal law institutions, I do not believe retributive theorists have any such tools.

scholar. His scholarship does not contain formal models. He uses little economic terminology and only rarely refers to the conflicts he discusses as principal–agent problems. Nevertheless, he leads other commendable noneconomist legal scholars[12] in identifying the incentives of the many public agents in the criminal justice system and how those incentives lead criminal justice agents to act against the public interest. In particular, Bill Stuntz identifies complex *interactions* between independent criminal justice agents, who sometimes produce unintended synergies that make a situation worse than the mere sum of its individual parts. Bill is not the only criminal law scholar who outperforms economists in applying the economic concept of agency costs to the field of criminal law. He is simply the best.

My chapter proceeds in two parts. The first part provides a critique of the economic literature on criminal law, explaining the severe principal–agent problems that infect American criminal law, why they deserve more attention than optimal punishment, and indeed why the agency problem limits the practical value of that literature. This part also attempts to supply an agenda for future economic scholarship, namely to describe in broad outline what is necessary to understand the obstacles that agency costs pose for optimal punishment. The second part turns to the criminal procedure scholarship of Bill Stuntz, interpreting it as an exploration of the agency problem in criminal law. What distinguishes Stuntz's work from the occasional economics paper or the more frequent legal paper on law enforcement agents is his focus on the big picture, his frequent insight that the explanation for some phenomenon is not a misalignment in the incentives of one particular agent – legislators or police or prosecutors – but on the dynamic relationship between those agents. Economists interested in addressing the agency problem in criminal law enforcement should start with Stuntz's work.

I. THE AGENCY PROBLEM IN CRIMINAL LAW

In their classic book on corporate law, Frank Easterbrook and Daniel Fischel state that "To understand corporate law you must understand how the balance of advantage among devices for controlling agency costs

[12] See, e.g., Rachel E. Barkow, *Administering Crime*, 52 UCLA L. Rev. 715 (2005); Stephanos Bibas, *Prosecutorial Regulation versus Prosecutorial Accountability*, 157 U Pa L Rev 959 (2009); Daniel Richman, *Prosecutors and their Agents, Agents and their Prosecutors*, 103 Colum. L. Rev. 749 (2003).

differs across firms and shifts from time to time.... Without answering difficult questions about the effectiveness of different devices for controlling agency costs, one cannot determine the appropriate allocation of rights."[13] It astonishes me that I can find no one who has said the same about criminal law and procedure, so let me (apparently) be the first: To paraphrase Easterbrook and Fischel, understanding criminal law enforcement requires understanding "how the balance of advantage among devices for controlling agency costs differs across" governmental functions and jurisdictions. "Without answering difficult questions about the effectiveness of different devices for controlling agency costs, one cannot determine the appropriate allocation" of governmental powers and individual rights.

Some may balk at the idea of applying a principal–agent model to the criminal justice system, but economists and political scientists long ago began to conceptualize government actors as agents of the public. As with the model of the firm, this framework has multiple principals as well as multiple agents. Shareholders or members of the public constitute the principals, whereas the agents are the firm's officers and employees or, respectively, the public's legislators, police, prosecutors, judges, chief executives, and so on. The idea that the latter are appropriately modeled as agents is old.

Because the idea is old, others may balk at my complaint that the economic literature slights the principal–agent relationships in criminal law. To repeat, my complaint is *not* that no one has ever thought of the idea before – I have cited several authors who have – but that the economic literature of criminal law does not take the idea seriously enough. There are a few scattered papers but no sustained attention; there is nothing like a comprehensive theory of criminal justice agents and nothing like the sophistication of the literature on optimal punishment. That literature grows increasingly refined while generally ignoring fundamental agency problems of implementing its recommendations. What I mean by this complaint will become clearer as I describe the severity of the overall agency problem, focusing on the whole rather than just some part of it.

Ultimately, we should want to explain why individuals in modern societies turn over the problem of antisocial behavior – crime – to a set of specialist agents. We also want to know why societies select government for the tasks of defining crimes, apprehending offenders, adjudicating guilt,

[13] See Frank H. Easterbrook & Daniel R. Fischel, The Economic Structure of Corporate Law 14 (1991).

and punishing criminals. Some literature addresses the related question of why informal sanctions or the tort system are individually or collectively not adequate to deter socially costly behavior. For present purposes, I merely note that modern societies do choose to have a separate system and to turn the tasks over to specialists, who are, for the most part, government officials. These are the public's agents.

As with shareholders in a firm, part of the principal–agent problem is that the public is inattentive. The other part of the problem is that agents lack the incentive to act in the public's interest. I explain each point in the following subsections, paying particular attention to the situations in which agents are not hierarchically arranged but exercise some independent final authority. The scope of the overall principal–agent problem emerges from this consideration of the individual problems.

A. An Inattentive Principal

In general, the public faces the same problems as do the shareholders in a firm. Individuals in the public have a collective action problem in monitoring and motivating their agents. First, no one has a strong incentive to be informed, given that an individual's ability to influence the agents is so small. For elected agents (legislators, mayors, district attorneys, sheriffs, and some judges), a citizen can influence the agent by threatening to vote against her or him in the next election. For unelected agents (police officers and some judges), the citizen can vote against the incumbent who could have fired or disciplined those agents. However, one vote will almost never affect the outcome. An individual might also incur costs to influence the votes of others, but this solution presents the collective action problem that each individual prefers to let someone else become informed and then organize voters to punish ineffective agents. Thus, it remains rational for most citizens to be fairly ignorant about crime rates, criminal law, and criminal processes, and the evidence suggests that most people *are* ignorant. Beyond rationality, citizens may be subject to the availability heuristic, among other biases, making them prone to generalize excessively from a few salient cases, such as those rare crimes or trials the media covers. Agents can then exploit the public's rational and irrational ignorance.

Nonetheless, there are several ways in which it is costlier for the public to monitor criminal law agents than it is for shareholders to monitor the corporation. One reason is that there is better information available about corporations than there is about criminal enforcers. Frequently, shareholders care only about movements in share price because their only concern with corporate behavior is financial. Under the efficient markets hypothesis, the best prediction of future share price is the present share price. Furthermore, there is little ambiguity about present share price; reliable data are reported in daily newspapers and online. Even if one rejects the efficient markets hypothesis and thinks it is possible to "beat the market," the law mandates a supply of useful information for making judgments about future share price. Securities regulations require various disclosures and create civil and criminal liability for misrepresentation.

For criminal law enforcement, not only is the information less available, there is ambiguity about the central criminal justice metric – the crime rate. Social scientists debate the merits of the FBI's *Uniform Crime Reports*, which certainly understate crime rates, versus the *National Crime Victimization Survey* series, which might overstate or understate them, depending on how well people remember and report victimization. City governments and police seem to think that the public relies on crime reports for judging the crime rate; there is evidence of such agents manipulating the numbers to create the appearance of improvement.[14] Unlike the manipulation of information about publicly traded stocks, "massaging" crime data creates no civil or criminal liability for criminal justice agents.

In any event, the evaluation of criminal law enforcers requires estimating the effect of their behavior on future crime rates. Even if *present* crime rates were reliable and unambiguous, there is no theory analogous to the efficient markets hypothesis, so there is no reason to believe that the best estimate of the future crime rate is the present crime rate. Moreover, the law does very little to supply citizens with information on which to base their estimates. The best analogue to the firm's underlying financial data might be the way police and prosecutors presently allocate their enforcement resources. There is no legal duty, though, to disclose such information, and there is some reason to keep it secret. If the police reveal the existing number of wiretaps for particular offenses or prosecutors publicize their policy not to prosecute certain offenses, they may aid criminals in structuring their crimes to avoid detection or prosecution.

[14] See, e.g., William K. Rashbaum, *Retired Officers Raise Questions on Crime Data*, New York Times, Feb. 6, 2010; Al Baker & William K. Rashbaum, *New York City to Examine Reliability of Its Crime Reports*, New York Times, Jan. 5, 2011.

Such matters are typically exempted from state Freedom of Information Act laws.[15]

Yet even if citizens had pristine data on crime rates and law enforcement strategies, the principal's job would remain exceedingly complex because most principals will not care about just one crime rate. Individuals have different concerns about different categories of crime and different geographical areas where crime occurs. Most individuals would agree to weight violent crime more heavily than nonviolent crime, but there is disagreement over how to rank the priorities of deterring white-collar fraud, environmental violations, safety violations, and illegal drug sales. Typically, individuals care more about their neighborhood's crime rate than their city's, and more about their city's crime rate than the national rate, but they still care somewhat about the latter (given that individuals travel outside their city and care about people who live elsewhere). Thus, instead of there being some simple crime index to observe, such as the Dow Jones Average or the S&P 500, citizens with multiple areas of concern need to create their own aggregation or to monitor multiple disaggregated dimensions of different criminal justice outputs.

This kind of heterogeneity matters in a more fundamental way. However it is aggregated, the crime rate is not the only output by which many citizens want to measure the performance of criminal law agents. Citizens also care about the taxes needed for criminal law enforcement; the rate of wrongful convictions (and not just as it may bear on the crime rate by its weakening deterrence); negative externalities of criminal investigations such as privacy intrusions, wrongful arrest, or excessive force; and inequalities in victimization, investigation externalities, or punishment. Probably some citizens care only about the crime rate and the costs of minimizing it, but some care about all of these other effects. For them, there is no observable index that measures all of these variables in the way that the price of a stock for shareholders. Instead, the principal needs to monitor all the dimensions of concern. This kind of citizen is like a shareholder who cares about his or her firm's environmental and labor policies, in addition to future share price. This is the problem of *multiplicity of objectives*.

In sum, the principals in criminal law – members of the public – are rationally inattentive to their agents, just like shareholders in a corporation. Magnifying this conventional problem, however, the diverse group

[15] See, e.g., 5 ILCS 140/7(d).

of citizen-principals also faces the problem of multiple objectives, creating the need to monitor different metrics of agency action rather than only one. The problem gets worse when we consider the multiplicity of independent agents that the principal needs to monitor.

B. Independent Agents

We might arrange governmental power over criminal law and enforcement very differently than we currently do. Following Jake Gersen, we might imagine a government in which powers are separated by subject matter instead of by function.[16] Currently, we divide powers into legislative, executive, and judicial functions, but we frequently "bundle" powers by giving each of those branches authority over all policy domains. We might instead unbundle power by policy area such as foreign affairs, economic policy, education policy, and crime policy. Within such a policy area, we could then aggregate across functions so that a single elected officer or policy board would possess all the governmental power. If we applied this idea to criminal law, we would allocate to one official or board all the power now held by different branches to create, adjudicate, and enforce criminal law. However lower-level agents were structured, they would all be subordinate to this plenary officer or board, which would have the power to reward and punish the subordinates, as, for example, by termination. If this were so, then this crime policy officer or board would be like a corporate board of directors. The public could exert its influence by selecting, monitoring, and rewarding or punishing the members of this board.

Obviously, the system we have is quite different because we divide governmental power by function. Indeed, in the criminal context many Americans would find such aggregation of power terrifying, as in the cliché of someone serving as a "judge, jury, and executioner." Perhaps for that reason, our system appears to divide power more finely in the policy domain of criminal law than any other. Part of the reason is that, in criminal law, we introduce governing institutions – the grand jury and a trial jury with the power to "nullify" the law (because criminal acquittals, unlike civil verdicts, are final) – that we use nowhere else. At many levels of government, we also split executive power, making police and prosecutors independent agents. At the state level, the governor may control the state police, but not the attorney general, who is separately elected. At the local

[16] See Jacob E. Gersen, *Unbundled Powers*, 96 Va. L. Rev. 301 (2010).

level, the mayor (or a legislative body such as the city council) may control the municipal police, but not the district attorney, who is separately elected. We also split the executive by state and local government. For example, only a governor can pardon an individual and he or she can do so independent of the wishes of the local police, prosecutor, and jury who arrested, charged, and convicted the individual. As a result, instead of a hierarchy, the criminal system has many horizontally aligned, independent agents, each exercising some discretion not subject to review by other agents.

As one way to understand this *multiplicity of independent agents*, consider what American agents have to do to bring about the criminal punishment of an individual. In most cases, seven sets of independent agents must assent; each holds a veto over the individual's punishment.

1. Prior to the individual's acts for which he or she is to be punished, *the legislature* must have defined the act to be criminal. No other agent can legally compel the legislature to enact a criminal provision. The legislature is also responsible for funding all the other agents subsequently discussed here.
2. In most cases, *the police* must make an arrest. Although the prosecutor can legally initiate prosecution without police assistance, in most cases she or he lacks the information to begin investigating a crime and the physical power to bring the individual into court. Thus, the prosecutor usually requires the police to investigate and make an arrest to initiate criminal proceedings. Neither the prosecutor nor any other agent can legally compel the police to make an arrest.
3. *The prosecutor* must bring charges against the individual. The crime victim and other enforcement agents lack the legal power to compel prosecution.
4. In most jurisdictions, *the grand jury* must indict the individual. Admittedly, this veto power is rarely exercised. Grand juries tend to do what prosecutors ask, and the refusal of one grand jury to indict does not prevent the prosecutor from seeking an indictment from another grand jury. Still, the grand jury's assent is (in most jurisdictions) legally necessary, and in rare cases its refusal blocks prosecution. No other agent can compel the grand jury to indict.
5. *The judiciary* must allow the trial against the individual to proceed and uphold any verdict of guilt. In some formal respects, the trial judge's authority to veto a prosecution is limited because the prosecutor can appeal certain decisions, such as quashing an indictment. However,

the judge has the formal power to terminate a case by entering a judgment of acquittal, which is not subject to prosecutorial appeal because of the double jeopardy clause.[17] Moreover, the trial court can render decisions on evidence and jury instructions that make conviction impossible as a practical matter, given that the prosecutor cannot appeal after a jury acquittal, even if the trial judge's erroneous rulings on evidence and instructions produced that acquittal (again, because of the double jeopardy clause). Appellate courts can reverse a conviction and allow no further trial. Other agents lack the power to compel the courts to permit the conviction.

6. *The petty jury* must convict the individual. The trial jury has the absolute power to acquit, even to the point of "nullifying" the law by acquitting against the evidence. The legal system has various ways to ensure that nullification rarely occurs. For example, the trial court can dismiss potential or sitting jurors for cause if they appear unwilling to follow the law. Nevertheless, no other agent can compel the jury to convict and, except for the possibility of a narrow exception for juror bribery or intimidation, acquittals are final.
7. *The chief executive* must not exercise the power to pardon the individual or fully commute his or her sentence. Separate from the local executive who controls the police and from the local prosecutor, the governor of most states and the president of the United States have the unilateral power to pardon individuals for crimes in their jurisdiction, fully voiding the conviction. They also have the power to commute the sentence to some lesser punishment, including no punishment. Except for the possibility of a narrow exception for bribery or coercion, no other agent has the power to prevent the chief executive from granting a pardon.

Thus, there are seven independent veto points over the criminal punishment of an individual. One might object to my characterizing all seven of these veto holders as "agents" of the public. First, the grand and petty juries consist of citizens, who are arguably principals rather than agents. Under the model, we might see jury duty as giving the principal an opportunity to monitor how various agents are operating, particularly prosecutors and trial judges. If so, jury service is a poorly designed mechanism, as the prosecutor can control what cases will be monitored and the judge can suspend the monitoring by ordering the jury out of the

[17] See United States v. Martin Linen Supply Co., 430 U.S. 564 (1977); Sanabria v. United States, 437 U.S. 54 (1978).

courtroom when certain important matters are to be discussed. The juries are better characterized as agents: A few members of the public to whom the larger public delegates some decision-making task. That juries are composed of citizens makes them no different than all the other citizen agents.

Still, there might be fewer than seven veto holders if we ignore those vetoes that are rarely exercised, such as the refusal by grand juries to indict and the granting of pardons by governors. We might even eliminate the petit jury because more than 90 percent of convictions occur by plea agreement without trial. Nonetheless, moving from the de jure to de facto independence of agents can increase as well as decrease the number of veto points. For example, from the aforementioned list I omitted prison officials and probation officers, who have substantial discretion over the actual conditions of punishment. Formally, governors can fire or demote such officials, but given civil service laws, they may do so as rarely as grand juries refuse to indict. Criminal law agents may also include individuals outside of government, such as witnesses and private police. If victims and other witnesses refuse to report crimes, then the police will never apprehend the offender. In some settings, such as firms and universities, private police (or their employers) exercise sufficient control over an area that, as a practical matter, the public police and prosecutor will never get involved for many crimes unless asked. Frequently, the law fails to impose any obligation on these citizens to report crime and cooperate with police, but even where the law does impose such requirements, these agents remain independent.

Moreover, punishment veto points are only one way in which criminal law agents operate independently of one another. Consider the public's need for information about how its agents are operating. To a significant degree, each agent has private information about itself that it is free not to share. The judiciary operates in a substantially public fashion, but the rest of the agents do not. Legislation is public, but the lobbying and logrolling behind the legislation is private. Much police work is secret. Prosecutorial bargaining is private. Grand jury proceedings are protected by requirements of secrecy, as are the deliberations of trial juries. Chief executives usually state some reasons for their pardon decisions, but, again, the lobbying, logrolling, and deliberations may remain secret. All of this means that, when it comes to the public's access to information about how its criminal agents perform, the public relies on those agents, such as the legislature, which can pry loose information by conducting hearings and enacting Freedom of Information Act laws. The public relies on prosecutors and grand juries to investigate criminal malfeasance by police and governors. In the end, however, the public's need for information is frequently met, if at all, by yet another agent, though a nongovernmental one: the media. The public relies on the media to collect, synthesize, and disseminate information about crime and the performance of other criminal law agents. The media too is not part of a hierarchy, and it is protected from government control by the First Amendment.

Finally, note that I omitted defense lawyers from the list. That might seem appropriate because, in the adversary system, defense lawyers are supposed to be the agents of the criminal defendant, not the public. However, the omission is not appropriate if we step back and ask why the public chooses to have an adversary process rather than one of the alternatives, such as an inquisitorial process. Presumably, if the adversary system is good for society, it is because it is more accurate and that accuracy depends on having defense counsel challenge the government's case. The theory is that defense counsel prevents the wrongful convictions that bureaucratic laziness or groupthink would otherwise produce. Therefore, the public has an interest in having defense counsel properly perform their role. In this view, defense lawyers are the public's agents (just as the Vatican's devil's advocate in beatification procedures is an agent of the Vatican). Defense counsel may then fail as agents by shirking, which fails to prevent false convictions, or by some types of excessive zeal, which produce false acquittals. Nonetheless, as with the others, defense lawyers are quite independent from other agents.

C. Weak Accountability

The predictable result of a busy and inattentive public and a series of independent agents is weak accountability. The citizen faces a final informational problem in measuring the causal responsibility of particular agents. Who is responsible for a good or bad outcome? Suppose a citizen cares only about a particular aggregated crime rate and has reasonably good evidence of what it is. First, it is difficult to determine from changes in the crime rate whether the public law enforcement agents are performing optimally, given that many other variables affect crime rates. The other variables include economic and demographic fluctuations, cultural and technological change, and the decisions of government actors in other domains, such as education, housing, and the economy. Second, if the public law enforcement agents are not performing optimally, it is difficult to determine if the problem arises at the federal, state, or local level. Third, if one identifies the jurisdictional level where the agents are underperforming, say municipal, it is difficult to determine whether the source is the city council, the mayor (by virtue of his or her selection of the police chief), the elected district attorney, local juries, or local judges. Crime control is a kind of "team production," so it is difficult to ascertain who is responsible for failure. Perhaps the police are misusing resources by staffing the night shift with too few officers in certain neighborhoods, or perhaps the prosecutor is plea bargaining too leniently in some cases and too aggressively in others. The problem is particularly acute when some police tactics, such as wiretapping, are inherently difficult to observe.

In sum, the agency problem in criminal law is severe; it is possibly more severe than it is in corporate law.

II. THE STUNTZIAN CONTRIBUTION

Enter Bill Stuntz. Bill brings the principal–agent problem in criminal law to the foreground. In a few instances Bill explicitly refers to agency costs. An example is his article *Unequal Justice*, where he invokes the 1932 work by Adolf Berle and Gardiner Means, who first noted that the separation of ownership and control in the modern corporation creates a governance problem. Bill notes the following:

> Contemporary American criminal justice faces the same governance problem, but in worse form. After all, managers have good reason to see that the corporations they run remain profitable: their jobs depend on it. The detached managers of urban criminal justice systems are in a different position.... Decisionmakers who neither reap the benefit of good decisions nor bear the cost of bad ones tend to make bad ones.

More pervasively, Bill addresses agency costs implicitly. He does this by relentlessly examining the incentives and information of the public and its agents – particularly legislatures, police, and prosecutors, but also judges, defense lawyers, and juries – as well as the *interaction* of these agents. I cannot cover all the insights Bill offers concerning the principal–agent problem in criminal law, but I will cover a few illustrative points.

As background, Bill takes seriously two key ingredients to a principal–agent analysis: the preferences of the agents and the information problems the principals face. Regarding the first, *The Pathological Politics of Criminal Law*[18] is the only article I know of that sets out to describe something like a utility function for not just one, but a wide set of criminal law

[18] See 100 Mich. L. Rev. 505 (2001).

agents: what elected legislators, prosecutors, and judges must do in the criminal law area to satisfy the public, as well as the goals of unelected agents, such as police, federal prosecutors, and federal judges. Bill writes, for example, about the prospects of prosecutorial shirking, about how plea bargaining minimizes their workload, and how prosecutors are an important lobbying group before legislatures, who wish to curb prosecutorial shirking by making it cheaper for the prosecutor to convict.

Bill also discusses information problems. An obvious but important point is that the public knows a lot more about cases resolved by trial than cases resolved by plea bargaining. In his article with Dan Richman, *Al Capone's Revenge*,[19] they make a more subtle and equally important point: the connection between the substance of criminal law and the information the public has about its agents. Bill and Dan reject the usual complaint about pretextual prosecutions – that they are unfair to the defendant – but identify this informational cost: Convictions are signals of the behavior of police and prosecutors, but the signals are noisier when the crimes of conviction are either (1) nonintuitive, technical offenses or (2) offenses other than those that motivate the prosecutor to target the defendant. The public has a reasonably good sense of the meaning and harmfulness of centuries-old crimes such as "burglary" and "robbery," and it can therefore evaluate the police for solving or failing to solve such a crime and evaluate the prosecutor for winning or losing such a trial. More difficult is deciding how well police or prosecutors are doing when they convict someone of mail fraud or federal program fraud. Most challenging is the problem of pretext: It is difficult for the public to evaluate government action when prosecutors convict an individual of a minor crime, say document fraud, but claim the person is a terrorist.

Besides these general points, Bill has a lot to say about the principal–agent problems of specific institutions. I will give three examples of his insights, the first being the principal–agent sources of the much discussed problem of overcriminalization. The public understands that prosecutors have discretion. As a result, if a prosecutor brings charges the public does not want brought, the public will blame the prosecutor and not the legislature for not having defined the crime more narrowly. By contrast, if the prosecutor cannot bring charges the public desires because there is no statutory offense, the public blames the legislature. As a result, there is a mostly one-sided incentive for legislatures to expand the scope of criminal

[19] See 105 Colum. L. Rev. 583 (2005).

law, giving prosecutors maximum discretion over what behavior should be punished.[20]

Second, Bill describes the connection between vice crimes and unequal enforcement. Within a category of crime, police seek to maximize arrests, which is a simple metric by which the public can measure the effort of police. For vice crimes, the police typically get more arrests per dollar if they direct their efforts against the poor. Part of the reason is that the poor, having fewer resources, have less effective means of evading apprehension. For example, wealthier individuals are less likely to buy drugs or solicit prostitution on the street. We see the same differential when we move from arrests to convictions – prosecutors are more likely to win against the lawyers representing the poor than the wealthy.[21]

Third, Bill emphasizes the different incentives that criminal enforcers face at the federal, state, and local level. Federal prosecutors, for example, have the most agency slack, because they are appointed rather than elected, have the most per capita resources, and are not held accountable by the public for street crime. Local prosecutors are elected, face enormous caseloads, and are blamed by the public for street crime. Federal prosecutors are therefore more likely to engage in arbitrary and vindictive prosecutions than are local prosecutors, who are less free to follow their personal preferences. To this point, Bill's most recent article links rising inequality in policing and punishment to the move away from local control of criminal justice.[22]

There are more examples and much more one could say about Bill's work. Certainly, the economics of criminal law will be greatly enriched if we follow Bill's lead in putting agency costs at the center of our analysis. But let me conclude with a more personal note. Bill Stuntz was my notes editor in law school and an inspiration and mentor, then and later, to my academic career. As others have noted, one marveled at discovering that a person so intellectually gifted could be so modest, generous, and funny, that a criminal law and procedure theorist on a grand scale could be so grounded in ordinary life. I am honored to have known Bill Stuntz and to be included in this volume on his work.

[20] See William J. Stuntz, *The Political Constitution of Criminal Justice*, 119 Harv. L. Rev. 780 (2006); William J. Stuntz, *The Pathological Politics of Criminal Law*, 100 Mich. L. Rev. 505 (2001).

[21] See William J. Stuntz, *Race, Class, and Drugs*, 98 Colum. L. Rev. 1795 (1998).

[22] See William J. Stuntz, *Unequal Justice*, 121 Harv. L. Rev. 1969 (2008).

3

Overcriminalization for Lack of Better Options: A Celebration of Bill Stuntz

By Daniel Richman

The unity of Bill Stuntz's character – his profound integrity – makes it easy to move from a celebration of his friendship (which I've treasured since we first met back in 1985) to one of his scholarship, for creativity, wisdom, and humility are strengths not just of Bill himself but of his work. Even as his broad brush strokes have fundamentally advanced our understanding of the interplay between substantive criminal law, criminal procedure, and criminal justice institutions over time, Bill's work – like Bill himself – welcomes and endures sustained engagement.[1] Humility is appropriate for me, too, as I offer some ruminations sparked by his scholarship. The academic's plight is to simultaneously worry about being uninteresting and about being wrong. My hope is to err on the side of error. My methodology here will be much the same as it has been in a lot of my other work: I seek to entertain Bill, and perhaps to bait him into telling me why I'm wrong.

* Thanks to Alexandra Bowie, Adam Carlis, David Garland, Niki Lacey, Maximo Langer, Jerry Lynch, Maren Messing, Bill Simon, Peter Strauss, Bill Stuntz, Carol Steiker, Jim Whitman, and participants at two lunches with my colleagues and students at Columbia for extremely helpful comments; to Carol, Mike Klarman, and David Skeel for putting on this celebration, and to Bill Stuntz for more than twenty-five years of friendship, inspiration, and humor.

[1] See William J. Stuntz, *Book Review: Christian Legal Theory*, 116 Harv. L. Rev. 1707, 1744 (2003) ("Imagine how differently most law review articles would read if their authors admitted the possibility that they might be mistaken"); cf. Letter from Oliver Cromwell to the General Assembly of the Kirk of Scotland (Aug. 3, 1650), in The Writings and Speeches of Oliver Cromwell 3022–03 (Wilbur Cortez Abbott ed., 1939) ("I beseech you, in the bowels of Christ, think it possible that you may be mistaken"). When speaking of Bill, I've not altered the present tense in which this chapter was written. Bill will always live in his written work, in the minds (including mine) that he challenged to think harder, and in the people (including me) who loved him.

As Bill has noted, "criminal law's breadth" – the sheer amount of conduct it subjects to penal sanctions – "has long been the starting point for virtually all the scholarship" in the field.[2] Back in 2001, he powerfully laid out the agency problems at the heart of the "pathologies" that inappropriately expand the range and depth of American criminal law: "Legislators gain when they write criminal statutes in ways that benefit prosecutors. Prosecutors gain from statutes that enable them more easily to induce guilty pleas. Appellate courts lack the doctrinal tools to combat those tendencies."[3] Thereafter, Bill elaborated his model, distinguishing between federal and local political dynamics[4] and explaining how the loss of local democratic control over the criminal justice system has led to racial inequality in criminal justice outcomes.[5]

Bill has never suggested that these actors make their moves within a closed universe. Indeed, voters' willingness to reward just about any legislation that increases the scope or depth of criminal law lies at the heart of his "pathology,"[6] and he notes how "interest group pressure only aggravates the tendency toward ever broader liability rules."[7] At the core of his diagnostic story, however, is a narrative of how the institutional purposes of these actors are served by more criminal law (and perhaps more criminal enforcement) than is appropriate for a well-functioning society. I suspect Bill's focus is quite right: More punitive and broader penal sanctions certainly tend to increase the discretion of police officers and prosecutors and, under a constitutional regime of largely unfettered bargaining, can be cashed out for search-and-seizure authority, cheaper adjudications, agency prestige, political capital, and the like. That these transactions occur in a regime in which monitoring is particularly difficult makes them even more attractive to enforcement actors, for whom increased criminalization can thus become an unalloyed good.

[2] William J. Stuntz, *The Pathological Politics of Criminal Law*, 100 Mich. L. Rev. 505, 507 (2001) [hereinafter Stuntz, *Pathological Politics*]; see also Douglas Husak, Overcriminalization: The Limits of the Criminal Law (Oxford 2008); Erik Luna, *The Overcriminalization Phenomenon*, 54 Am. U. L. Rev. 703 (2005); John Coffee, *Does "Unlawful" Mean "Criminal"?: Reflections on the Disappearing Tort/Crime Distinction in American Law*, 71 B.U. L. Rev. 193 (1991); Sanford H. Kadish, *The Crisis of Overcriminalization*, 7 Am. Crim. L. Q. 17 (1968).

[3] Stuntz, *Pathological Politics*, supra note 2, at 528.

[4] See Daniel C. Richman & William J. Stuntz, *Al Capone's Revenge: An Essay on the Political Economy of Pretextual Prosecution*, 105 Colum. L. Rev. 583 (2005).

[5] William J. Stuntz, *Unequal Justice*, 121 Harv. L. Rev. 1969 (2008); see also William J. Stuntz, The Collapse of American Criminal Justice (2011).

[6] Stuntz, *Pathological Politics*, supra note 2, at, 529–533.

[7] Id. at 553.

Nonetheless, one might profitably supplement Bill's insights into why institutional actors oversupply criminal law by exploring another, more perverse, reason why Americans are all too quick to resort to criminal statutes and actual prosecutions: Because criminal law offers a unique and unnecessarily bundled set of institutional and procedural characteristics for which there are no noncriminal substitutes, it frequently becomes a recourse – not a preferred choice – when more effective and durable alternatives just aren't available. It is troubling enough when a society overcriminalizes (by some unspecified metric) and overpunishes (by some unspecified metric). It is even more troubling when we use criminal law not necessarily because we affirmatively want to but because it is easier and cheaper than less punitive options.

To be sure, criminal law comes with some expensive appurtenances – also known as "fundamental constitutional rights" – that tend to limit recourse to it. As Carol Steiker has so insightfully explained, by raising "the cost to government of using the criminal process," the "revolution in criminal procedure" spearheaded by the Warren Court gave state and federal legislators good reason to devise civil avenues for attacking "what might be more plausibly classified as criminal conduct."[8] The chance to avoid adjudicative costs attributable to such criminal procedure rights as trial by jury and proof beyond a reasonable doubt will give a legislator or state official good reason to characterize a sanction or restraint as merely "regulatory" when all things are equal. However, all things are rarely equal, particularly when institutional context is considered. My goal here is to explore the powerful countervailing forces that often make the criminal route more alluring – the forces that push legislators and enforcers to use criminal law in lieu of other possible interventions, not those that lead them to circumvent criminal protections by proceeding civilly. (In a semiperfect world, these countervailing forces would balance each other out. We don't live in that world.)

In addition to honoring Bill by adding a few brush strokes to his wonderful picture, I want to suggest that the solution to overcriminalization lies outside criminal law processes as well as within them. The focus here will be to sketch out what moves in that external direction would look

[8] Carol Steiker, *Punishment and Procedure: Punishment Theory and the Criminal-Civil Procedural Divide*, 85 Geo. L. J. 775, 780 (1997); see also Carol Steiker, *The Limits of the Preventive State*, 88 J. Crim. L. & Crim. 771 (1998); Daniel Richman, "United States v. Salerno: The Constitutionality of Regulatory Detention," in Criminal Procedure Stories 413, 442 (Carol Steiker, ed. 2006); Erin Murphy, *Paradigms of Restraint*, 57 Duke L. J. 1321 (2008).

like.[9] Insightful and provocative work by David Garland, John Simon, Jim Whitman, and others[10] has quite properly focused on the cultural roots of our recourse to criminalization – and highly punitive criminalization at that. Like Bill, however, I think institutional dynamics (spurred by cultural preferences that are not necessarily related to punishment itself) have far more explanatory power than is often appreciated.

THE INSTITUTIONAL "DEFINITION" OF WHAT IS "REALLY" CRIMINAL

Had we an accepted metric for figuring out when conduct can properly be subjected to criminal sanctions and to what degree, then guarding against overcriminalization would be a lot easier. Having one would perhaps not produce more reasoned decision making in our punishment of core crimes – murders, rapes, robberies, and the like – but it would at least anchor our decisions about when criminal sanctions should be used as a tool of government power at the border between "mere" regulation and prosecution. Unfortunately, we lack any such metric. Markus Dubber has plausibly suggested that the fault lies (at least in part) in the Anglo-American conflation of law and police power.[11] Picking up on this point, Niki Lacey has noted the contrast with our more discerning cousins on the Continent, who worked hard to keep criminal law preoccupied with wrongdoing and culpability and relied on regulation to advance other state goals such as risk creation or public health.[12] We made no effort in that regard and quietly allowed the police power to be

[9] Although the focus here is on the United States, the argument that overcriminalization in the United States is partially a function of peculiar doctrinal and institutional arrangements not found in, say, Europe, may, in passing, offer some comfort to Europeans scared that they are on the verge of taking "the punitive turn" down the American or English path. See Nicola Lacey, The Prisoners' Dilemma: Political Economy and Punishment in Contemporary Democracies (2008).

[10] For an excellent review essay, see James Q. Whitman, *The Comparative Study of Criminal Punishment*, 1 Ann. Rev. Law Soc. Sci. 17 (2005).

[11] See Markus Dirk Dubber, The Police Power: Patriarchy and the Foundations of American Government (2005).

[12] Lacey, supra note 9, at 104: On the Continent "this location of regulatory offenses within the framework of criminal law 'proper' would be regarded as most unsatisfactory. Rather than drawing the old police power within the modern framework of criminal justice, the modern governmental settlements of European codification of the early nineteenth century were inclined to separate out this form of social regulation within a discrete framework, leaving regulatory offenses as a more visible and autonomous manifestation of state power."

"absorbed" within "law."[13] The result is intellectual chaos. As Douglas Husak recently noted, "The absence of a viable account of criminalization constitutes the single most glaring failure of penal theory as it has developed on both sides of the 14Atlantic."[14]

The scant attention Anglo-American legal development gave to drawing clear distinctions between the province of criminal law and that of civil regulation was partly a function of our general preference for procedural justice over a priori principles of substantive law. As Bill has often noted, our Constitution has a lot to say about how criminal law should be enforced but little about what criminal law should be. Our substantive criminal law therefore developed first through the case-by-case pronouncements of common law judges and then by the varied articulations of incensed legislators. The Model Penal Code eventually offered theoretical rigor to receptive jurisdictions (a category that certainly does not include the federal system).[15] Even in those states, however, the Model Penal Code has had only limited effect on the "special part" of the penal code.[16] To be sure, Continental systems – such as those in Germany, France, and Italy – will occasionally criminalize what we leave to regulation or tort, as the French have done with employment discrimination.[17] Moreover, the coherence I see may just come from my distance and ignorance. Nevertheless, one discerns an integrity in the substantive penal law of those countries that is sorely absent here. Perhaps the same institutional self-confidence behind the commitment of inquisitorial systems to seek the "real truth" in their courts also supports an effort to systematically discern what really should be criminal.[18] Here, in contrast, we make it up as we go along.

[13] Lacey, supra note 9, at 102.

[14] Douglas Husak, Overcriminalization: The Limits of the Criminal Law 58 (2008).

[15] See Dixon v. United States, 548 U.S. 1, 15 (2006) (when setting contours of the duress defense under federal criminal law, Court gives "no weight" to the Model Penal Code formulation).

[16] Gerard E. Lynch, *Towards A Model Penal Code, Second (Federal?): The Challenge of the Special Part*, 2 Buffalo Crim. L. Rev. 297, 299 (1998) (noting that the "Model Penal Code is a significantly less potent guide to the 'special part' of the criminal law today," in part because "state legislatures have poured out new criminal statutes undreamed of by [that Code's] drafters").

[17] See Julie C. Suk, *Procedural Path Dependence: Discrimination and the Civil-Criminal Divide*, 85 Wash. U. L. Rev. 1315 (2008); Gabrielle S. Friedman & James Q. Whitman, *The European Transformation of Harassment Law: Discrimination Versus Dignity*, 9 Colum. J. Eur. L. 241 (2003).

[18] See Richard S. Frase & Thomas Weigend, *German Criminal Justice as a Guide to American Law Reform: Similar Problems, Better Solutions?*, 18 Boston College Int'l and Comp. L. Rev. 317, 353, 357 (1995) (noting the "[n]arrower scope of the criminal

Our tolerance for theoretically unrestricted criminal law and our readiness to rely on criminal enforcement to advance a wide range of public policies is also a function of what some have contestably called our historically "weak state"[19] and the paucity of our institutional structures, namely the lack of regulatory actors other than cops, prosecutors, and judges. From the Founding – and long before in Britain[20] – criminal justice institutions (however part time) offered the promise of local control (through juries, venue rules, and decentralized enforcers) and the capacity for accepting new responsibilities on a discretionary basis.[21] These characteristics made them the perfect recourse for political and social entrepreneurs who believed in minimal government, disdaining the interventionist Weberian bureaucracies of some other Western polities,[22] but who periodically desired a law for "just this one bad thing" with an off-the-rack enforcement regime. Darryl Brown recounts that "[t]he early decades of the American republic continued earlier English and colonial practices of employing criminal law routinely as a means of local regulation."[23] Thereafter, efforts to identify and target vice in its many forms have played a remarkably large role in the growth of the criminal docket. As Bill notes in his masterful

law" in Germany as well as the commitment of tribunals to "finding the truth"); see also Richard S. Frase, *Comparative Criminal Justice as a Guide to American Law Reform: How the French Do It, How Can We Find Out, and Why Should We Care?*, 78 Cal. L. Rev. 539, 568 (1990) (similarly noting narrower scope of French criminal law).

19 For insightful counsel on how the term *state* should be used when referring to the United States in comparative terms, see Desmond King & Robert C. Lieberman, *Ironies of States Building: Comparative Perspective on the American State*, 61 World Politics 547 (2009); see also William Novak, *The Myth of the "Weak" American State*, 113 Amer. Hist. Rev. 752 (2008).

20 See J. M. Beattie, Policing and Punishment in London 1660–1750 (2002); J. M. Beattie, Crime and the Courts in England, 1660–1800 (1986); P. King, Crime, Justice and Discretion in England 1740–1820 (2000).

21 Eric Monkkonen notes how the Boston sewer department was essentially spun out of the city marshal's service in 1837. Eric H. Monkkonen, Police in Urban America, 1860–1920, at 47 (2004 ed.) (noting how when Boston incorporated in 1822, the city marshal was given general responsibility for matters affecting the "health, security, and comfort of the city," and that "[t]he only change in the power of the Boston marshal came in 1837, when the city created a separate department of sewers, run by a former deputy marshal").

22 See Desmond King & Robert C. Lieberman, supra note 19, at 573–574 ("A well-rehearsed motif in American political culture is that of being a strong nation with a weak state whose citizens prize decentralization and localism, that is, a political system less centralized, less interventionist, and less Weberian than that found in comparable advanced democracies, including some with strong federal systems such as Australia or Germany").

23 Darryl K. Brown, *Yick Wo and the Constitutional Regulation of Criminal Law*, 2008 U. Ill. L. Rev. 1405, 1407.

book, "Between the late 1870s and 1933, America's criminal justice system fought a series of cultural battles in which criminal law – especially federal criminal law – was a key weapon: against polygamy, state lotteries . . . , prostitution, various forms of opium, and, last, but definitely not least, alcoholic drink."[24]

Vice is not the whole story, though. One also sees an easy creep from more mundane regulation to criminalization in *United States v. Grimaud*,[25] the watershed case upholding the constitutionality of administrative crimes.[26] It arose out of the 1908 federal criminal prosecution of a California shepherd for violating the Interior Department's national forest grazing rules. The 1897 legislation authorizing the Interior Department to promulgate regulations to protect the lands under its stewardship had left it free to use either civil or criminal sanctions.[27] Thereafter, when the newly created Forest Service – led by the able Gifford Pinchot, who carefully nurtured his ties to the Attorney General[28] – assumed the Interior Department's responsibilities and found civil injunctions inadequate, it simply prevailed on the Justice Department to replead the regulatory violations in grand jury indictments.[29] And so the shepherd found himself charged with a crime, not a rule violation. Although the New Deal and the growth of the administrative state brought a conspicuous proliferation of public welfare offenses within the federal system, that proliferation thus had begun decades before. As early as 1933 a canny observer such as Francis Sayres could already worry about the upcoming flood that threatened to erase what was left of the civil–criminal divide.[30]

Lacking any commonly accepted intellectual basis for distinguishing the appropriate realm of criminal prosecutions from that of other government interventions, we ended up, by default, with an institutional

[24] William J. Stuntz, The Collapse of American Criminal Justice, 158–59 (2011).

[25] 220 U.S. 506 (1911).

[26] See Thomas W. Merrill & Kathryn T. Watts, *Agency Rules with Force of Law*, 116 Harv. L. Rev. 467, 501–502 (2002) ("*Grimaud* thus established what Congress could do: it could delegate power to an agency to adopt regulations subject to criminal penalties, provided that Congress itself legislated the penalties").

[27] See Logan Sawyer, *Grazing, Grimaud, and Gifford Pinchot: How the Forest Service Overcame the Classical Nondelegation Doctrine to Establish Administrative Crimes*, 24 J. L. & Pol. 171, 184 (2008).

[28] Id. at 193.

[29] Id. at 184–202.

[30] See Francis Bowes Sayre, *Public Welfare Offenses*, 33 Colum. L. Rev. 55, 84 (1933) ("With respect to public welfare offenses involving light penalties the abandonment of the classic requirement of mens rea is probably a sound development. But courts should scrupulously avoid extending the doctrines applicable to public welfare offenses to true crimes. To do so would sap the vitality of the criminal law").

definition. Over time, criminal law in the United States became what criminal justice actors did, nothing more.

WHY CRIMINALIZATION WILL BE SOUGHT BY THOSE WHO MIGHT PREFER SOMETHING ELSE

Conceptually, we thus have an inexhaustible supply of criminal law in the United States – a supply largely unrestrained by the Constitution, thanks to the Framers' preoccupation with criminal procedure. Although Bill has given us a provocative glimpse of "a kind of criminal substantive due process" that would ensure that "the conduct criminalized was serious enough to justify *some* criminal punishment,"[31] this is not a doctrinal dog likely to bark in the foreseeable future (although every so often, it gets up and walks around).[32] As a result, the federal government and the states are thus substantially free to impose the same stigma and sanctions on the violator of any social policy that they impose on the robber, rapist, or murderer (with the exception of capital punishment). They can also use the same cops, prosecutors, and courts to do so.

The supply of actual criminal enforcement is of course not inexhaustible. Cops and prosecutors are expensive, as are prisons. (Particularly prisons, when you think about it.) However, these very limits, when combined with the strong norms of police and prosecutorial discretion that characterize American criminal enforcement and the opacity that insulates prosecutorial decision making from scrutiny,[33] have ended up promoting the extension of criminal law's domain. Like those magic bags that seem to hold everything the magician puts in them without getting bigger, criminal justice institutions seem able to assume any number of new assignments without necessarily acting on them. Such is the value of decentralized and highly discretionary authority. In addition, because of our reliance on general jurisdiction criminal enforcement institutions, the mere bringing of a criminal case entails a powerful statement of the condemned conduct's worthiness for criminal treatment.

That a single institution at each level of government should – with notable exceptions – have responsibility for all criminal prosecutions is

[31] William J. Stuntz, *Criminal Procedure and Criminal Justice*, 107 Yale L. J. 1, 66 (1997).

[32] See Lawrence v. Texas, 539 U.S. 558 (2003); California v. Lambert, 355 U.S. 225 (1957).

[33] See James Q. Whitman, *Equality in Criminal Law: The Two Divergent Western Roads*, 1 J. Legal Analysis 119 (2009).

something we take for granted, but shouldn't. Our readiness to extend criminal law beyond "core" harm-based concerns[34] did not necessarily (at least as an a priori matter) have to be accompanied by the assignment of these extended criminal functions to the same general jurisdiction enforcement agencies that handle regular crimes. One could imagine a system of subject-specific investigators bringing cases to "special" prosecutors housed in stand-alone agencies with limited missions. In such a world, specialized enforcement agencies could be equipped with specialized investigative and enforcement tools keyed to their particular subject matter; prosecutors could even bring cases in special courts. We have largely rejected or ignored that model, however.[35] Within the federal system, most prosecutions are brought by generalist U.S. Attorneys. Even the Justice Department's specialized litigating divisions (such as those for Antitrust, Civil Rights and Tax) are housed within an agency that has general federal criminal jurisdiction. Similarly, in state and local systems, the vast majority of prosecutors are in general jurisdiction district attorneys' offices and bring cases before general jurisdiction criminal judges.[36] Sure, prosecutors within the larger offices sometimes specialize – sometimes in units that proclaim their dedication to particular kinds of cases – and at the local level, some jurisdictions have experimented with specialty drug, gun, and domestic violence courts.[37] Nevertheless, it is a fundamentally generalist system. Moreover, everywhere, trials (to the extent they occur) will be before the ultimate general jurisdiction players: lay jurors whose

[34] See generally Douglas Husak, *Crimes Outside the Core*, 39 Tulsa L. Rev. 755 (2004) (discussing ways to distinguish the "core" of criminal law from its "periphery"); see also Douglas Husak, *Gardner on the Philosophy of Criminal Law*, 29 Oxford J. Legal Stud. 169, 171 (2009) (referring to "offences such as murder, rape, theft and the like" as the "core of the criminal law").

[35] But see Luis A. Aguilar, Speech at North American Securities Administrators Association's Winder Enforcement Conference, "Empowering the Markets Watchdog to Effect Real Results," Jan. 10, 2009 (SEC commissioner argues "that Congress could greatly enhance enforcement of the securities laws by authorizing the Commission to prosecute criminal violations of the federal securities laws where the Department of Justice declines to bring an action"), available at http://www.sec.gov/news/speech/2009/spch011009laa.htm.

[36] For a survey of the degree to which state attorneys general get involved in what otherwise would be local prosecutions, see Rachel E. Barkow, *Federalism and Criminal Law: What the Feds Can Learn from the States*, 109 Mich. L. Rev. 519 (2010).

[37] See generally Michael C. Dorf & Jeffrey A. Fagan, *Problem-Solving Courts: From Innovation to Institutionalization*, 40 Am. Crim. L. Rev. 1501 (2003); Phyllis Skloot Bamberger, *Specialized Courts: Not a Cure-All*, 30 Fordham Urb. L. J. 1091 (2003).

response to the evidence (and readiness to convict) will be substantially driven by their views of the "seriousness" of the offense (or offender).[38]

Consider how this institutional design affects the prosecution of offenses outside core criminality: A fraud or "public welfare" offense will usually be pursued with resources (and by prosecutors) that could just as easily be used against rapes, robberies, and murders, and by prosecutors and enforcement personnel who may have just gone after such obviously "real" crimes.[39] Moreover, the reputational capital that an agency develops going after "real" crimes gets deployed – consciously or not – across all the criminal cases it brings.[40] No prosecutor would be so stupid as to explicitly analogize a securities fraud or environmental crime to murder, rape, or terrorism at a press conference, arraignment, or trial. Nor will anyone confuse Martha Stewart with Matty "the Horse" Ianniello of the Genovese Family. Nevertheless, the announcement that an indictment has been issued in a securities fraud case is made from the same podium as an announcement that a mob boss has been convicted. The police or federal agents will wear the same bedizened raid jackets as they cart boxes out of a hedge fund or counterfeit handbag plant as they do at a hostage "situation" or murder scene. And all handcuffs look alike.[41]

38 See Daniel C. Richman, Old Chief v. United States: *Stipulating Away Prosecutorial Accountability?*, 83 Va. L. Rev. 939, 971–973 (1997) (citing studies).

39 See Alice Ristroph, Criminal Law in the Shadow of Violence, from The Law of Violence (forthcoming, Oxford University Press) ("In the criminal law, violent crime seems to verify the need for, and justice of, the state's own violence in policing and punishment"), available at www.law.berkeley.edu/img/Ristroph(1).pdf; see also James Q. Whitman, *The Comparative Study of Criminal Punishment*, 1 Ann. Rev. Law Soc. Sci. 17, 29–30 (2005) (discussing relationship between criminal punishment and social traditions of violence).

40 The same sort of cross-subsidy has historically supported extensions of federal criminal jurisdiction. See Kathleen J. Frydl, *Kidnapping and State Development in the United States*, 20 Stud. in Am. Pol. Dev. 18, 20 (2006) ("The quintessential crime against the person, kidnapping, furnished opportunity to those eager to project the formal power of the state").

41 See Caldarola v. County of Westchester, 343 F.3d 570 (2d Cir. 2003) (dismissing civil claim of corrections officers complaining about videotaped "perp walk" following their arrest for disability benefit fraud). The court noted:

> The "perp walk," that is, when an accused wrongdoer is led away in handcuffs by the police to the courthouse, police station, or jail, has been featured in newspapers and newscasts for decades. The normally camera-shy arrestees often pull coats over their heads, place their hands in front of their faces, or otherwise attempt to obscure their identities. A recent surge in "executive perp walks" has featured accused white-collar criminals in designer suits and handcuffs. Whether the accused wrongdoer is

In this world, the decisions that prosecutors and other enforcers make and the actions they take speak far more loudly than legislative criminalization. This difference in expressive capacities arises for a number of reasons. For one thing, because criminal laws are not self-executing, and we lack the German "principle of legality" that compels prosecution, a penal provision may never have a life beyond the penal code. Yes, a legislator's campaign literature will tout her sponsorship of the "Get Tough on [Fill in the Blank] Act," but that marginal contribution to the thickness of the statute book likely has little more salience than a bridge funded or defense contract obtained. It is often only after a prosecutor takes action that a statute – particularly one drafted some years earlier – enters the public consciousness. Moreover, when a prosecutor invokes a provision, she will always do so in the context of facts that she can select for their moral appeal.[42] This both enables the prosecutor to shape the contours of the doctrine and ensures maximum pressure behind the expansion of the criminal law. In the end, though, much of the power of the speech comes from the identity of the speaker: Although generalist prosecutors may lack the specialized knowledge of their regulatory brethren across the civil–criminal divide, they are far better placed to make trans-substantive claims of moral blameworthiness.[43] In addition, because prosecutors have more "skin" in the game and must face the opportunity costs of their cases, their claims of "criminality" have far

> wearing a sweatshirt over his head or an Armani suit on his back, we suspect that perp walks are broadcast by networks and reprinted in newspapers at least in part for their entertainment value. Yet, perp walks also serve the more serious purpose of educating the public about law enforcement efforts. The image of the accused being led away to contend with the justice system powerfully communicates government efforts to thwart the criminal element, and it may deter others from attempting similar crimes.

Id. at 572–573.

[42] See Dan M. Kahan, *Is Chevron Relevant to Federal Criminal Law?*, 110 Harv. L. Rev. 469, 480 (1996) ("By paying close attention to the facts of the cases they select as vehicles for novel statutory readings, federal prosecutors can highlight the benefits and suppress the costs of the interpretations that they favor").

[43] See Gerard E. Lynch, *The Role of Criminal Law in Policing Corporate Misconduct*, 60 L. & Contemp. Probs. 23, 54 (1997) ("The EPA or SEC lawyer may be better able to compare each case with other violations of securities or environmental laws, in terms of its importance to operating honest capital markets or protecting environmental quality, but the prosecutor is better equipped to compare the violation with other types of crime in terms of the moral blameworthiness of conduct, the degree of departure from general standards of citizenship, and the equity of imposing stigmatizing punishment").

more power to transform social norms than the assertions of a legislature that has an infinite supply of such epithets.[44]

The unique expressive capabilities of those who actually bring cases can be misused. As Bill has pointed out, prosecutors may have reasons for deploying the "criminal" label that have little do with culpability or social harm and much to do with building institutional or political capital. There may be short-term political gains – to the prosecutor personally or to her office – from putting all sorts of temporary "public enemies" on the same moral plane as "other" criminals. Moreover, the implicit or explicit claim that "crimes are crimes" can end up being a bridge too far. Early in the New Deal – a time when criminal law was increasingly used as the leading edge for federal regulatory regimes – the A. L. A. Schechter Poultry Corporation in Brooklyn emerged as a serious threat to the National Recovery Administration's program for the notoriously corrupt kosher poultry business. Government inspectors found serial violations of the Live Poultry Code's wage and hour provisions, sales of unfit and uninspected poultry, and they were themselves threatened with violence as they pursued these problems.[45] The Justice Department obtained an indictment against the four Schechter brothers and their firm on sixty criminal counts, and gained a conviction on nineteen counts and then an affirmance on appeal.[46] When the case reached the Supreme Court, Justice McReynolds got defense counsel to explain the poultry's code's "straight killing" requirement – the seller was supposed to put his hand in the coop and take the first chicken he touched – then commented "And

[44] See Mariano-Florentino Cuéllar, "The Institutional Logic of Preventive Crime," in Prosecutors in the Boardroom: Using Criminal Law to Regulate Corporate Conduct 131, 139 (Anthony S. Barkow & Rachel E. Barkow, eds., 2011) (noting relative political insulation of criminal law enforcement bureaucracies).

[45] See Peter H. Irons, The New Deal Lawyers 87 (1982).

[46] United States v. A.L.A. Schechter Poultry Corp., 76 F.2d 617 (2d Cir. 1935), rev'd, 295 U.S. 495 (1935). The Second Circuit opinion in *Schechter* was written by Judge Martin Manton, who had just missed being appointed to the Supreme Court, and who later became the first federal judge convicted of receiving bribes. United States v. Manton, 107 F.2d 834 (2d Cir. 1939) (affirming conviction); see also David R. Stras, *Pierce Butler: A Supreme Technician*, 62 Vand. L. Rev. 695, 710 n. 112 (2009). Bill *loved* these sorts of details and recently reminded me that another of his favorite New Deal cases, the "Hot Oil" case, *Panama Refining Co. v. Ryan*, 293 U.S. 388 (1935), arose out of a National Industrial Recovery Act regime that threatened code violators with criminal prosecution. For a lovely tour of the criminal law in the midst of changes brought by its deployment for regulatory purposes, see Livingston Hall, *The Substantive Law of Crimes: 1887–1936*, 50 Harv. L. Rev. 616, 618 (1937).

it was for that your client was convicted?" Counsel replied: "Yes, and fined and given a jail sentence."[47] The rest is history.[48]

Still, the idea that a prosecutor's office – not the courtroom or the criminal code[49] – is the place for discussions about what is "really" criminal runs deep. Particularly in the rarified world of white-collar enforcement that Kenneth Mann and Jerry Lynch have captured so insightfully,[50] the standard defense pitch starts by explaining how the alleged conduct, though technically covered by a criminal provision, does not rise to the level of a real crime. Indeed, this tack is pursued to a fault.[51]

The thickness of the prosecutorial portfolio, the privileged status of certain of its component parts (violent crime, treason, et al.), and the opacity of the criminal enforcement regime can have material, as well as expressive, consequences. Consider the effects on investigative or prosecutorial tactics. A standard story starts when some technique or tactic is rolled out and authorized for an especially egregious offense – terrorism or child pornography, for instance. Over time, the argument "isn't [some other] offense just as bad" gains power, particularly when accompanied by the assumption that enforcers will pick out only the really "bad" instances of the new offense. Prosecutors (or agents or police) who move from one unit to another will tout the virtues of the new tool, but word will get out even without personnel shifts because of the common hierarchy and culture. Before long, the extraordinary tactic becomes just another criminal enforcement tool. Outside the federal system, the vehicular stops that the police make for felonies soon get made

[47] Irons, supra note 45, at 99.

[48] See A. L. A. Schechter Poultry v. United States, 295 U.S. 495 (1935) (finding poultry industry regulations to be outside Congress's Commerce Clause authority and to be unconstitutional delegations of congressional power).

[49] The federal system doesn't even have a formal criminal code, because codifiers have never been able to wrangle all the U.S. Code's penal provisions into a single title.

[50] See Kenneth Mann, Defending White-Collar Crime (1985); see also Gerard E. Lynch, *Our Administrative System of Criminal Justice*, 66 Ford. L. Rev. 2117 (1998).

[51] Two former executives at the Southern District of New York U.S. Attorney's office recently noted: "In our experience, it is not uncommon for defense counsel to seek non-criminal or deferred resolutions when, in view of the charging precedent of the office, prosecutorial practice and the facts and circumstances of the case, such request is not realistic." See Lev L. Dassin and Guy Petrillo, Pre-Charge Presentations to a U.S. Attorney's Office and the Department of Justice (2010) (unpublished draft).

for misdemeanors.[52] Within the federal system, USA PATRIOT Act subpoenas get used in cases having nothing to do with terrorism,[53] and insider trading cases get investigated with the sort of electronic surveillance previously reserved for mobsters and drug traffickers.[54] Although none of these tactics is necessarily inappropriate on the facts, the pooling of criminal cases without the slightest concern for proportionality can be disconcerting. This is doubly true when the criminal law has expanded beyond realms traditionally enforced by civil law.

Showing a causal link is difficult, especially when one tries to connect constitutional development to political change and bureaucratic choice. Nevertheless, I wonder whether the creep of enforcement tactics from one offense to another not just mirrors, but is actually promoted by, the "trans-substantive" state of criminal procedure doctrine that Bill has rightfully highlighted.[55] That courts draw no "distinctions among crimes . . . when it comes to regulating criminal investigations"[56] surely affects the calculus of enforcers deciding whether to import a tactic from one area to another.

The ability of agencies that pursue so-called real crime to attract and maintain funding and resource commitments also has repercussions outside the core. Public safety is not exactly a nonnegotiable part of governmental budgets. Indeed, it has been interesting to watch state and local governments cut back on their criminal justice expenditures in the wake of

[52] See Atwater v. City of Lago Vista, 532 U.S. 318 (2001); Wayne A. Logan, *Street Legal: The Court Affords Police Constitutional Carte Blanche*, 77 Ind. L. J. 419, 458 (2002) ("[B]y disavowing any need to correlate reasonableness with offense gravity, the *Atwater* majority missed an opportunity to provide legislatures with an incentive to undertake critical reexaminations of their criminal codes, a task that is long overdue."); see also Sameer Bajaj, *Note: Policing the Fourth Amendment: The Constitutionality of Warrantless Investigatory Stops for Past Misdemeanors*, 109 Colum. L. Rev. 309 (2009).

[53] See, e.g., Eric Lichtblau, "U.S. Uses Terror Law to Pursue Crimes from Drugs to Swindling," *New York Times*, Sept. 28, 2003 (detailing federal government expansive application of investigatory powers granted to it under the USA PATRIOT Act); see also Risa Berkower, *Sliding Down a Slippery Slope? The Future Use of Administrative Subpoenas in Criminal Investigations*, 73 Fordham L. Rev. 2251 (2005) (explaining the increasing availability of administrative subpoenas to criminal investigators).

[54] See Peter J. Henning, "White Collar Watch: Using Drug War Methods to Look for Insider Trading," *New York Times*, Sept. 30, 2010, at F7.

[55] William J. Stuntz, *O. J. Simpson, Bill Clinton, and the Transsubstantive Fourth Amendment*, 114 Harv. L. Rev. 842 (2001).

[56] Id. at 843.

the recent economic downturn.[57] However, support for general criminal enforcement agencies – local police and prosecutors; the FBI and federal prosecutors – certainly has a durable strength that agencies lacking their core crime portfolio can only envy. Furthermore, the relative opacity of those agencies, the high fixed cost of the informational networks (i.e., the local police patrol beat; the federal relationships with local enforcers), and the apparently low marginal cost of extending beyond the core crime mission means that even when funding for some government mission lags (perhaps because of shifting political preferences), criminal prosecutors will remain potential actors.

Notice the two steps of the problem: Lacking any clear understanding of what ought to be criminalized, we have opted for an institutional definition. This is not in and of itself indefensible. However intellectually unsatisfying this approach may be to moral retributivists or adherents to Becker and Posner,[58] there is something to be said for creating criminal options and leaving prosecutors to make the granular determinations not amenable to easy legislative specification: Although crack houses are usually targeted civilly, the owner of this particular one should face criminal charges; although the Securities and Exchange Commission (SEC) generally brings civil enforcement actions against insider traders, this particular group should be prosecuted for criminal securities fraud. However, in combination with a second aspect of our system – our reliance on relatively high-status general criminal jurisdiction institutions – we end up with a dangerous political dynamic that makes criminal enforcement the envy of anyone with a policy agenda – even a policy agenda that, all things being equal, they would have preferred to pursue with some other form of governmental action. The intervention of agencies that, as a result of legislative and theoretical abdication, we have placed in charge of sorting for so-called real criminality will thus often be sought less for features intrinsic to criminalization than for those that have been bundled into criminal enforcement only contingently.

[57] See Judith Greene & Marc Mauer, Downscaling Prisons: Lessons from Four States (Sentencing Project 2010); Pew Center on the States, Prison Count 2010: State Population Declines for the First Time in 38 Years (March 2010).

[58] Compare John C. Coffee, Jr., *Corporate Crime and Punishment: A Non-Chicago View of the Economics of Criminal Sanctions*, 17 Am. Crim. L. Rev. 417 (1980), with Richard A. Posner, *Optimal Sentences for White-Collar Criminals*, 17 Am. Crim. L. Rev. 409 (1980), and Gary Becker, *Crime and Punishment: An Economic Approach*, 76 J. Pol. Econ. 169 (1968).

The problem occurs at all levels of government and is not new. Decades ago, Sanford Kadish (writing from California) bemoaned how the criminal process had become "overburdened" by the imposition on prosecutors and police of the duty to provide various "social services to needy segments of the community."[59] Although the obligation to pursue nonsupport complaints, he noted, "is performed by police and prosecutors with some success, it is done reluctantly and usually less effectively than by a civil agency especially designed to handle the service. In addition, it is performed at a sacrifice to those primary functions of protecting the public against dangerous and threatening conduct which only the criminal law can perform."[60] As Kadish surely recognized, however, any such civil agency would face vagaries of public funding and political support that criminal justice agencies would never face. Perhaps the relative sanctity of criminal justice expenditures (at least until the current recession) is endemic to California. Exploring how California prosecutors have been using statutory rape charges as leverage for child support payments, Kay Levine recently noted, "In an age where funding for social services is constantly on the decline and law and order programs seem to be the only measures garnering bipartisan support, criminal justice agencies may be the only institutions with the financial resources to take on seemingly intractable social problems."[61] California is probably not unique, however. Jonathan Simon (writing from California) has plausibly suggested the phenomenon is national, reporting that "prosecutors operating mainly at the local level have found themselves pulled to act in a wider sphere of governance that was largely abandoned by the retreat of welfarism."[62]

Not only will funding be stickier when a policy is pitched as a criminal enforcement project, but it will come with institutional and fiscal multipliers because of the priority that other organizations, public and private, give to cooperation with crime-fighting institutions. Consider Nancy Wolff's account of mental health courts: "By invoking the court's power and legitimacy [and presumably that of the prosecutors bringing the cases], mental health courts may more effectively jump queues

[59] Sanford H. Kadish, *The Crisis of Overcriminalization*, 7 Am. Crim. L. Q. 17, 27–28 (1968).

[60] Id. at 30.

[61] See Kay Levine, *The New Prosecution*, 40 Wake Forest L. Rev. 1125, 1211 (2005).

[62] Jonathan Simon, Governing Through Crime: How the War on Crime Transformed American Democracy and Created a Culture of Fear 72 (2007).

or circumvent access barriers and, as such, be more successful in getting mentally ill offenders into treatment."[63] Also consider the allure of "community prosecutors," whose status often allows them to leap bureaucratic boundaries and deploy (without themselves providing) social services in the name of public safety.[64]

We see the same phenomenon on the federal side, particularly in the white-collar area. Even as the Bush (II) Administration's ambivalence about financial regulation led to diminished numbers and zeal among frontline investigators at the SEC,[65] federal prosecutors were racking up convictions in financial fraud prosecutions, and the Justice Department was touting their successes.[66] To be sure, prosecutors faced competing criminal enforcement priorities[67] and had to do some backpedaling in response to congressional concerns about overaggressive enforcement.[68] Nonetheless, they were far more insulated from deregulatory pressures than were their SEC cousins. Anyone wanting more zealous public enforcement in the capital markets during the Bush years (the lack of which we are now coming to regret) would therefore have reached for

[63] Nancy Wolff, *Courts as Therapeutic Agents: Thinking Past the Novelty of Mental Health Courts*, 30 J. Am. Acad. Psychiatry L. 431, 433 (2002).

[64] See Cecelia Klingele, Michael S. Scott, & Walter J. Dickey, *Reimagining Criminal Justice*, 2010 Wisc. L. Rev. 953, 981 (2010) (noting that "prosecutors possess a level of credibility and moral authority within many communities that could enable them to engage members of the community in active partnerships and to garner support for new initiatives"); Elizabeth Glazer, *Thinking Strategically: How Federal Prosecutors Can Reduce Violent Crime*, 26 Fordham Urb. L. J. 573, 605 (1999) ("It is not that the prosecutors will run the after-school programs, but rather they have the wherewithal to bring to the table the front-line service providers who know how to make the world of legitimate work more attractive to . . . children than the world of their drug-dealing friends").

[65] See General Accountability Office, "Securities and Exchange Commission: Greater Attention Needed to Enhance Communication and Utilization of Resources in the Division of Enforcement," 17–24 (March 2009), available at www.gao.gov/new.items/d09358.pdf; Securities and Exchange Commission, Office of Inspector General, "Program Improvements Needed Within the SEC's Division of Enforcement" (Sept. 29, 2009), available at http://www.sec-oig.gov/AuditsInspections/Reports.html. See also Donald C. Langevoort, *The SEC and the Madoff Scandal: Three Narratives in Search of a Story*, 2009 Mich. St. L. Rev. 899.

[66] See Daniel Richman, *Political Control of Federal Prosecutions*, 58 Duke L. J. 2087 (2009).

[67] See Daniel Richman, *Decisions About Coercion: The Corporate Attorney-Client Privilege Waiver Problem*, 57 DePaul L. Rev. 295, 314 n. 90 (2008) (highlighting sketchy and somewhat contradictory evidence as to the extent of criminal resources committed to white-collar prosecutions during the Bush Administration).

[68] Id. at 297–302 (recounting the Bush Administration's response to congressional concerns about the Justice Department's corporate attorney–client privilege waiver policies).

criminal sanctions far more than any rational sanction model would dictate.[69]

Then there are the cheerleaders for criminal enforcement that come from the ranks of those who want less government intervention, not more. Take public corruption. The mantra of opponents to campaign finance or lobbying reform – whether in Washington, D.C. or a state capital – is that the bad behavior that reform proposals would target through prophylactic regimes can simply be prosecuted, should actual instances occur.[70] These regulatory opponents drive the point home by regularly passing overlapping criminal statutes that explicitly target the bad behavior. So too with gun regulation, where the need for state and federal prosecutions of gun-toting felons has been a key plank of anti-firearms-regulation forces.[71] Note how the best-case scenarios for a regulatory regime can thus be picked off and assigned to the criminal process.

Criminalization – not just symbolic legislation but actual prosecutions – has thus become a sweet spot for both those favoring maximal government action and those favoring minimal. Rather than offering an extreme option in a graduated spectrum of sanctions and regulatory

[69] See John C. Coffee, Jr., *Law and the Market: The Impact of Enforcement*, 156 U. Pa. L. Rev. 229 (2007) (highlighting value of public enforcement).

[70] See, e.g., Colorado Republican Federal Campaign Committee v. FEC, 518 U.S. 604, 642 (1996) (Thomas, J. concurring), quoting with approval the argument by appellants in *Buckley v. Valeo*: "If a small minority of political contributions are given to secure appointments for the donors or some other *quid pro quo*, that cannot serve to justify prohibiting all large contributions, the vast majority of which are given not for any such purpose but to further the expression of political views which the candidate and donor share. Where First Amendment rights are involved, a blunderbuss approach which prohibits mostly innocent speech cannot be held a means narrowly and precisely directed to the governmental interest in the small minority of contributions that are not innocent" (Quoting Brief for Appellants in *Buckley v. Valeo*, O. T. 1975, Nos. 75–436 and 75–437, pp. 117–118). See also Testimony of Roger Pilon, Cato Institute, before the House Committee on House Administration: Constitutional Issues Related to Campaign Finance Reform (July 22, 1999) ("If there is quid-pro-quo corruption, then let the Justice Department investigate it. All the evidence suggests, however, that money buys access, it does not buy votes"), available at http://www.cato.org/testimony/ct-rp072299.html; see also Citizens United v. Federal Election Comm'n, 130 S. Ct. 876, 908 (2010) (in the course of striking down campaign finance restrictions, Court notes that bribery laws cover quid pro quo arrangements).

[71] See Daniel C. Richman, *"Project Exile" and the Allocation of Federal Law Enforcement Authority*, 43 Ariz. L. Rev. 369 (2001); see also Jackie Calmes, "Administration Invites N.R.A. to Meet on Gun Policies, But It Declines," *New York Times*, Mar. 15, 2011, at A24 (noting, in connection with efforts by the White House to reach out to the NRA, that President Obama's recent column had "emphasized, 'First we should begin by enforcing laws that are already on the books' – a line long used by the gun lobby").

choices, criminal prosecution ends up as the natural point of first resort for all too many players of this perverse political game. The odds become slim that actual enforcement patterns – the result of institutional choices that we rely on in lieu of serious thinking about the criminal–civil divide – will reflect a serious engagement with overcriminalization concerns.

One can argue that criminal prosecutions are simply the gold standard for state action in the United States, and that the centrality (and severity) of penal sanctions are just features of the larger "culture of control" that David Garland has so insightfully explored.[72] Nonetheless, as Garland himself has noted, we should attend to the structural and political sources that contribute to our distinct culture.[73] The (tentative) suggestion here is that the historically contingent institutional arrangements I have highlighted are more a cause than an effect of that culture (though they are probably both). At the very least, we should recognize how our distinct institutional mechanisms reinforce the social dynamics that social theorists have sketched out. One certainly ought to do so before making broad claims that American penal policy is "but the pretext and springboard for a broader remaking of the perimeter and functions of the state."[74]

RELIEVING THE DEMAND

Just as consideration of how criminal law and its enforcement become a resort for those for whom the stigma and punishment are but side effects of an institutional preference makes the pathologies of criminal law seem even worse than Bill has portrayed, so too might it offer new avenues for relief. Bill has suggested that the overcriminalization problem could be solved either by deregulating criminal procedure or by constitutionalizing the borders of criminal law.[75] Perhaps there is another avenue, more true

[72] David Garland, Culture of Control (2001).

[73] See David Garland, Concepts of Culture in the Sociology of Punishment, 10 *Theoretical Criminology* 419, 437 (2006).

[74] Loïc Wacquant, "The Place of the Prison in the New Government of Poverty," in After the War on Crime: Race, Democracy, and a New Reconstruction 23, 24 (Marie-Louie Frampton, Ián Haney López and Jonathan Simon, eds., 2008); see also Loïc Wacquant, *Ordering Insecurity: Social Polarization and the Punitive Upsurge*, 11 Radical Philosophy Rev. 9 (2008). I'm grateful to Jim Whitman and David Garland for pointing me toward Wacquant's work.

[75] William J. Stuntz, *Substance, Process, and the Civil-Criminal Line*, 7 J. Contemp. Legal Issues 1, 29 (1996).

to our process orientation: reducing the allure of criminal law by providing institutional alternatives to prosecution, and giving those institutions sufficient insulation from the ebb and flow of political preferences that they remain effective alternatives even in the lean years.

Criminal enforcers (tautologically) have a monopoly over the state's harshest coercive sanctions. Against whom should this sanction be deployed? That question – extended to include all instrumental uses of criminal sanctions, including information gathering – ought to be at the heart of any discussion about which conduct should be criminalized and to what extent. If we are not going to be systematic in having such a discussion, we might still – at least in theory – obtain a regime reflecting revealed societal preferences by relying on the choices made by accountable enforcement agencies. Yet when criminal sanctions are simply the second-best preference of those who would prefer a regulatory, social services, or some other noncriminal regime but cannot obtain it, that regime is unattainable, and overcriminalization – however normatively measured – is bound to occur. That our harshest sanctions are used only because less harsh alternatives are unavailable – that certain securities fraud cases are prosecuted because public and private civil enforcement are underfunded or procedurally obstructed,[76] or that drug treatment is more easily provided to addicts who are prosecuted than to those who simply seek help – makes no sense at all. We therefore ought to try to reduce this overuse by addressing the ways in which criminalization can crowd out and displace noncriminal processes and institutions.

One key to such demand reduction lies in recognizing the features we have bundled together with criminal sanctions that need not be exclusive to that regime. Sometimes unbundling will be particularly hard because of the relationship that Bill has highlighted between criminal defense rights and exercises of government power. Because criminal defendants have speedy trial rights that civil parties lack, criminal cases will be on a fast adjudication track that regulatory action cannot match. Criminal proceedings will also dominate when potential informational sources can invoke their Fifth Amendment right against self-incrimination, because the threat of prosecution (or the promise of immunity against prosecution) will be a powerful information-forcing tool. Nonetheless, we could do a lot more to bridge the huge gap between civil information-gathering mechanisms and the search warrants, grand jury subpoenae, and other such tools currently available only to prosecutors.

[76] See Christine Hurt, *The Undercivilization of Corporate Law*, 33 J. Corp. L. 361 (2008).

I suspect, for example, that a truly independent ethics commission with adequate resources and subpoena power would not be able, by itself, to clear up the self-dealing in Albany, Springfield, or any other state capital in the intense competition for "most corrupt."[77] Because the most troubling transactions are those about which participants are least likely to tell the truth, even under oath, only the threat or reality of criminal prosecution and imprisonment will likely shake this information loose. (Bill would probably have argued that antisnitching norms are now stronger in state capitals than in some Mafia families. But he could be harsh.) Nonetheless, subpoena power and the manpower to analyze compelled disclosures might well make recourse to the criminal law less necessary, particularly if given to an agency with the esprit and professionalism to make use of them. Although those who would starve regulatory agencies will indeed get less regulation, they will likely end up with more criminal prosecutions as well, in cases that might otherwise have been pursued without the threat of prison. The precise distribution of cases in an institutionally richer system is of course uncertain: In the course of its regulatory work, an effective ethics commission might kick up evidence of serious offenses meriting prosecution – as a result of direct referral by the commission or otherwise – frequently enough that we end up with more criminal cases than before. One can equally imagine fewer criminal cases. The goal here should simply be to create a number of institutional halfway houses – instead of a desert with criminal sanctions as the only shelter.[78]

Consider the citizen seeking recourse for some "wrong," perhaps done to her, perhaps to others; perhaps one for which the law creates a private cause of action, perhaps not. Although the line operator – the jaded desk sergeant or eye-rolling agent – to whom she brings this information may well do exactly nothing with it, a set of positive gatekeeping decisions by criminal enforcers will trigger a cascade of publically funded actions that will likely impose penal sanctions on the wrongdoer and, should he have any money, recompense for anyone actually harmed (via restitution or facilitated civil recovery). How far would the citizen have to look for noncriminal attention, and to what extent will the state subsidize that alternative process? Obviously the answer to that question will vary greatly by context and jurisdiction. In some contexts, because

[77] See Gail Collins op ed., *New York Times*, Feb. 14, 2010.

[78] See also Robert A. Kagan, American Legalism: The American Way of Law (2003) (suggesting that even in its civil mode, American-style regulation has too much in common with criminal prosecutions).

of, say, the nature of the targeted conduct or the value in developing a public norm, it might make sense to flatten out the landscape short of criminal sanctions and to give the citizen fewer substitutes.[79] In many others, however, it is worth thinking more about the gap between the satisfaction offered by a prosecution – if enforcers decide to pursue one – and that offered by alternatives (which might be as simple as regulatory outreach). Against the obvious net-widening risks whenever opportunities for recourse are increased (more litigation or regulatory responses to more complaints), we should weigh the distorting effect that the absence of such opportunities has on criminal enforcement.

We have similarly given too little attention to the development of efficient public institutions charged with finding facts and inflicting stigma outside of the criminal justice process. Because of defamation laws and the prohibitive cost of civil litigation, a person's criminal record is often the only source of public information about his past; it is certainly the most frequently consulted.[80] The private or public official who wants a record of someone's misdeeds maintained in the public domain will therefore often see criminal prosecution as the only solution. Moreover, civil service or other employment protections can often make it far easier (and cheaper for the employer) to have someone prosecuted than to terminate him with cause.[81] This is not to say that libel and employment law don't have social benefits. The point is simply that these and other institutional limitations of the civil process funnel close cases to the criminal side.

Even public discourse has become impoverished. Consider how many discussions of the morality of a public figure's behavior soon degenerate into arguments about whether the behavior constitutes a "crime," with the implication that what's not criminal is acceptable. Also consider how often criminal procedure's foundational "presumption of innocence"

[79] This may be one justification for the no-drop policies and other such institutions and procedures that have been explored in domestic violence cases. See Andrew R. Klein, "Practical Implications of Current Domestic Violence Research: For Law Enforcement, Prosecutors and Judges," National Institute of Justice Report, 2009, available at http://www.ojp.usdoj.gov/nij/topics/crime/intimate-partner-violence/practical-implications-research/welcome.htm; see also Michelle Madden Dempsey, Prosecuting Domestic Violence: A Philosophical Analysis (2009) (exploring moral dimensions of prosecutorial policies in this area).

[80] See Shawn D. Bushway, *Labor Market Effects of Permitting Employer Access to Criminal History Records*, 20 J. Contemp. Crim. J. 276 (2004).

[81] See Nicole B. Porter, *The Perfect Compromise: Bridging the Gap Between At-Will Employment and Just Cause*, 87 Neb. L. Rev. 62, 78–84 (2008).

drives debates about a candidate or appointee's qualifications.[82] Moreover because recourse to the criminal process leads to the underdevelopment of the very noncriminal norms that would condemn behavior without declaring it worthy of prosecution, the funnel widens over time.

Jonathan Simon suggests that the state has deployed the rubric of crime itself as a tool of governance: "When we govern through crime, we make crime and the forms of knowledge historically associated with it – criminal law, popular crime narrative, and criminology – available outside their limited original subject matter domains as powerful tools with which to interpret and frame all forms of social action as a problem for governance."[83] Perhaps. Ours is indeed a culture that has become all too quick to criminalize what we do not like. However, if we decoupled certain criminal enforcement privileges from the criminal label we might substantially reduce recourse to the criminal process, and to the sanctions and stigma that attend it.

As Bill has long noted, the degree to which we rely on criminal enforcers to sort out conduct that is "really" criminal from that which is not challenges standard rule-of-law notions. Judges and legislators ought to take on a lot more of this responsibility. While we are waiting for these reluctant actors, though, we should give more thought to the sociolegal vacuums that criminal enforcers will rush in or be recruited to fill. Recognizing the degree to which diverse institutional and political factors push toward overuse of the criminal process should push us to design effective alternatives to it.

[82] Dennis E. Curtis, *Gender, Race, and the Politics of Supreme Court Appointments: The Import of the Anita Hill/Clarence Thomas Hearings: The Fake Trial*, 65 S. Cal. L. Rev. 1523, 1525 (1992).

[83] Simon, supra note 62, at 17.

4

Stealing Bill Stuntz

David Alan Sklansky

George Orwell began his celebrated essay on Charles Dickens by remarking that Dickens was "one of those writers who are well worth stealing.... The Marxist claims him as 'almost' a Marxist, the Catholic claims him as 'almost' a Catholic, and both claim him as a champion of the proletariat." Even Chesterton, Orwell pointed out, "credit[ed] Dickens with his own highly individual branch of medievalism."[1] Everyone wanted Dickens as an ally; everyone saw in him a sympathetic soul.

Bill Stuntz is the Charles Dickens of criminal procedure scholars. Burkean skeptics praise him as a model Burkean skeptic.[2] Law-and-order conservatives enlist him in arms against the legacy of the Warren Court.[3] Liberals embrace him as a critic of overcriminalization, excessive punishment, and inequality.[4] Even scholars assigned to critique Stuntz's work have usually paused first to make clear that, really, on the important matters, they see eye to eye with him.[5]

* I thank Erin Murphy for helpful feedback on an earlier draft.

1 George Orwell, *Charles Dickens*, in 1 COLLECTED ESSAYS, JOURNALISM AND LETTERS OF GEORGE ORWELL 413, 413–414 (Sonia Orwell & Ian Angus eds., 1968).

2 See, e.g., Ronald J. Allen & Ross M. Rosenberg, *The Fourth Amendment and the Limits of Theory: Local Versus General Theoretical Knowledge*, 12 ST. JOHN'S L. REV. 1149, 1184–1189 (1998).

3 See, e.g., Paul G. Cassell, *A Tribute to Joe Grano: He Kept the Flames Alive*, 46 WAYNE L. REV. 1215, 1219 (2000).

4 See, e.g., Jonathan Simon, *Positively Punitive: How the Inventor of Scientific Criminology Who Died at the Beginning of the Twentieth Century Continues to Haunt American Crime Control at the Beginning of the Twenty-First*, 84 TEX. L. REV. 2135, 2169 (2006); Andrew E. Taslitz, *Judging Jena's D.A.: The Prosecutor and Racial Esteem*, 44 HARV. C.R.-C.L. L. REV. 393, 435 (2009).

5 See, e.g., Carol S. Steiker, *"How Much Justice Can You Afford?" – A Response to Stuntz*, 67 GEO. WASH. L. REV. 1290 (1999); Louis Michael Seidman, *The Problems with Privacy's Problem*, 93 MICH. L. REV. 1079 (1995); David Alan Sklansky, *Killer*

Having so many fans can be disreputable. We often say of writers with such broad appeal that they are "hard to pigeonhole" – meaning, usually, that they are mercurial or vacuous. However, it is hard to think of scholars whose ideas were more orderly and reflective than Stuntz's, or scholars who thought harder and deeper than he about our system of criminal justice. Stuntz was open-minded, and his thinking evolved over the years – but he didn't change course lightly.

The reason that different people find different things to like in Stuntz's work is not that he was inconsistent and certainly not that he had little to say. It is that there are several distinct and important themes in his work – three at least. One is that criminal justice must be understood as a complicated system, and that changing any part of that system inevitably affects the rest of the system in complex, often unintended ways. This is the theme that appeals to Burkeans – although Stuntz had little faith that systems, left to themselves, gradually perfect themselves in anything but the very long run. A second strand of his work is that criminal justice has a political economy: that the system involves allocation of resources through markets and pricing, and that there is no free lunch. This is the strand that appeals to conservative critics of the criminal procedure revolution – although Stuntz was hardly an unqualified foe of judicial activism. The third theme of his scholarship is egalitarianism, or more precisely an overriding concern for the least well off. He was a persistent critic of inequality, in the criminal justice system and elsewhere – although he argued again and again that some traditional responses to inequality, particularly in the criminal justice system, may do more harm than good.

Part of what I want to do here is to say a bit about each of these three themes of Stuntz's work, why Stuntz was right to stress it, and how it helps to make his body of scholarship so illuminating. I also want to draw some broader lessons from the crosscutting appeal of the work. One of those lessons has to do with the possibilities for enlightened politics and meaningful reform: the possibilities that issues of criminal justice, in particular, can be addressed democratically in ways that are thoughtful and deliberative, rather than just becoming another battlefront in a never-ending culture war. A second lesson has to do with the significance of leadership, idealism, and personal decency – a theme that, ironically enough, is largely missing from Stuntz's rich account of

Seatbelts and Criminal Procedure, 119 HARV. L. REV. F. 56 (2006); Robert Weisberg, *First Causes and the Dynamics of Criminal Justice*, 119 HARV. L. REV. F. 131 (2006).

criminal justice as a dynamic system of political economy. It shows up in some of his other writings, though, and it is richly demonstrated by his own career.

CRIMINAL JUSTICE AND COMPLEXITY

The claim about criminal justice that surfaces most often in Stuntz's work is that the system is complicated. It's complicated to describe, it's complicated to assess, and it's complicated to reform intelligently. Not only did Stuntz repeatedly make this claim – policing and criminal adjudication, he kept insisting, are more multifarious and complex than we think[6] – but he repeatedly demonstrated it. This is what makes summarizing any of Stuntz's articles so difficult: The account he offered was rarely simple, because the world, as he saw it, was a complicated place.

Here, for example, is the argument Stuntz made in 1992 about the way the Supreme Court had applied the Fourth Amendment in "special needs" cases (i.e., cases involving some government interest beyond the

[6] See, e.g., William J. Stuntz, *Self-Incrimination and Excuse*, 88 COLUM. L. REV. 1227, 1228, 1289 (1988); William J. Stuntz, *Warrants and Fourth Amendment Remedies*, 77 VA. L. REV. 881, 901, 916, 935, 942 (1991) [hereinafter *Warrants and Fourth Amendment Remedies*]; Robert E. Scott & William J. Stuntz, *Plea Bargaining as Contract*, 101 YALE L. J. 11909, 1936 (1992) [hereinafter *Plea Bargaining as Contract*]; William J. Stuntz, *Lawyers, Deception, and Evidence Gathering*, 79 VA. L. REV. 1903, 1928, 1943, 1955 (1993); William J. Stuntz, *Privacy's Problem and the Law of Criminal Procedure*, 93 MICH. L. REV. 1016, 1027 n. 43, 1076 (1995) [hereinafter *Privacy's Problem*]; William J. Stuntz, *The Uneasy Relationship Between Criminal Procedure and Criminal Justice*, 107 YALE L. J. 1, 13, 22, 36, 49, 51 (1997) [hereinafter *Uneasy Relationship*]; William J. Stuntz, *Terry's Impossibility*, 72 ST. JOHN'S L. REV. 1213, 1216, 1218 (1998); William J. Stuntz, *Race, Class, and Drugs*, 98 COLUM. L. REV. 1795, 1798 n. 7, 1833, 1835, 1841 (1998) [hereinafter *Race, Class, and Drugs*]; William J. Stuntz, *The Distribution of Fourth Amendment Privacy*, 67 GEO. WASH. L. REV. 1265, 1266 (1999) [hereinafter *Distribution of Fourth Amendment Privacy*]; William J. Stuntz, *Self-Defeating Crimes*, 86 VA. L. REV. 1871, 1891 (2000) [hereinafter *Self-Defeating Crimes*]; William J. Stuntz, *The Pathological Politics of Criminal Law*, 100 MICH. L. REV. 505, 531, 541, 573, 575 (2001) [hereinafter *Pathological Politics*]; William J. Stuntz, *Terrorism, Federalism, and Police Misconduct*, 25 HARV. J. L. & PUB. POL'Y 665, 667 (2002) [hereinafter *Terrorism, Federalism, and Police Misconduct*]; William J. Stuntz, *Reply: Criminal Law's Pathology*, 101 MICH. L. REV. 828, 836 (2002); William J. Stuntz, *Christian Legal Theory*, 116 HARV. L. REV. 1707, 1743 (2003) [hereinafter *Christian Legal Theory*]; William J. Stuntz, *Plea Bargaining and Criminal Law's Disappearing Shadow*, 117 HARV. L. REV. 2548, 2554 (2004) [hereinafter *Disappearing Shadow*]; William J. Stuntz, *The Political Constitution of Criminal Justice*, 119 HARV. L. REV. 780, 786 (2006) [hereinafter *Political Constitution*]; William J. Stuntz, *Unequal Justice*, 121 HARV. L. REV. 1969, 1970 (2008) [hereinafter *Unequal Justice*].

usual aims of law enforcement).[7] A series of Supreme Court decisions in the 1980s and 1990s invoked the concept of special needs in the course of upholding drug-testing programs, sobriety checkpoints, searches of schoolchildren, searches of parolees, and searches in government workplaces. By the time Stuntz wrote, these cases had a bad reputation. Most scholars who had written about them thought they watered down Fourth Amendment protections without justification.

Stuntz thought the results made sense, but the justification he gave was subtle and multifaceted. In an ordinary criminal investigation, if the police are prevented from carrying out a particular search or seizure because, say, they lack probable cause, then they generally will not be able to substitute something equally intrusive. They *would* have that ability if the state could expand substantive criminal liability without limits; then probable cause requirements could be circumvented simply by widening what counts as criminal. However, a combination of political constraints and constitutional restrictions significantly limits the scope of substantive criminal liability. (This is a judgment Stuntz later revisited, but more about that below.) So probable cause requirements meaningfully restrict the police. The situation is different, though, when the government has some kind of preexisting relationship with the subject of the search – a teacher–student relationship, for example, or an employer–employee relationship. Then if the government is prevented from carrying out a search or seizure, it will typically be able to take some other, even more intrusive step – such as suspending the student, or firing the employee. Everyone may be better off if the government is allowed to carry out the search or seizure – well, everyone except suspects with something to hide, and *their* interests are not the ones that should control. That means that searches or seizures of suspects with whom the government has some kind of preexisting relationship should be permissible as long as they are of a kind that innocent targets would agree to, if the rules were negotiated in advance. Criminal procedure in this setting is not tort law for the police; it is contract law for the police. This explains the results the Supreme Court had reached for school searches, government workplace searches, parole searches, and searches of regulated industries. It *does not* explain the decisions in which the Supreme Court upheld suspicionless drug testing and sobriety checkpoints. Here there is a different explanation, though. Because these programs impose blanket burdens on large

[7] See William J. Stuntz, *Implicit Bargains, Government Power, and the Fourth Amendment*, 44 STAN. L. REV. 553 (1992) [hereinafter *Implicit Bargains*].

groups of people, politics provides an adequate remedy for excessive zeal on the part of the police. We don't need the Fourth Amendment.

That is only a rough outline of the argument, and this is an article Stuntz wrote relatively early in his career. The later articles are even harder to summarize. Notice, though, that even in this early article, there is no unitary explanation, no single, grand theory – not even of what might be thought a narrow, specialized subcategory of search-and-seizure law.

As time went on, Stuntz's accounts of criminal procedure grew even more nuanced. As an illustration, here are just the bullet points from an article he published in 2006.[8] The Warren Court's criminal procedure revolution regulated policing and trial procedures aggressively, but left substantive criminal law largely untouched. That has meant that rules of criminal liability and sentencing are easier for legislators to monkey with than rules regulating police and the trial process, so legislatures have been willing to spend more money on prisons, and on lengthy terms of incarceration for convicted criminals, than on policing and criminal adjudication. This series of incentives has reinforced the tendency that legislators would have in any event to worry more about the interests of criminal suspects than the interests of criminal defendants, and more about the interests of criminal defendants than the interests of defendants who have been convicted and sentenced to prison, because as targets proceed through the criminal justice pipeline, they become fewer, less sympathetic, and less politically powerful. Those natural tendencies on the part of legislators mean that, left to their own devices, legislators are more likely to devise fair rules for policing and for the trial process than reasonable rules of criminal punishment. Thus the criminal procedure revolution attacked the wrong end of the process. The criminal justice revolution also had another pernicious effect: It widened the gap between the cost of investigating and prosecuting wealthy targets and the cost of investigating and prosecuting targets with fewer resources. That has made the system even more tilted against the poor and even more racially skewed. Also, by focusing legislative attention on punishment rather than policing and adjudication, the criminal justice revolution may have exacerbated the tendency toward racism in criminal justice politics, because it has made minority convicts more politically salient than minority suspects, and convicted criminals are less sympathetic than people the police just suspect may have committed crimes. Remedying this state of affairs requires the following: (a) shifting control over criminal

8 *Political Constitution*, supra note 6.

procedure from appellate courts to trial courts, in part by giving trial judges broad discretion to acquit whenever they think it appropriate; (b) shifting the concern of criminal procedure from conduct (such as police practices) to outcomes (such as erroneous convictions); (c) making more use of default rules (which encourage elected officials to craft their own, substitute rules for police conduct and criminal trials), data collection and disclosure requirements (which help unclog channels of democratic accountability), and structural injunctions (which function, in effect, as a system of bankruptcy for underperforming criminal justice agencies); (d) focusing constitutional regulation of the police on violence, discrimination, and corruption, rather than on privacy; (e) mandating adequate funding for indigent criminal defense; (f) requiring prosecutors to prove that the criminal statutes they invoke are applied systematically, not just sporadically or selectively, and that the sanctions they recommend in any particular case are in keeping with past practices; (g) subjecting sentencing rules to serious equal protection review; and (h) promoting accountability by drawing clear lines between crimes that should be investigated and prosecuted locally and those that should be handled by the federal government. The odds are against reform of this type, but if it happens it will be because the Supreme Court begins to think of itself as working *with* politicians in the area of criminal justice, rather than against them. Whenever the Supreme Court tries to impose rigid rules of conduct, in criminal justice or elsewhere in constitutional law, it winds up triggering a political backlash.

Anyone who has read *The Political Constitution of Criminal Justice* will recognize how inadequately this summarizes Stuntz's argument there, and how hopeless it is to try to capture the argument in a paragraph – even a long paragraph. Stuntz's arguments resist summary because he saw the world as full of twists and turns.

Among the great virtue of this view is that it is faithful to reality. The world *is* full of twists and turns, and so is criminal procedure. Anyone who writes about the criminal justice system, including Stuntz, falsifies by simplification. Stuntz did less of that than just about anyone else writing in the field, though. And he was surely right to warn, again and again, that well-intentioned reforms of complicated systems can wind up backfiring, because complicated systems can react to changes in unanticipated ways.

Nonetheless, if there are virtues in acknowledging complications, there are also risks. The chief risk is that an embrace of complexity can easily descend into fatalism, or into a paralyzing form of uncertainty.[9] It

[9] Cf. C. Wright Mills, The Power Elite 27, 245 (1956).

is instructive that this never happens in Stuntz's work. He did preach humility,[10] and he practiced it – but not by retreating into bewilderment or indecision. There is never any shrugging of the shoulders in a Stuntz article. He knew what he thought. "[A]voiding hard predictions," he warned, "has its own downside."[11] Even "educated guesswork" is better than throwing up our hands.[12] He was a believer in humility, but he was also deeply committed to the project of rationalist reform.

The humility that Stuntz practiced did not entail irresolution. It did entail listening carefully to what others had to say and being willing to reconsider his own views. Two signal strengths of Stuntz's work are, first, the wide range of scholars whose work he read and drew upon – a group remarkable for both its ideological diversity and its disciplinary diversity – and, second, his willingness to reconsider positions he had previously staked out. I have noted, for example, Stuntz's appeal in a relatively early article to the strong constitutional restrictions on substantive criminal law. Much of his later work, in contrast, argued that constitutional restrictions on substantive criminal law are virtually nonexistent, and that we are the worse for that.[13] An early and influential article Stuntz wrote with Robert Scott argued, famously, that plea bargaining is not as bad as it was often made out to be; the practice had, they said, many of the virtues and vices of contracts more broadly.[14] Later Stuntz was, to say the least, considerably less sanguine about plea agreements.[15] What is more, on moralism in criminal law – the use of criminal statutes to endorse and to reinforce contested moral commitments – Stuntz completely reversed course, changing from a strong fan to a committed opponent.[16]

It is clear that the kind of humility Stuntz practiced was intentional, and in part a matter of personal commitment. In Stuntz's writings about Christianity, he spoke explicitly not only about the general importance of humility but also, and more specifically, about the importance of seeing things with other peoples' eyes – of imagining and stepping inside

[10] See, e.g., *Christian Legal Theory*, supra note 6, at 1729; David A. Skeel, Jr. & William J. Stuntz, *Christianity and the (Modest) Rule of Law*, 8 U. PA. J. CONST. L. 809, 831 (2006); William J. Stuntz, "Faculty Clubs and Church Pews," *TCS Daily*, Nov. 29, 2004, available at www.tcsdaily.com [hereinafter *Faculty Clubs and Church Pews*].

[11] *Implicit Bargains*, supra note 7, at 570. [12] Id.

[13] See, e.g., William J. Stuntz, *Substance, Procedure, and the Civil-Criminal Line*, 7 J. CONTEMP. LEGAL ISSUES 1 (1996) [hereinafter *Civil-Criminal Line*]; *Uneasy Relationship*, supra note 6.

[14] See *Plea Bargaining as Contract*, supra note 6.

[15] See *Disappearing Shadow*, supra note 6.

[16] See infra notes 38–44 and accompanying text.

their mental universes.[17] As we will see later, this particular dimension of humility had a lot to do with Stuntz's change of heart about moralism in criminal law. For now I want to make two more general comments about the role of humility in Stuntz's work. The first is that among the many things Stuntz's work teaches is that humility doesn't have to mean meekness or compliance – and that a "Mr. Fix-it mentality" (to borrow Justice Scalia's famous putdown of common-law judging)[18] is not necessarily a sign of arrogance. The second is that the kind of humility seen in Stuntz's work – which strikes me as a particularly appealing kind of humility – is not *just* a matter of personal commitment. It is also a scholarly strategy, linked, in important ways, to Stuntz's embrace of complexity. A simple world could be understood, maybe, from a single perspective, with a unified set of ideological presuppositions, and using a limited disciplinary toolkit. But that is not the world Stuntz wrote about. The very complexity of the problems he described demanded a kind of intellectual triangulation.

The complexity stressed in Stuntz's accounts of the criminal justice system has another important implication. It also underscores the importance of designing systems of government accountability – a theme Stuntz repeatedly stressed. The more complicated a system is, the harder it becomes to pinpoint the people responsible for what the system does and to hold them to account. And the criminal justice system, as Stuntz described it, is *very* complicated. So he argued again and again for designing rules and institutions in ways that would clarify which government officials, which sets of institutions, and which bodies of law are responsible for what. Much of his critique of the criminal procedure revolution had to do with the ways in which the Warren Court's constitutionalization of criminal procedure short-circuited the systems of accountability provided by local politics.[19] The worry that he and Dan Richman raised about pretextual prosecutions was not that they are unfair but that they make it harder for the public to monitor what the government is doing.[20] Similarly, their concern about the federalization of criminal law was not

[17] See William J. Stuntz, "Turning Faith into Elevator Music," *TCS Daily*, July 1, 2005, available at www.tcsdaily.com; More on Lewis' Uniqueness–Stuntz, blog post to Less than the Least, Aug. 16, 2008, available at www.law.upenn.edu/blogs/dskeel/.

[18] Antonin Scalia, A MATTER OF INTERPRETATION: FEDERAL COURTS AND THE LAW 14 (1997).

[19] See, e.g., *Pathological Politics*, supra note 6; *Political Constitution*, supra note 6; *Unequal Justice*, supra note 6.

[20] Daniel C. Richman & William J. Stuntz, *Al Capone's Revenge: An Essay on the Political Economy of Pretextual Prosecution*, 105 COLUM. L. REV. 583 (2005).

that the federal government is getting involved in matters that are inherently local, but that we lack clear lines dividing federal criminal responsibility from local criminal responsibility. The jurisdictional restrictions the Supreme Court has placed on federal criminal statutes are not too restrictive or too loose; they are too arbitrary and unpredictable.[21]

That is an important lesson, particularly when combined with another of Stuntz's great themes. Part of what makes criminal procedure complex, Stuntz showed, is the way that it intersects with other things – politics,[22] substantive criminal law,[23] government budgets,[24] and the constitutional law of the welfare state.[25] The boundaries separating criminal procedure from other dimensions of government activity have, of course, grown even more porous and less distinct since September 11, 2001. The most obvious way this has happened is by the blurring of the frontier between criminal law enforcement and counterterrorism – a subject on which Stuntz wrote perceptively, both alone and with Dan Richman.[26] Equally if not more important, though, is the increasingly indistinct boundary between criminal justice and immigration. These used to be almost entirely distinct realms of governance: local police departments stayed out of immigration enforcement not just because it was a federal responsibility, but because they wanted the trust of the millions of people in the United States without proper documentation. Many departments still maintain that policy, but immigration enforcement and criminal justice are far more intertwined than they used to be; practitioners increasingly see themselves as working in the merged field of "crimmigration."[27] This is a process that began before September 11, 2001, but it accelerated dramatically after that date. Immigration cases are now not just the largest category of federal criminal prosecutions; they are a *majority* of federal

[21] See id. at 634–636.

[22] See, e.g., id.; *Self-Defeating Crimes*, supra note 6; *Pathological Politics*, supra note 6; *Political Constitution*, supra note 6; *Unequal Justice*, supra note 6.

[23] See, e.g., William J. Stuntz, *The Substantive Origins of Criminal Procedure*, 105 YALE L. J. 394 (1995); *Uneasy Relationship*, supra note 6; *Civil-Criminal Line*, supra note 13.

[24] See, e.g., *Uneasy Relationship*, supra note 6; *Political Constitution*, supra note 6.

[25] See, e.g., *Privacy's Problem*, supra note 6.

[26] See, e.g., William J. Stuntz, *Local Policing After the Terror*, 111 YALE L. J. 2137 (2002) [hereinafter *Local Policing After the Terror*]; *Terrorism, Federalism, and Police Misconduct*, supra note 6; Richman & Stuntz, supra note 20; see also Daniel C. Richman, *The Right Fight: Local Police and National Security*, BOSTON REV., Dec. 2004.

[27] See, e.g., Jennifer Chacón, *Managing Migration Through Crime*, 109 COLUM. L. REV. SIDEBAR 135 (2009); Juliet Stumpf, *The Crimmigration Crisis: Immigrants, Crime, and Sovereign Power*, 56 AM. U. L. REV. 367 (2006).

criminal prosecutions.[28] Meanwhile administrative deportations of immigrants because of criminal convictions have risen steeply, the "criminal alien" has become the central, overriding concern of immigration authorities, and immigration proceedings increasingly borrow the tools and standards of criminal cases.[29] Local police agencies increasingly cooperate with federal immigration officials. In addition, a vast network of administrative detention facilities has emerged for immigration violations, paralleling – and regularly transferring prisoners to and from – the jails, prisons, and other criminal correctional institutions operating at the federal, state, and local levels.[30] All of this tends to make the criminal justice system, and the immigration system, more complicated and less transparent.[31] Here as elsewhere, greater complexity and reduced transparency have meant less accountability, in ways that closely parallel the accountability deficits Stuntz highlighted elsewhere in the criminal justice system.

How should we think about and respond to the rise of crimmigration? One lesson of Stuntz's work is that we should start by recognizing the sheer complexity of the merged system of criminal and immigration enforcement, and by doing our best to understand all its nuances, traps, and hidden opportunities. A second lesson is that the very complexity of the system, with its blurred boundaries, overlapping responsibilities, and intersecting processes, may pose threats to transparency and accountability. We should be alert to ways in which the proliferating interconnections between immigration enforcement and the criminal justice system make it hard to know which agencies and which officials are responsible for which goals, which processes, and which consequences.

These seem to me, in fact, to be precisely the dimensions of crimmigration most worth worrying about – not whether illegal entry is really

[28] See Transactional Records Access Clearinghouse, FY 2009 FEDERAL PROSECUTIONS SHARPLY HIGHER: SURGE DRIVEN BY STEEP JUMP IN IMMIGRATION FILINGS (2009), available at trac.syr.edu; Joanna Lydgate, Chief Justice Earl Warren Institute on Race, Ethnicity & Diversity, ASSEMBLY-LINE JUSTICE: A REVIEW OF OPERATION STREAMLINE (2009).

[29] See. e.g., Stephen H. Legomsky, *The New Path of Immigration Law: Asymmetric Incorporation of Criminal Justice Norms*, 64 Wash. & Lee L. Rev. 469 (2007); Teresa A. Miller, *Citizenship & Severity: Recent Immigration Reforms and the New Penology*, 17 Geo. Immigr. L. J. 611 (2003).

[30] See William J. Sabol, Heather C. West & Matthew Cooper, U.S. BUREAU OF JUSTICE STATISTICS, PRISONERS IN 2008 (2009); Transactional Records Access Clearinghouse, HUGE INCREASE IN TRANSFERS OF ICE DETAINEES (2009), available at trac.syr.edu.

[31] See David Alan Sklansky, *Crime, Immigration, and Ad Hoc Instrumentalism*, NEW CRIM. L. REV. (forthcoming 2012), http://ssrn.com/abstract=1912518.

a crime or a civil violation, not whether criminal law concepts are inherently inappropriate in immigration proceedings, but what kind of systemic complexities have been created by the greater integration of the criminal justice and immigration systems, and how to ensure that those complexities do not obscure what the system is doing and who is responsible for it. The fact that Stuntz's scholarship points us in precisely these directions – even though Stuntz never wrote directly about these new sets of problems – is a nice indication of the power and the importance of his body of work.

CRIMINAL JUSTICE AND POLITICAL ECONOMY

The criminal justice system that Stuntz described is not just a complicated system; it is a particular kind of complicated system: in essence, a collection of interconnecting markets. It allocates resources – notably time, money, and attention – by pricing alternative strategies available to politicians, prosecutors, and defense attorneys. Changes in the system operate, intentionally or unintentionally, as changes in prices and reallocations of resources. Everything has a cost; nothing comes for free.

This is a strong and persistent theme in Stuntz's work – maybe the strongest and most persistent. The tools of political economy came naturally to him, and he repeatedly used them to generate sharp and important insights. When he thought about warrants, for example, the first thing he noticed was that they are a form of prescreening, and prescreening is costly. In a variety of ways, after-the-fact review is cheaper and more efficient. That is why the law usually does not make use of prescreening. Why, Stuntz asked, should the rules governing searches and seizures be different?[32] The answers he ultimately suggested are interesting – and characteristically multifaceted. (Warrants serve one function, he proposed, in a damages regime, and a different set of functions in a regime that relies for enforcement on evidentiary exclusion.) In some ways, though, the best and most valuable part of the inquiry is the initial framing of the question.

That might be said as well of Stuntz's later, more famous argument that criminal procedure rights draw resources and attention away from the substance of criminal cases – the adjudication of guilt or innocence.[33] Stuntz argued persuasively that this trade-off occurred through (no

[32] *Warrants and Fourth Amendment Remedies*, supra note 6.
[33] *Uneasy Relationship*, supra note 6.

surprise) a series of intricate pathways, but the most valuable contribution he made may have been simply to pose a question of political economy that no one before had thought seriously about: Do procedural protections in criminal cases draw on any resources that might otherwise be devoted to assessing guilt or innocence?

One can quarrel about some of the market processes Stuntz found at work in criminal justice.[34] One can quarrel, too, about whether trade-offs are in fact as ubiquitous as Stuntz sometimes suggested. He sometimes treated restrictions on the police as reflecting a straightforward trade-off "between the social need for order and individuals' desire for privacy and liberty" – a balance that will and should be recalibrated as crime rates and the threat of terrorism go up or down.[35] But the trade-off really isn't straightforward, and sometimes there isn't a trade-off at all. Restrictions on law enforcement can be loosened in ways that do little to make us safer; there are reasons to think a good amount of this happened over the past decade. Furthermore, Stuntz himself argued, in many contexts, that law enforcement can be constrained in ways that provide little meaningful protection of the dimensions of privacy and liberty most worth protecting.[36]

Still, although the trade-offs may be neither perfect nor ubiquitous, they surely exist, and they are important. Stuntz was right to emphasize them. Moreover, the focus on political economy does more than focus attention on compromises and balances. It serves to frame questions of criminal procedure as questions about what sorts of rules, practices, and institutional arrangements will best advance society's overall interests. That framing may seem obvious, even banal, but it is not. It runs contrary to two strong themes over the past few decades in criminal procedure jurisprudence and in criminal procedure scholarship: originalism and expressivism. Originalists, in the academy and on the Supreme Court, frame questions about criminal procedure as, first and foremost, historical questions: What rules governed criminal investigations and criminal prosecutions in the late eighteenth century?[37] Expressivists suggest that rules of criminal procedure and substantive criminal law are often important less because of what they *do* – and what balance they strike, in their

[34] I have done so. See Sklansky, supra note 5.

[35] *Local Policing After the Terror*, supra note 26, at 2138, 2145.

[36] See, e.g., id.; Miranda's *Mistake*, 99 MICH. L. REV. 975 (2001); *Privacy's Problem*, supra note 6.

[37] On originalism in criminal procedure, see, e.g., David Alan Sklansky, *Hearsay's Last Hurrah*, 2010 SUP. CT. REV. 1 (2010); David A. Sklansky, *The Fourth Amendment and Common Law*, 100 COLUM. L. REV. 1739 (2000).

operation, between safety and public order, on the one hand, and liberty and privacy on the other – but because of what the rules *communicate*: what norms and values the rules appear to endorse or to reject.[38]

The theme of political economy running through Stuntz's scholarship is, among other things, a way of taking a pragmatic approach to criminal justice pretty thoroughly at odds both with originalism and with expressivism. Stuntz never showed any attraction to originalism or had anything good to say about it, and although he was, in his youth, a full-throated expressivist – what the law did best, he argued, was "to state basic norms, to reinforce principles that can guide people in how to order their lives"[39] – he later repented. It is a fool's errand, Stuntz concluded, to try to send signals through the criminal justice system.

This was partly, for Stuntz, a consequence of the system's complexity. Because, for example, the "law-as-written" is not the "law-as-enforced," the system delivers signals "different from the messages one could find in the statutes."[40] More fundamentally, though, it was a matter of overreaching. It is hard enough for laws themselves to be fair and just; remaking hearts and souls is not something we have any reason to believe the law can do well, or even half-competently. Therefore, "law governs best when it seeks *only* to govern, not to teach people how to live."[41] The term "best" in that maxim – drawn from a wonderfully thoughtful essay Stuntz wrote with David Skeel – does double duty, referencing not only pragmatic considerations but also matters of... well, morality. Stuntz's turn against "moralism" in criminal law reflected more than his growing conviction that, as a practical matter, moralistic laws tend to be undone by the political backlashes they trigger.[42] It reflected, too, his sense that, on contested moral issues, a decent degree of humility is called for – a recognition by those in the majority that they might be wrong.[43]

38 See, e.g., Dan M. Kahan, *The Secret Ambition of Deterrence*, 113 HARV. L. REV. 413 (1999); Richard H. McAdams, *A Focal Point Theory of Expressive Law*, 86 VA. L. REV. 1649 (2000).

39 William J. Stuntz, *Pride and Pessimism in the Court*, FIRST THINGS, Feb. 1997, at 22, 22–23; see also William J. Stuntz, *When Rights Are Wrong*, FIRST THINGS, Apr. 1996, at 14.

40 *Self-Defeating Crimes*, supra note 6, at 1897; see also *Christian Legal Theory*, supra note 6, at 1740 n. 98.

41 Skeel & Stuntz, supra note 10, at 829; see also *Christian Legal Theory*, supra note 6, at 1737–1746.

42 See *Self-Defeating Crimes*, supra note 6; *Christian Legal Theory*, supra note 6, at 1740.

43 See, e.g., *Self-Defeating Crimes*, supra note 6, at 1896 (arguing that "a system accustomed to using criminal law as a weapon in contested cultural and moral battles... is a system bound to produce not justice, but its opposite").

So hostile did Stuntz grow to the use of the criminal justice system to send messages that – despite his great, overarching concern about racial inequity in criminal justice – he was visibly uncomfortable with Randy Kennedy's argument that racial profiling should be banned in order to make clear "that as a society we think race-conscious policing is wrong."[44] Stuntz recognized the argument and was not prepared to dismiss it, but he relegated it to a footnote. All his instincts were that racial profiling "is a *complicated* thing"[45] and that it must be addressed pragmatically, with an eye toward the overall political economy of criminal justice. What is important here, he suggested, are practices, consequences, and practical alternatives – not symbolism. This was notwithstanding the great emphasis Stuntz came to place on racial inequity and on *perceptions* of racial inequity in the criminal justice system – a topic to which we will turn shortly.

It is one thing to worry about the appearance of fairness. Stuntz was all in favor of that, and he fully endorsed Tom Tyler's conclusions about the importance of procedural fairness in securing respect for and compliance with the law.[46] One reason he thought it important for criminal law and criminal procedure to *be* just was so that they will be *perceived* as just. Stuntz, however, grew to have little sympathy for the idea that the criminal justice system should be used to send messages other than messages about its own fairness and effectiveness – messages that the system sends by actually *being* fair and effective.

Stuntz's emphasis on the political economy of the criminal justice system was thus a way of focusing attention on the system's practical consequences. The normative commitment underlying this focus was that both criminal law and criminal procedure should be shaped in the manner that, over the long term, will best advance the collective goals and interests of society as a whole. That is not a novel position. It was probably the consensus position of legal scholars in the 1960s and 1970s, and it was a position they shared for much of that time with the Supreme Court. (Unlike many critics of the Warren Court's "criminal procedure revolution," Stuntz sympathized with what the Justices were trying to do; he just thought they made a bad job of it.) Nonetheless, it is a position at odds

44 *Christian Legal Theory*, supra note 6, at 1744 n. 111, discussing Randall Kennedy, Race, Crime, and the Law 165 (1997).

45 *Christian Legal Theory*, supra note 6, at 1743.

46 See, e.g., *Political Constitution*, supra note 6, at 797 & n. 92; *Local Policing After the Terror*, supra note 26, at 2173–2174; *Self-Defeating Crimes*, supra note 6, at 1871 & n. 1.

with both originalism and expressivism, two of the strongest and most influential themes in criminal procedure jurisprudence and scholarship over the past three decades.

There may be a lesson here about originalism and expressivism. Some (although certainly not all) of the extraordinary power and the broad, crosscutting appeal of Stuntz's work – even among scholars who never themselves use the language or conceptual tools of political economy – likely has to do with Stuntz's heavy focus on practical consequences. This may not mean that originalism and expressivism are dead ends, but it does suggest that they are, at best, radically incomplete ways of thinking about criminal procedure. They leave out a whole range of considerations – considerations of practical consequences – that are at least of great importance, even if they are not *all* that we should care about.

CRIMINAL JUSTICE AND EQUALITY

I alluded briefly, a few paragraphs back, to Stuntz's overarching concern about racial inequity in the criminal justice system. This is, in fact, one of the dominant themes, if not *the* dominant theme, of Stuntz's scholarship during the last decade of his life, and it represents one of the biggest changes in his scholarship over the course of his career. Stuntz's early articles were keenly attentive to the complexity of the criminal justice system, and they stressed, repeatedly, the political economy of that system. They did not worry much about equality, though. That began to change in the late 1990s,[47] and by 2008 Stuntz was squarely focused on "unequal justice" – and, more particularly, racially disparate treatment – as the great scandal of American criminal justice.[48] He was reluctant to call the system "racist," because he did not think the disparities could be blamed on prejudice, plain and simple.[49] Instead, he thought, the inequality stemmed from the political "pathologies"[50] hardwired into our current system, mainly by "the decline of local democratic control

47 See *Uneasy Relationship*, supra note 6; *Race, Class, and Drugs*, supra note 6; *Distribution of Fourth Amendment Privacy*, supra note 6.

48 *Unequal Justice*, supra note 6.

49 See, e.g., *Race, Class, and Drugs*, supra note 6, at 1798 (arguing that "[c]ontemporary drug policy is not fundamentally racist, at least not in the usual sense of the word 'racist'"); *Unequal Justice*, supra note 6, at 1972 (suggesting that "[o]fficial racism is an unlikely explanation for a massive rise in black punishment that took hold in the generation *after* the civil rights movement)."

50 *Pathological Politics*, supra note 6, at 512, 591.

over criminal justice outcomes"[51] – a decline that he blamed in part (but only in part) on the Warren Court's "criminal procedure revolution." He was clear, though, that the massive racial disparities in America's criminal justice system represented not only an enormous obstacle to the system's effectiveness, but a grave moral failure. It is hard to think of a scholar who has written more powerfully in recent years about the gap between our system's putative commitment to "equal justice under law" and the system's actual operation.

Fundamentally, though, Stuntz's concern was not so much with inequality as with indecency. What bothered him most about how the criminal justice system treated members of racial minorities, and particularly African-American men, was not that it is worse than the treatment of whites, but that it is *so much* worse – or, more precisely, that it is so harsh, not just in relative terms but in absolute terms. What was lacking was a sense of moderation, of decency. This was one reason he favored approaching the problem of racial profiling, for example, with something of a sidestep: deemphasizing disparities in stop rates, and focusing instead on how members of racial minorities are treated when they are stopped.[52]

Seeing the problem as one of decency, rather than one of formal equality, influenced the solutions to which Stuntz was drawn. At bottom, he thought, what we need is not more law but more collective sympathy, more fellow feeling. Because he was a reformer and not a moralist, he was interested in how sympathy can be engineered into our social arrangements, and the answer for him was local democracy: allowing and encouraging criminal justice officials "to listen to those who live in the places we call 'war zones' and heed their wishes."[53] "Make criminal justice more locally democratic," he urged, "and justice will be both more moderate and more egalitarian."[54] The path to equality was through moderation, and the path to moderation was through a certain kind of democracy – the kind that involves having public officials treat crime-ridden neighborhoods as *their* neighborhoods, not as foreign "war zones."

I said a moment ago that Stuntz was a reformer and not a moralist, but that is not quite right. The moralism he opposed was the use of the law to settle contested questions of morality: debates over such matters as temperance, birth control, abortion, or assisted suicide. He did not argue

51 *Unequal Justice*, supra note 6, at 1973.
52 See *Local Policing After the Terror*, supra note 26, at 2162–2180.
53 *Unequal Justice*, supra note 6, at 2040. 54 Id. at 1974.

that criminal law can or should be morally neutral – that would be nonsensical – and there was plainly a moral component to his attacks on the racial disparities in American criminal justice. The prescription he offered for "unequal justice" in 2008 – less law, more local democracy – was prefigured in his writings about law and Christianity. There he suggested that law does a relatively poor job of changing behavior; what really changes behavior is relationships: "family attachments that . . . motivate us to do good for the sake of the household."[55] Family life is largely beyond the reach of the law, and precisely for that reason, Stuntz suggested, the family is the "sphere of ordinary life" that "sees the most behavior that is not just prudent or nonnegligent, but actually loving – behavior that genuinely treats the other as more valuable than the self."[56] Stuntz stressed the parallel between family bonds and our bond with God; he was interested in the household as the earthly image of the relationship "between us and our Creator."[57] But local communities, too, can be and often are understood as a kind of household – intermediate in scale between actual families and the realm of God.[58] This seems to be how Stuntz saw them, and it helps to explain why he was more sanguine than many other scholars that democracy can produce moderation in criminal justice. He read American history, so he knew that local democracy can take the form of lynch mobs and Jim Crow, just as he knew that family households can be the site of "cruelty, violence, and exploitation."[59] Ultimately, though, he believed that relationships, not rules, bring out the best in us.

Of course he didn't ask readers to take that, as it were, on faith. The dichotomy that Stuntz drew between rules and relationships was rooted in a particular religious tradition, and an argument explicitly resting on that dichotomy would be of necessarily limited appeal. The appeal would not be narrow, because Stuntz's faith was anything but idiosyncratic, but the appeal would not be universal, either, and it is a hallmark of Stuntz's criminal procedure scholarship that it aims to engage all readers

[55] *Christian Legal Theory*, supra note 6, at 1748; cf. Skeel & Stuntz, supra note 10, at 818 (contrasting legal codes with definitions of relationships).

[56] *Christian Legal Theory*, supra note 6, at 1747.

[57] Id. at 1748–1749; cf. Skeel & Stuntz, supra note 10, at 839 (invoking Christ's criticism of the Pharisees for their "tendency to focus on rules rather than relationships with the one true God").

[58] For a critical take on one particular strand of this rhetorical practice, see Markus Dirk Dubber, The Police Power: Patriarchy and the Foundations of American Government (2005).

[59] *Christian Legal Theory*, supra note 6, at 1747.

of goodwill. So it is no accident that Stuntz's argument for local democracy in criminal procedure is secular, pragmatic, and empirical: It is an argument of political economy.

Still, the secular, pragmatic form of the argument should not blind us to the faith that motivates it. Another prominent theme of Stuntz's writings on Christianity, complementing and building on the emphasis on relationships, is the spiritual imperative of helping those individuals who are worse off than oneself. For evangelicals, he emphasized, redistribution is, or should be, "a passion and a spiritual obligation, not just a political preference."[60] Stuntz made plain his view that this should have large and immediate consequences for evangelicals who, like him, spend time thinking about criminal justice. Prisons may be necessary, he suggests, but "those of us who live outside those awful warehouses have good reason to be penitent for what we have done to, and failed to do for, those inside."[61]

CRIMINAL JUSTICE AND DELIBERATION

Stuntz's arguments about racial disparities in the criminal justice system, and about what is to blame for them, are rooted in faith but couched in pragmatic terms. That quality of the argument – the bridge between the religious and the secular – is significant for at least two different reasons. The first, and less important, is that by bridging two different kinds of appeals Stuntz may have helped to bridge two different communities. His work offers evangelical Christians a point of entry into academic concerns about the uneven and excessive severity of American criminal justice, and it provides academics with a window into aspects of evangelical thought that may be unfamiliar.

This bridging project clearly mattered to Stuntz, and it should. It was important to him strategically, to help build a coalition for refocusing American politics on "how a loving society should treat its poorest members."[62] It was a moral matter for him, as well. The imperative to see the world through others' eyes includes the need for the religious to understand, and even to empathize, with the outlook of nonbelievers.[63] Vice versa, too – although Stuntz was generally too polite to say that.

[60] *Faculty Clubs and Church Pews*, supra note 10; see also, e.g., *Christian Legal Theory*, supra note 6, at 1729–1733.
[61] *Christian Legal Theory*, supra note 6, at 1733.
[62] *Faculty Clubs and Church Pews*, supra note 10.
[63] See sources cited supra note 17.

Even more significant is the particular *way* in which Stuntz's arguments bridge religion and reason: by taking commitments that may be rooted in faith (such as the primacy of relationships over rules) and arguing for them with appeals to reason and evidence. In this way, Stuntz's work is a testament to, and a validation of, another kind of faith: a faith in the possibilities of discourse and reasoned deliberation in a diverse society.

Orwell closed his essay on Dickens with a portrait of Dickens as "a man who is always fighting against something, but who fights in the open and is not frightened, the face of a man who is *generously angry* – in other words, of a nineteenth-century liberal, a free intelligence, a type hated with equal hatred by all the smelly little orthodoxies which are now contending for our souls."[64] No one hated *Dickens*, of course; Orwell's point was that the middle-of-the-road thinking running through Dickens's novels, and helping to explain his broad popularity, was more radical than it appeared. The portrait Orwell painted of Dickens applies pretty well to Stuntz: a "free intelligence," fighting in the open and "generously angry." Just as with Dickens, the crosscutting appeal of Stuntz's work can hide some of its edgier implications. What I have in mind here is not the controversial nature of many of Stuntz's conclusions: about the failure of *Miranda*, or the damage done by criminal procedure law more generally, or the moderating influence of local democracy. I have in mind Stuntz's methodology, which has generally *not* been thought controversial. But it is. For that reason, the broad popularity of his work is significant – and, I want to suggest, encouraging.

Debates about criminal justice can sometimes have the feel of ships passing in the night. This is infamously the case with respect to debates in political campaigns and the popular media, where stories about violent criminals receiving lenient sentences are met with accounts of innocent suspects brutalized by the police. But it is true even of judicial opinions and academic treatments of the subject; these, too, can have the stylized feel of kabuki. It is easy to become pessimistic about the possibilities for real dialogue. Arguments often seem aimed less at persuading those of opposite views than at reassuring those of similar mind that they have the moral high ground.

What makes the situation even more depressing is that there is a case for thinking it is inescapable. That case is rooted in the expressive theory of criminal law – the idea that criminal law and its enforcement functions in large part to endorse and to reinforce particular values. This is an idea

[64] Orwell, supra note 1, at 460.

with a long history, and one that is currently experiencing renewed popularity. It is sometimes suggested that whether people support a particular aspect of the criminal justice system, or any other aspect of public policy, depends mostly on their cultural values and affiliations, and that debates over criminal law and criminal procedure are, inevitably, battlefields in larger cultural conflicts. The best we can hope for, this view suggests, is rules and rhetoric that can offer something to all of the various camps; the objective should be to find ways of talking about criminal justice that do not devalue the cultural commitments of significant parts of the population.

This was no part of Stuntz's approach. It is not just that, after expressing sympathy for the expressive theory of criminal law early in his career, Stuntz later repudiated it. More to the point, he did not act on it. His work was not about finding ways of talking about criminal justice that would resonate, in different ways, with different world views. He focused relentlessly on concrete results: crime rates, incarceration rates, police behavior, and so on. What is more, his language, almost always, was the language of public choice – hardly a language that seems to aim at, or to reflect, cultural compromise.[65] It is therefore all the more remarkable that Stuntz's work has such broad, crosscutting appeal, and that so many scholars, of such varying perspectives, have wanted to embrace Stuntz as an ally.

Part of this, of course, is a matter of Stuntz's skill and intelligence. It obviously matters that the work is . . . well, really good. I will argue shortly, in fact, that Stuntz's singularity, his atypicality, is itself important, and that there are lessons to be drawn from it. That is not the whole story, though. Stuntz's work is broadly praised, and broadly adopted, not just because it is well executed – and not just because Stuntz himself was so admirable (another matter to which I'll return shortly). It is popular in part because it offers the promise that criminal justice can be the subject of open dialogue across ideological divides, dialogue that operates through evidence and inference rather than through cultural appeals. More than that, it provides a model for that kind of reasoned discourse, and a starting point.

[65] Cf. Dan M. Kahan, *The Logic of Reciprocity: Trust, Collective Action, and the Law*, 102 MICH. L. REV. 71, 100 (2003)(warning that "[p]olicies designed to counteract public choice pressures do more than change political actors' incentives to engage in rent-seeking; they also broadcast to citizens and their representatives that we expect political actors to engage in rent-seeking behavior whenever it is in their interest to do so").

CRIMINAL JUSTICE AND VIRTUE

Because Stuntz's approach to criminal justice was, essentially, the approach of public choice, there are some things it left out, notwithstanding his embrace of complexity. The criminal justice system, as Stuntz described it, is a series of incentives and constraints, and its operation can be predicted and understood by thinking about how those incentives and constraints are likely to shape the behavior of judges, prosecutors, police officers, elected officials, defense attorneys, and citizens. The dimensions of human behavior largely left out of public-choice theory – leadership, idealism, personal decency – are also largely left out of Stuntz's accounts of the criminal justice system, and also out of his analysis of potential reforms.

In his essay on Dickens, Orwell noted that "[t]wo viewpoints are always tenable. The one, how can you improve human nature until you have changed the system? The other, what is the use of changing the system before you have improved human nature?"[66] Dickens took the second viewpoint; for all his railing against backward institutions, he was essentially a moralist. Stuntz took the first viewpoint, at least in his thinking about the law. He certainly cared about improving human nature, but he believed this was a matter to be accomplished not through law but through relationships – interpersonal relationships, and relationships between individuals and God.[67] In the meantime, reformers must work with human beings as they find them.

There is nothing wrong with this. It may be the best way to proceed. There is a good deal to be said for designing legal institutions so that they do not depend on heroism or sagacity. Nonetheless, it leaves out much of what anyone who has worked in the criminal justice system knows is important: the commitments and personal qualities that judges, lawyers, and law enforcement officers bring to their work.

Add scholars and teachers to that list. I suggested a moment ago that the broad popularity of Stuntz's work and the diversity of the scholars who want to associate themselves with it owe something to the kind of dialogue in which Stuntz was engaged. Very plainly, though, they also owe much to Stuntz himself – to the excellence of his work, and to the kind of teacher, colleague, friend, and mentor he was. If it would be a

[66] Orwell, supra note 1, at 427.

[67] See *Christian Legal Theory*, supra note 6, at 1746–1749; Skeel & Stuntz, supra note 10, at 831–839.

mistake to make too much of Stuntz's atypicality, it would be just as large a mistake to ignore the ways in which he truly was extraordinary – and not only in the intelligence and creativity of his work, but also in his infectious enthusiasm, his limitless curiosity, and his unfailing generosity. It is easy to imagine the dizzying complexity of the criminal justice system described in Stuntz's work leaving a reader discouraged about how much difference any one person can make. But only a reader not fortunate enough to have known the author.

PART II

Police Investigations

5

The Accidental Feminist

Anne M. Coughlin

It is impossible to capture in a few (or even many) words the magnitude of Bill Stuntz's influence on the mainstream scholarly literature on criminal procedure and criminal law. To be sure, the inventory of his books, papers, and essays does offer some insight into the breadth and depth of his individual contributions. Bill has coauthored textbooks on criminal procedure, federal criminal law, and substantive crime definitions. Among his too-numerous-to-count scholarly publications are articles about topics ranging from the substantive origins of criminal procedure, the perverse effects of the exclusionary rule, the distribution of Fourth Amendment privacy, the value and function of the Fifth Amendment privilege against self-incrimination, the pathological politics of criminal law, race and racism in the criminal justice system and especially in the war on drugs, local policing in the wake of the 9/11 terrorist attacks, plea bargaining, habeas corpus, gambling, and beyond. Even this monumental bibliography does not do full justice to the power of Bill's achievements, because it does not reveal the extent to which his insights have fundamentally reshaped the work done by a whole generation of criminal justice scholars. Nor does the bibliography disclose how profoundly Bill's contributions have influenced and motivated the work of still other authors, including those who, like me, tend to employ methodologies and pursue political objectives that often are quite different from his own.

For me, one of Bill's most powerful and liberating intellectual moves was his injunction to cease thinking about substantive criminal law and criminal procedure as operating within separate practical domains or as occupying separate curricular and scholarly spheres. Rather, as Bill

* Georgina Shepard provided me with magnificent research assistance and substantive advice, for which I thank her.

instructed, criminal justice must be studied as a system in which outcomes are determined by the constant interplay of, or by the sometimes fractious and sometimes friendly relations between, these two ostensibly distinct bodies of law. One measure of the genius of Bill's insight is that it now seems to us to be obvious – so obvious that it goes without saying, let alone citing to any particular Stuntzian article – that we may make sense of the work performed by substantive criminal prohibitions on the one hand and by criminal procedure on the other, only if we take account of the work that they do together.

This insight has profoundly influenced my teaching of criminal law and criminal procedure courses, and, in recent years, it has provided the inspiration – the scholarly eureka moment, if you will – for two research projects on police interrogations and confessions. The first paper, *Interrogation Stories*,[1] recommends that we scrutinize police interrogation techniques not merely to determine whether they comply with the rules of criminal procedure as embodied in the well-known *Miranda*[2] warnings, but also to investigate the extent to which they are serving the substantive mandates embodied in the criminal statutes that authorize the police to interrogate people in the first place. In that initial foray, I studied the strategies that police are trained to use when interrogating accused rapists. Among other things, I argued that the police persuade these men to talk by feeding them "victim-blaming narratives," which construct the truth of rape confessions in ways that are inconsistent with the political and substantive objectives of the rape reforms sponsored by feminist legal scholars and activists, and adopted in recent years in statutes in virtually every state in the country. The second project, which I will sketch in this essay, retrieves yet another set of insights from the terrain that Bill discovered, which is that frontier where criminal procedure (sometimes, for me, wholly unexpectedly) meets criminal substance. In this project, I return to the police interrogation room, this time to explore the connections between the rules governing the admissibility in evidence of criminal confessions, as embodied in the Supreme Court's criminal procedure cases requiring that such confessions must be voluntary, and those governing the lawfulness of sexual intercourse, as embodied in the substantive law of rape.[3]

[1] See Anne M. Coughlin, *Interrogation Stories*, 95 Va. L. Rev. 1599 (2009).

[2] See Miranda v. Arizona, 384 U.S. 436 (1966).

[3] See Anne M. Coughlin, *The Intercourse of Interrogations* (draft on file with author).

The analogy between police interrogations and sexual intercourse – and, particularly, between the rules governing the lawfulness of each transaction – might seem forced or fanciful but for the fact that interrogators themselves use it when describing just what it is that they do to get a suspect to squeal on himself. In the first place, a few expert interrogators use erotic language to describe the kicks they get from participating in an interrogation that culminates in an admission of guilt from the subject.[4] The police interrogators whom one meets in the literature tend to be respectful and reticent when recounting "how it was" for them, but many nonetheless use language that implies that their objective going into the interrogation room is to have sex with their suspects. That is, they explicitly refer to the process through which they procure a confession as a "seduction."[5] According to this figure of speech, the verbal intercourse between interrogator and suspect is flirtatious and not forcible. The exchange may be somewhat clumsy, even ham-handed, but the cop puts his or her energy into cajoling, rather than coercing, the suspect into talking. The analogy between police interrogations and one-night stands has left its mark on judicial rhetoric as well. As (then) Justice Rehnquist put it in his concurring opinion in *Dunaway v. New York*, there likely are numerous cases in which a suspect "agrees voluntarily to answer questions that the police wish to put to him . . . and later regrets his willingness to answer those questions. However, such morning-after regrets do not render involuntary responses that were voluntary at the time they were made."[6] By slightly teasing out Justice Rehnquist's metaphor and announcing less delicately his doctrinal bottom line, we may infer that the good interrogators – the ones who elicit confessions that are admissible in evidence – are those who *seduce*, but do not *rape*, their suspects into incriminating themselves. This essay will offer some preliminary

[4] Arthur S. Aubry, Jr., & Rudolph R. Caputo, Criminal Interrogation 78 (3d ed. 1980) (describing the "close, personal relationship" that develops between interrogator and subject, which "rapidly peaks up as it does, to the tremendous crescendo of the confession of guilt, and then is abruptly and completely severed").

[5] See, e.g., "Senator Leahy Presses FBI Director for Answers on Questionable Interrogation Techniques," *U.S. Fed. News*, May 20, 2004 ("A recent issue of the FBI Law Enforcement Bulletin stated that felons are more likely to confess to an investigator who treats them with respect, and the interview should be a 'seduction, not a showdown'"); Peter Carlson, "You Have the Right to Remain Silent . . . ," *Washington Post Magazine*, September 13, 1998 (quoting police interrogators who describe their work as "seduction," with one elaborating that "[i]t's like trying to pick somebody up in a bar").

[6] Dunaway v. New York, 442 U.S. 200, 222 (1979) (Rehnquist, J., concurring).

observations that suggest that, as a positive matter, the analogy between interrogation and seduction promises to be a robust one, and it will identify some of the complex themes, issues, and normative speculations that I cover in the larger project.

Justice Rehnquist was onto something important when he compared the dynamics of a police interrogation to a sexual one-night stand. The parties often commence their encounter as perfect strangers – at most, they tend to be slight and superficial acquaintances – and their assignation is intense, highly charged, and fleeting. The outcome of the exchange is consequential for each of the parties, although each is understood to have different priorities for and stakes in it. According to the rich literatures on police interrogations[7] on the one hand and sexual seductions[8] on the other, which consist of judicial opinions, advice manuals, and literary texts both high and low, each transaction is structured along lines that are hierarchical and adversarial. In both contexts, we are meant to believe that one of the parties (the interrogator, or the man) has power over the other (the suspect, or the woman). In both contexts, the dominant party's aim is to get the subordinate to do something – to implicate himself in a crime, to acquiesce to sexual intercourse – that is or may be contrary to the subordinate's legal, political, social, or psychological interests. But, of course, as the latter condition implies, the power relations between the actors are far more complex than a simple hierarchy of dominant over subordinate, of top over bottom. Because the subordinate party has something – his guilty secret, her sexual compliance – that the dominant actor desperately wants to get, the subordinate has a hold over the dominant, at least up and until, and, perhaps, after the moment when the subordinate gives up that thing which the dominant wants.

Then too, we must evaluate carefully the assertion that the parties to an interrogation, like the partners to a seduction, are always already adversarial, that they are locked in a game in which there are perennial winners and losers. First, let's contemplate the dynamics of a seduction that

[7] I describe this literature in detail in *Interrogation Stories*. See Coughlin, supra note 1, at 1635–1651.

[8] The advice literature on seductions includes texts such as Logan Edwards, Secrets of the A Game: How to Meet and Attract Women Anywhere, Anyplace, Anytime (2009); Robert Greene, The Art of Seduction (2003); Mystery, The Mystery Method: How to Get Beautiful Women into Bed (2007). I describe these manuals, together with additional literary sources, as well as juridical ones, in *The Intercourse of Interrogations* (draft on file with author).

culminates in sexual intercourse. Some feminist commentary, as well as the male-authored advice literature on the art of the pickup, uses rhetoric that suggests that when the encounter culminates in sexual intercourse the man inevitably is a winner and the woman a loser. To put it crudely, he scores, which implies that she does not. To say the least, this crude and thoroughly one-sided account fails to capture the complexity, the risks and rewards, the costs and benefits, of sexual encounters. The exchange of sex is not – at least, it need not be – a zero-sum game because sexual intercourse may confer a substantial benefit on each of the participants. Sex is – at least, sex can and should be – a win–win situation because the woman, as well as the man, gets something – for one thing, the sex! the pleasure of sex! – from the exchange. Next, consider the stakes of the parties to the interrogation game, which at first glance appears to be a straightforward win–lose contest. When a suspect confesses, the cop scores, and the suspect loses big time. However, when we characterize a suspect's decision to confess as a win–lose proposition for the parties, we are relying exclusively – as criminal defense lawyers almost certainly do and usually should – on the parties' litigation positions and legal interests. If the suspect confesses, the state will win and the suspect will lose the criminal case.

However, there are other perspectives from which to evaluate confessions, ones from which we may be inclined to think of police confessions as having the potential to be win–win transactions. Some judges and criminal justice commentators argue that confessions are beneficial for guilty suspects because, by expressing remorse and taking responsibility for their misconduct, they begin the process of rehabilitation and reintegration into the community of law-abiding people.[9] According to some religious traditions, the primary benefit of a confession accrues not to the community or to law enforcement but to the confessing subjects themselves, as it cleanses their souls and restores them to a state of grace. Likewise, some secular institutions endorse the notion that confession is a beneficial thing for troubled or fallible parties to undertake. Some forms of therapy (whether applied to criminal or noncriminal clients)

[9] For example, in his dissenting opinion in *Miranda*, Justice White faulted the Supreme Court for failing to recognize the numerous benefits conferred by police interrogations, some of which may accrue to the accused person who incriminates himself or herself. As Justice White put it there, "it is by no means certain that the process of confessing is injurious to the accused. To the contrary it may provide psychological relief and enhance the prospects for rehabilitation." Miranda v. Arizona, 384 U.S. 436, 538 (1966); see also Minnick v. Mississippi, 498 U.S. 146, 166–167 (Scalia, J., dissenting).

exhort subjects to confess their faults or weaknesses – or, what might be the same thing, to cease engaging in denial – for psychic healing purposes. Police interrogators reinforce these religious and secular messages about the value of confessions by admonishing suspects that they will feel much better only if and when they make a clean breast of it. No less than sexual intercourse, therefore, it is possible to argue that confession is a mutual exchange, one in which both participants are winners of the game.

Police interrogations and sexual seductions share yet another structural feature: Each transaction takes place in private. Why? Of course, it seems goofy to ask why sexual encounters are private. Sexual intercourse just is – and it seems to go without saying that sexual intercourse should be – private activity. But it is worth remarking that the kind of privacy that we expect for sex today – the kind of privacy supplied by bedrooms and similar spaces, the kind of privacy that we enjoy behind closed doors – is a relatively recent development, a luxury (if one owned by many people in this country) made possible by architectural innovations and economic prosperity. As for police interrogations, the experts insist that the enterprise can be successful, in the sense that it can be expected to produce inculpatory statements, only if the questioning occurs in private. The presence of third parties threatens to break the mood, to rupture the human connection, to snap the psychological bond that must develop before a suspect is willing to spill his or her guts to, of all people, the cops. So too for religious confessions and for therapeutic techniques that rely on confessional practices. The private character of police interrogations and sexual intercourse can make it excruciatingly difficult to evaluate any given transaction after the fact. When one of the parties steps forward and claims that the transaction was not a mutual one, we often have no external account of the encounter; we must rely exclusively on the participants' often conflicting perceptions of what transpired between them. Thus, in the end, our judgments about police interrogations, just as our judgments about sexual intercourse, may come down to contests over credibility. The trials are what, in the rape context, we like to call "he said, she said" proceedings. This evidentiary difficulty may be ameliorated, if not eliminated altogether, thanks to developments in technology. By now, a number of police departments have begun to videotape interrogations, presumably in order to have an accurate record of the content of the confession as well as to prove that they are administering adequate *Miranda* warnings and otherwise complying with the rules of criminal procedure.[10]

[10] See Brandon L. Garrett, *The Substance of False Confessions*, 62 Stan. L. Rev. 1051, 1113–1114 & nn. 363, 364 (2010).

Likewise, seducers who are worried about potential litigation arising from their sexual conquests might be inclined to begin recording some of their exploits. For example, fraternity brothers have been known to videotape sexual encounters that occur in their houses.[11] In addition to creating pornography, the men might plan to use the videotape as evidence that will refute complaints by women who come forward to claim that the intercourse was forced on them.

These reflections begin to move us toward contemplating the doctrinal questions that arise when a party does complain about the lawfulness of an interrogation or of a sexual encounter, and he or she petitions a court for some sort of redress, remedy, or revenge. It goes without saying – but why? – that the complainant in court always is the suspect, always is the woman. By that point in the game, the complainant is in a bit of a pickle. The cat is out of the bag, as courts put it in the interrogation context, and, alas, no one, not even a judge, can cajole it to get back in.[12] Still, the courts will scrutinize the transactions to be sure that the confession was voluntary,[13] the intercourse consensual,[14] and, if they find that the exchange was neither of those things, they will suppress the confession or toss the man in jail. The fact that we use these different terms to judge the legality of each transaction – confessions must be voluntary, whereas sex must be consensual – might correspond to significant practical differences in the legal regulation of these proceedings. For example, the term *voluntary* might be thought to demand proof that the suspect chose to confess. The suspect who makes a good confession was not one who was pressed into the state's service; rather, he was a volunteer. He came forward to make the statement or, at the very least, initiated the conversation in which he confessed. By contrast, the term *consent* seems to call for a showing not that the woman initiated the intercourse or volunteered to have sex, but only that she agreed to cooperate, that she acquiesced in or went along with a course of sexual conduct that the man

[11] See Missy Diaz, Lawsuit Against UF Frat Brothers Who Secretly Videotaped Woman Settled Out of Court, available at http://articles.sun-sentinel.com/2010-01-23/news/fl-uf-videotape-20100122_1_delta-tau-delta-ben-farias-lauren-highley.

[12] See United States v. Bayer, 331 U.S. 532, 540 (1947) ("Of course, after an accused has once let the cat out of the bag by confessing, no matter what the inducement, he is never thereafter free of the psychological and practical disadvantages of having confessed. He can never get the cat back in the bag. The secret is out for good").

[13] The Supreme Court confirmed in Dickerson v. United States, 530 U.S. 428 (2000), both that the *Miranda* warnings are required by the federal constitution and that the warnings supplement, but do not displace, the due-process line of cases that command that criminal confessions must be voluntary to be admissible in evidence.

[14] See, e.g., Richard A. Posner, Sex and Reason 388 (1992) ("[A]ll that distinguishes [rape] from ordinary sexual intercourse is lack of consent").

proposed. These differences in nomenclature could be a reflection of the different attitudes and aspirations by which we evaluate the lawfulness, not to mention the morality, of our practices in one context as opposed to the other. Still, when these definitions are applied by the courts, *voluntary* and *consensual* seem to mean one and the same (negative) thing: the absence of physical violence or threats thereof. Cops are prohibited from beating statements out of suspects, and men are forbidden to get sex by beating it out of women. As far as the law is concerned, (almost) anything else goes.

In particular, fraud goes. As the interrogators' seduction trope implies, fraud is *de rigueur* in the interrogation room, just as it is in the case of a sexual seduction itself. In both contexts, the dominant party is well-advised to develop strategies that make his or her target forget, at least momentarily, about the imbalance of power between them. Then too, he or she must deploy techniques that have the effect of obfuscating or discounting the parties' adversary interests. How does the dominant character pull this wool over the subordinate's eyes? It is said to be simple. The dominant works to persuade the subordinate that he is her friend, that he is one who cares about her welfare, when he is no such thing. Surely, I am not the only person who has heard it alleged that one (almost) foolproof way for men to get sex from reluctant women is to make false professions of love, insincere protestations about affection enduring and respect abiding after the sex act is completed. Likewise, police interrogators are trained to adopt friendly postures toward suspects. Let's forget about Mutt for the moment, okay? These days, the police training manuals have demoted that bad cop, even written him entirely out of many interrogation scripts. These days, that is, most interrogators are trained to be Jeff. This good cop chats with his suspect in rhetoric that is familiar, respectful, comforting, and consoling, even when and especially when the suspect is a person whom the interrogator might otherwise be inclined to shun or to treat with outright contempt and loathing. A good interrogator sympathizes with the suspect's plight and declares that the offense was an understandable, even forgivable, act of human folly. Moreover, the good interrogator reassures his or her suspect that, by and through the act of confessing, he or she will earn the interrogator's admiration and respect, and possibly even that of the prosecuting authorities.

To be fair, the courts have insisted that police detectives scrub some kinds of fraud from their interrogation scripts. Thus, when officers decide to put suspects through custodial interrogation, they are not permitted to deceive them about *anything* and *everything* under the sun. No, indeed. The suspects must be aware of what they are doing – they are making statements to police interrogators – and they must be aware of the potential consequences of doing so – their statements may be used against them in court. And, just in case these facts are lost on suspects who find themselves being questioned by police interrogators, *Miranda v. Arizona* requires the officers to bring them to their attention by offering the customary advice of rights. The courts have been willing to condone virtually any other kind of deception, however, and the leading interrogation manuals helpfully identify the various scams that are most likely to induce various kinds of suspects to spill the beans. For example, police interrogators are counseled to misrepresent the strength of the evidence they've collected against the suspect, to minimize the moral seriousness of the crime for which the suspect is being questioned, and to falsely empathize with the suspect, even to the point of expressing admiration for the suspect's criminal misbehavior. The interrogator who performs this particular good-cop role may seem to be verging on committing one of the kinds of fraud that the law (probably) does disapprove of, that is, police deception as to the identity of the person to whom the suspect is confessing. After all, this interrogator aims to make the suspect believe that it is safe to confess because the suspect is confiding in a friend, albeit a new one. However, as long as the interrogator does nothing to suggest that he or she is not really a police officer, this type of deception is tolerated by the courts and encouraged by the training manuals.

When sexual intercourse, rather than an incriminating statement, is at stake, the case law and the advice manuals on dating and sex seem to tell the same story. The law sometimes punishes sex by fraud, but again, almost nothing here counts as illegal fraud, and the only deceptions that might be criminalized are almost identical to the deceptions we forbid interrogators. Sex by fraud is a crime only in unusual, even somewhat improbable, circumstances, to wit, a man dupes a woman into having sex by persuading her that she, in fact, is doing something *other than* having sex. As for exactly what *that* would be, the cases tend to involve physicians who sexually touch or even penetrate their patients under the guise of giving them a medical examination. The law also might be willing to punish the cheat who gets sex from a woman by masquerading as her husband. But that is pretty much it. As long as the woman knows what she is doing – she is having sexual intercourse – and she knows whom she is doing it with – the man is anybody other than her husband – rape law tolerates fraud.[15]

[15] For a discussion of the rare cases in which the criminal law punishes sex by fraud, see Anne M. Coughlin, *Sex and Guilt*, 84 Va. L. Rev. 1, 32–33 (1998).

In both domains, moreover, participants and courts seem inclined to abide by a rule of construction under which the word *no* sometimes or, even, often, means *yes*. At least during the opening phases of the encounter, the subjects' bodies – not their words – speak the truth. Up until the latter part of the twentieth century, for example, courts routinely and explicitly insisted that the woman who refused sex by saying the word *no* should be treated as if she had said *yes* and thereby consented to the connection. As the Supreme Court explained in a late-nineteenth-century case, "though she object verbally, if she make no outcry and no resistance, she by her conduct consents, and the act is not rape in the man."[16] To be sure, feminists have lobbied to change this (to them) peculiar canon of construction, and, insofar as courts and legislatures are concerned, they have achieved some success. However, popular culture still endorses the notion that the word *no* may and, perhaps, often does mean *yes*, and it encourages men (and women?) to look for interpretive clues, such as their sexual targets' tone of voice or body language, that suggest that *no* expresses assent, not dissent. Likewise, the authors of interrogation manuals train officers to ignore the actual substance of the suspect's initial statements – not surprisingly, suspects frequently say *no* in response to questions intended to elicit the answer *yes* – and to search for evidence of the truth in the suspect's demeanor, posture, facial expression, tone, and so forth. In other words, to ferret out the truth concerning their suspects' involvement in the crime, officers are advised to place more emphasis on the physical form in which suspects embody their answers – their bodies are nervous or worried or distracted or defensive or subdued or tense or sweating or combative – than on the content of what they say. Why does this mode of interpretation – this preoccupation with ascertaining the truth spoken by the body – govern our evaluations in both contexts? Should it apply in both?

With these and other questions, I begin moving to the conclusion of this essay of thought experiments inspired by my decision to walk along some of the trails blazed for me by Bill Stuntz. If my preliminary impressions are correct – in particular, if the force and the fraud norms governing sexual intercourse are virtually identical to those governing interrogations – by what account may we justify them? Why would we evaluate the lawfulness of sex by reference to the same construct of voluntariness that we use to judge the admissibility of a criminal suspect's confession? More polemically, why would the substantive criminal law treat rape victims,

[16] Mills v. United States, 164 U.S. 644, 648 (1897).

almost always women, as if they were criminal suspects? And why would the law of criminal procedure treat men (most criminal suspects) as if they were women (most rape victims)?

Some of my prior research may provide a useful vantage point from which to begin developing answers to at least some of these questions.[17] The insight is that the contemporary feminist critique of rape law is enriched when we investigate rape doctrine, not in isolation, but in conjunction with the fornication and adultery prohibitions with which it formerly resided in the substantive criminal law and, perhaps in our cultural imagination, continues to reside. When we recall that the rape prohibition emerged from a system that outlawed consensual nonmarital intercourse for both women and men, we obtain a more nuanced explanation for the narrow definition of rape – one in which the crime is limited to intercourse obtained through physical violence by a man that overcomes physical resistance by a woman – that feminists have aimed to revise and expand. Consider, for a moment, the position of the rape victim in a world that punishes consensual nonmarital intercourse. In particular, consider the way in which law enforcement officials would react to her claim that she was raped as opposed to the way in which they would respond to her claim that she was the victim of some other crime, say, robbery. In a legal system that criminalizes adultery and fornication as well as rape, the woman who comes forward to report that she has been raped is *not* in the same position as the person who comes forward to report that she has been robbed, because someone who gives away sex, unlike someone who gives away money, is herself committing a crime. For the authorities working within such a system, the appropriate analogy would be to compare the situation of the rape complainant to that of a person who implicated herself in the commission of a crime, albeit one in which another perpetrator also was involved. If this analogy is the persuasive one, we then must wonder, how would those authorities react to a person who, for example, confessed that she had been involved in carrying out a robbery? Law enforcement officials confronted with such a malefactor today – and, we may speculate, then – almost surely would punish her for her misconduct, unless she was able to establish that her participation came about under circumstances that afforded her a defense to criminal liability. Viewed from this perspective, the traditional elements of rape begin to mimic the substantive arguments that we would expect a woman to make if she were trying to defend herself against an accusation

[17] See Coughlin, supra note 15.

of fornication or adultery. She would be expected to demonstrate that she had acquiesced in the criminal sex act under duress or, more vividly, that she had participated in the intercourse only after and because her partner threatened to beat it out of her. In other words, law enforcement officials in that system would be inclined to treat the rape complainant as if she were a criminal suspect, rather than a crime victim, and, according to the law and norms of that system, it would be proper for them to do so.

Not so today. Prosecutorial inaction, legislative repeal, and judicial disapproval have swept (all of?) those consensual sex crimes away, which makes it unfair, even cruel, to continue to require rape complainants – and no one else – to offer excuses for perpetrating them. Contemporary lawmakers have an urgent obligation to reconfigure the law of sexual assault so as to eliminate this patent double standard. In this moment of transition, it may be useful for feminist legal scholars to identify transactions whose legality is judged according to consent norms that seem to be analogous to those that have been employed in the rape context. At the same time, it is essential to acknowledge the limitations of these analogies. When we examine the intercourse of interrogations, we discover the way in which legal constructs of voluntariness and consent, by focusing exclusively on the methods used to procure a subject's act or acquiescence, tend to flatten the parties' lived experience and to force the subject into one of two roles. In law, the suspect and the woman must be either spotless innocent or filthy reprobate. In life, they almost certainly are neither, both at the same time, or some shifting combination of those things.

6

The Distribution of Dignity and the Fourth Amendment

Tracey L. Meares

There is a great deal to admire about Bill Stuntz's work. It is smart, hard-headed, almost always surprising, and so right. I often find when I read his articles that I have a smile on my face. It is one of those expressions you find yourself making when thinking to yourself, "Man, I wish I wrote that."

Of the many occasions I found myself thinking this while reading Bill's work, one is prominent. That occasion is the first time I read *The Distribution of Fourth Amendment Privacy*.[1] There, Bill wrote the following:

> There seems to be widespread agreement on the twin propositions that (1) Fourth Amendment law should protect privacy and (2) the protection should tend to increase as the privacy invasion increases.... These obvious propositions may be wrong.[2]

At this point, I sat up and started to smile.

In his piece, Stuntz begins with the idea that perhaps the central problem of criminal justice administration in the late twentieth century was its distributional impact on poor and black people. Recognition of this fact is a problem for a Fourth Amendment jurisprudence that tends to "make wealthier suspects better off than they otherwise would be, and make poorer suspects worse off."[3] This is true, Stuntz explains, because the Fourth Amendment protects only some spaces and not others. Furthermore, it tends to protect the spaces to which the wealthy have greater access than do the poor. This means that the rich have greater Fourth Amendment privacy in their large homes surrounded by ample lawns than do the poor, urban residents of crowded, thin-walled apartment

[1] William J. Stuntz, *The Distribution of Fourth Amendment Privacy*, 67 Geo. Wash. L. Rev. 1265 (1998).

[2] Id. at 1265.

[3] Id. at 1266.

buildings. Moreover, because the Fourth Amendment tends to enhance protection of privacy interests by making certain police tactics more costly for police to pursue than others, police naturally respond to legal pressures by choosing to engage in the tactics that are least expensive for their agencies. Consider this: It is cheaper for police to enforce drug laws in open-air drug markets in poor, often minority urban neighborhoods than it is to police clandestine suburban drug bazaars.[4]

To me, there was an obvious connection between Stuntz's thesis in the *Distribution of Privacy* piece and the trajectory of my own work regarding the Fourth Amendment, which at that time was written primarily with my colleague, Dan Kahan. Our target of investigation was not solely the Fourth Amendment but rather the modern corpus of constitutional criminal procedure. We were concerned about the ways in which modern constitutional criminal procedure failed to address the importance of mechanisms of political accountability of local law enforcers to the communities they policed.[5] The Fourth Amendment is, of course, a wonderful text to subject to this kind of analysis, given that one ready interpretation of the notion of reasonableness is an idea of representation reinforcement.[6]

Kahan and I worked through this idea with respect to two principles: community burden sharing and guided discretion.[7] We argued that it was no longer appropriate for courts to assume that communities will not share in the burdens of law enforcement, given the political strength of minorities in the current age. Instead, courts should simply ask whether the relevant community has internalized the burden that a particular law imposes on individual freedom. If the community has internalized the burden of law enforcement as opposed to shifting those costs to communities or groups that lack political power both to resist an easy laying on of hands by police and also to shape such power,[8] we argued that the court

[4] See id. at 1282, and see William J. Stuntz, *Race, Class and Drugs*, 98 COLUM. L REV. 1795 (1998), where he develops this argument with greater detail.

[5] See Tracey L. Meares and Dan M. Kahan, URGENT TIMES: POLICING AND RIGHTS IN INNER CITY COMMUNITIES (1999); Tracey L. Meares and Dan M. Kahan, *The Wages of Antiquated Procedural Thinking*, 1998 U. CHI. L. REV. 197 (1998); Dan M. Kahan and Tracey L. Meares, *The Coming Crisis of Criminal Procedure*, 86 GEO. L. J. 1156 (1997).

[6] See Meares and Kahan, *Coming Crisis*, cited in note 5 at 1172. See also John Hart Ely, DEMOCRACY AND DISTRUST (1980).

[7] See Meares and Kahan, *Antiquated Procedural Thinking*, cited in note 5 at 209–210.

[8] Kahan and I argued that the enforcement of loitering laws in the period before the Civil Rights Era provides the paradigmatic example of the *lack* of law enforcement burden

should presume that the law does not violate individual rights. Guided discretion, too, represents a modern alternative to the Warren Court's discretion skepticism. That skepticism was appropriate when people of color were formally and functionally disenfranchised. In that world, political establishments could be counted on to *reward* law enforcers who harassed minorities. In the modern era of wider political accountability, discretion skepticism is unwarranted, but insistence on guided discretion – requiring communities to adopt mechanisms, which may be statutory or administrative to reduce the risk of burden concentration – is appropriate, we argued.

The work Kahan and I did, given its concern with the political realities of criminal procedure on the ground, obviously is in conversation with much of Bill Stuntz's oeuvre.[9] However, we missed something that Bill so perceptively identified in the *Washington Law Review* piece. Although we were attuned to the contextual nature of rights ("Rights have histories"),[10] we paid inadequate attention to the distributional consequences of rights as a benefit.

It is ten years later, and I am still thinking about that point.

To place constitutional benefits in proper context, it is useful to begin with constitutional harms. It is commonly said that there are at least two potential harms of an individual's engagement with a law enforcement officer: privacy invasion and autonomy incursion. However, Professor Sherry Colb of Cornell Law School has identified at least one additional harm associated with public law enforcement encounters. She points out that when police stop or arrest someone in public and the police turn out to be wrong – that is, the person did not really do anything – that person is likely to experience what she calls a "targeting" harm.[11] This harm is a function of constitutional standards because police action is justified only when police have a "good reason" to stop, arrest, or search a person. Courts have names for these good reasons. "Probable cause," "individualized suspicion," and "reasonable suspicion" are the names we call some of them. Typically these reasons are defined in such a way that allows the police to act to interfere with an individual's interest in privacy or autonomy only when they have enough information to believe that the

internalization. See id. at 202; also see William O. Douglas, *Vagrancy and Arrest on Suspicion*, 70 YALE L. J. 1 (1960).

9 See generally William J. Stuntz, *Unequal Justice*, 121 HARV. L. REV. 1969 (2008).

10 See Meares and Kahan at note 6.

11 See Sherry F. Colb, *Innocence, Privacy, and Targeting in Fourth Amendment Jurisprudence*, 96 COLUM L. REV. 1456 (1996).

person to be interfered with has committed or is about to commit a crime. This means, of course, that when police actually encounter and interfere with someone in public, people watching the encounter should be able to say to themselves, "That person must have done X. Otherwise, the police wouldn't be bothering her." At least this *should* be true.

In a new article, Bernard Harcourt and I criticize the prevalent manner of justifying police action with reference to individualized suspicion.[12] We argue that Fourth Amendment jurisprudence has been constructed by using an inaccurate model of suspicion. The model prevalent in the jurisprudence is inaccurate in at least two ways. The term "individualized suspicion" is misleading in that it implies suspicion is either individualized and meets constitutional requirements, or it is not. The term implies that the process of suspicion-based judgments is *binary*. In reality, suspicion is a probabilistic concept. It is, in technical terms, a *continuous* variable, not a *categorical* one. The term is misleading in another way because it suggests that law enforcers come to judgments about individuals by evaluating unique individual traits. In reality, most individuals become suspicious because of the group-based type of behavior that they exhibit or the fact that they belong to readily identifiable groups – sex and age are two examples – rather than because of unique individual traits. Importantly, by modeling suspicion with respect to a binary standard rather than to the more realistic probabilistic one, courts have created a mismatch between Fourth Amendment jurisprudence and everyday police work.

As a response to this problem, Harcourt and I contend that the model of checkpoint, with its attendant randomization mechanism, should serve as the lodestar for reasonableness under the Fourth Amendment. We believe that randomization is critical to promote the value of evenhandedness, which is necessary to promote the goal of discretion control at the heart of Fourth Amendment reasonableness. We also argue that randomized searches, by definition, are accompanied by a certain level of suspicion. The constitutional issue, we maintain, should not turn on the question of suspicion-based versus suspicionless police encounters with individuals, but on the *level of suspicion* that attaches to any search program *and* on the evenhandedness of the program. In essence, we argue for a new paradigm of randomized encounters that satisfy a base level of suspicion that will capture the benefits of *both* privacy protection by

[12] See Bernard E. Harcourt & Tracey L. Meares, *Randomization and the Fourth Amendment*, 78 U. Chi. L. Rev. (forthcoming 2011).

ensuring a minimum level of suspicion, *and* evenhandedness by cabining police discretion.

We also think that the concept of individualized suspicion should be abandoned. We could, of course, simply urge that courts use a more honest metric of suspicion and stop there. We promote the concept of randomization for two reasons: The first is that suspicion predominantly attaches to groups, at least in the ordinary policing context. When we require a certain level of suspicion, it turns out, we have identified a group of individuals – generally, a group that contains individuals of different races, ethnicities, gender, and so on. To pick individuals from within that group – all of whom satisfy the required level of suspicion – we ought to use a neutral sorting mechanism. We must pick fairly from the group. Once we have decided to search within any category, then we are in effect searching within the group. The only way to do that without injecting bias and prejudice is to randomly search the group, because randomization allows us to select from the group while avoiding illegitimate criteria to discriminate within the group.

The notion of reasonableness at the core of the Fourth Amendment has a few aims. Two of the most important are controlling police discretion and avoiding discrimination, whether political, racial, or other. A second reason to promote randomization, then, is that it has great potential to control the exercise of state power exercised against individuals as a function of the discretion of individual police officers. Primarily, we want to claim that the Fourth Amendment ought to be interpreted in a way that best constrains police power and makes it politically accountable to those against whom it is being deployed. In emphasizing discretion and discrimination we do not mean to slight privacy protection. We think randomization protects privacy by ensuring an honest and open evaluation of the level of suspicion necessary to trigger the possibility of police intervention and coercion.

This argument is, of course, responsive to the concerns Stuntz lays out in *Distribution of Privacy*. He notes that to solve privacy's bias, we must change privacy's meaning. He states quite clearly that "the change must be dramatic.... [T]he law would have to focus not on the interest in keeping things secret or being free from observation, but on the interest in being free from humiliation or indignity, or the interest in avoiding the stigma that comes from being publicly identified as a criminal suspect, or the interest in avoiding police harassment or discrimination."[13]

[13] Stuntz, cited in note 1 at 1273.

Harcourt and I do not give up entirely on privacy, but we make avoidance of the targeting harm central to the interpretation of the Fourth Amendment. It does not take a rocket scientist to see the value of a randomization mechanism if the harm to be averted is Professor Colb's targeting. The reason is that each encounter an officer makes in the checkpoint context is made with reference to *no reason* at all as opposed to the an individualized suspicion-based "good reason." According to *Sitz v. Michigan*,[14] a checkpoint search is justified with reference to the entire program and not with respect to each individual search or stop. Consider again the public law enforcement encounter. If observers watch a person stopped and searched at a checkpoint, they would never say to themselves, "That person must have done X." Indeed, it would make no sense for the observers to wonder to themselves why the person had been stopped. In the checkpoint world, all are aware that there is no reason at all. That is the beauty of the approach. As opposed to searching for so-called good crime-behavior-based reasons for police action, we are instead satisfied that there is an absence of bad reasons for police actions. Another way to describe this regime is simply to say that it is a particular manifestation of guided discretion.

There is another benefit of randomization. Because police do not exercise their discretion to pick out those whom they believe are lawbreakers in the cheapest manner in the way that Stuntz describes, their incentive to prefer poor minorities is lessened. Thus, they should randomly encounter individuals from more varied demographic groups, and the consequence is that political accountability should be enhanced when the burden of the incidence of law enforcement intrusions is shifted to a more varied demographic group. Another way of describing the shift is to say that it is more likely with a randomization mechanism to govern police encounters as opposed to an individual-suspicion-based one that the police will encounter the "median voter."

So far I have said nothing about the connection between this idea and the distribution of constitutional benefits. It turns out to be quite straightforward once one considers the mechanism together with recent work in social psychology. There is a benefit of randomization that is not simply the absence of the targeting harm but the potential conferral of a dignity benefit. To understand why, a brief survey of the social psychology of procedural justice is necessary.

[14] See 496 U.S. 444 (1990).

Individuals care about how they are treated by legal authorities because that treatment provides them with important information regarding how authorities view the group to which the individual evaluator perceives herself or himself to belong. A complex collection of factors matter to people, but researchers have grouped them into three categories: standing, neutrality, and trust.[15] By standing, researchers mean indications that an authority recognizes an individual's status and membership in a valued group, such as polite treatment or treatment that otherwise accords a person dignity and respect. Neutrality means signals regarding decision making and actions that do not convey bias, discrimination, and incompetence to a perceiver. Trust is the most amorphous of the three. Individuals look for signals in the behavior of legal authorities indicating to them that they can count on the authority in question to behave fairly and benevolently in the future.

Psychologists Allan Lind and Tom Tyler have shown that people care about procedural justice because it provides them with important informational signals that they view as relevant to their identities. For example, if a police officer treats a person rudely during an encounter, that person will process that treatment as information relevant to how legal authorities tend to view her or him, as well as the group to which she or he belongs. And, it turns out, these signals are much more important to people when evaluating the behavior of the legal officials with which they deal than even favorable (or unfavorable) outcomes people receive at the hands of these same folks.

The conclusion is one that Bill Stuntz might have anticipated. The legality of encounters – at least when defined in terms of suspicion requirements – may not matter very much to people, but the qualitative details of the encounter such as how polite an officer is when talking to a person he or she stops and questions are paramount. The recent arrest of Henry Louis Gates at his home in Cambridge well illustrates this intuition. The following are two excerpts of a report in which Professor Gates describes the encounter.

1. Gates said he asked for the officer's name and badge number on several occasions, but that the officer never responded or asked him if he was all right. Gates said that "the silence was deafening." Gates said he then said to the officer, "You're not responding because I am a black man and you're a white officer."

[15] See Tracey L. Meares, *Norms, Legitimacy and Law Enforcement*, 79 Ore. L. Rev. 391, 402–404 (2002).

II. Professor Gates said he was greatly disturbed that Sergeant Crowley refused to formally give him his name and badge number. He interpreted this refusal as an insult and an abuse of power.[16]

Gates concluded on the basis of his experience that he was racially profiled. Note that Gates's highlighting of the negative aspects of his experience clearly is in accord with the procedural justice account. Note also that official treatment of individuals that conveys a message regarding the individual's dignity is central to the account.

The distributional point is this: Because Fourth Amendment privacy is biased in the way that Stuntz explained, seemingly against the individual interests of those who are poor, black, and urban dwelling, police work has followed suit. That is, police will find it easier to choose to engage members of these demographic groups on the street. And because nothing in Fourth Amendment law today encourages police to attend to the factors that social psychologists tell us are critical – such as polite treatment – then poor, urban-dwelling people of color bear the brunt not only of privacy and autonomy intrusions, but also of the constant stream of official messaging they interpret as insulting.

It does not have to be this way.

Harcourt and I have offered an approach that could potentially help to lessen, if not erase, the negative distributional consequences of targeting. It is important to note, however, that the approach can do more. Because randomization does not depend on an officer's investing in attributing a criminal identity to a person she or he stops as the current regime does, it is reasonable to predict that there will be less animosity between officers and people encountered on the street. Less animosity will, in turn, lead to more positive encounters. More positive encounters will, one hopes, lead to more polite treatment. An abundance of polite, dignity-filled encounters between police and people of color on the street should do more than take the sting of the former negative encounters away. Positive encounters actually *confer* dignity. That is a conclusion that I hope Bill Stuntz would applaud.

[16] Gates Commission Report, at 21.

7

Why Courts Should Not Quantify Probable Cause

Orin Kerr

INTRODUCTION

Probable cause is a basic tool of Fourth Amendment law. It appears prominently in the constitutional text: "no warrants shall issue, but upon probable cause."[1] Police power often depends on it. In a range of settings, searches and seizures are constitutional if the police have probable cause but unconstitutional if they don't. But just how "probable" is probable cause?

The Supreme Court has declined to say. The Supreme Court has described probable cause as a "nontechnical conception"[2] that requires proof of a "fair probability."[3] The Court has also said that probable cause exists when "a man of reasonable caution" would believe an offense has been committed.[4] But the Court has refused to quantify probable cause. "The probable-cause standard is incapable of precise definition or quantification into percentages," the Court recently declared, "because it deals with probabilities and depends on the totality of the circumstances."[5]

This is no explanation at all, of course. The fact that the standard deals with probabilities is exactly why it might be quantified. The question remains: What probability is a "fair" probability? Does it require 50 percent likelihood? Or perhaps 40 percent? Scholars and lower-court judges occasionally have tried to guess, without reaching a

This chapter honors the late Professor William Stuntz. It is dedicated to his memory.

[1] See U.S. Const. Amend. IV.

[2] Brinegar v. United States, 338 U.S. 160, 176 (1949).

[3] Illinois v. Gates 462 U.S. 213, 238 (1983).

[4] Safford Unified School Dist. No. 1 v. Redding 129 S. Ct. 2633, 2639 (2010), quoting Carroll v. United States, 167 U.S. 132, 262 (1925).

[5] Maryland v. Pringle, 540 U.S. 366, 371 (2003).

consensus.[6] The Supreme Court's refusal to quantify probable cause raises a puzzle. Why has the Court left the concept so vague? Are the Justices simply afraid of math? More broadly, should probable cause be quantified to help lower-court judges apply this foundational concept more accurately?

This chapter argues that courts should not quantify probable cause because quantification would lead to less accurate probable cause determinations. This sounds odd at first. It's natural to expect that judges will assess probable cause more accurately if they know more about it. But that is not true, because the warrant process is a fertile ground for cognitive biases. When judges apply the probable cause standard to review ex parte warrant applications, they know only the limited picture of the facts provided in the government's affidavit. Intuitions about unknown facts play a critical role in assessing probable cause. Quantification would block those intuitions and instead provide a fertile ground for cognitive biases that would distort the probable cause assessment. Leaving probable cause unquantified is therefore critical to ensuring accurate probable cause determinations.

The basic problem is that assessments of probable cause require information typically left out of warrant affidavits. Affidavits explain the officer's affirmative reasons to think probable cause exists. However, they exclude two critical pieces of information. They generally leave out what steps the police took that failed to provide evidence, and they always leave out what steps the police did not take and why they didn't take those steps. These excluded facts are often highly relevant to the likelihood that the government's affirmative evidence amounts to probable cause. In some cases, these facts are critical. Because affidavits generally don't report those facts, judges must make intuitive estimates of them to accurately assess probable cause. Qualitative legal standards such as "fair probability" let judges account for these missing facts intuitively.

Quantifying probable cause would eclipse those intuitions and instead facilitate distortions of probability resulting from cognitive biases. By reducing probable cause to numbers, quantification would allow the

[6] In one study, 166 federal judges were asked to quantify probable cause. Their answers ranged from 10 percent certainty to 90 percent certainty, with an average of 44.52 percent certainty. See C. M. A. McCauliff, *Burdens of Proof: Degrees of Belief, Quanta of Evidence, or Constitutional Guarantees?*, 35 Vand. L. Rev. 1293, 1327–1328 (1982). See also Christopher Slobogin, *Let's Not Bury Terry: A Call for Rejuvenation of the Proportionality Principle*, 72 St. John's L. Rev. 1053, 1082–1085 (1998), estimating probable cause at about 50 percent.

representativeness heuristic and anchoring effects to play a major role in assessing probabilities. The limited information in the affidavit would seem like the entire picture, allowing the government to make very-low-probability events appear to be very-high-probability events. In short, quantification would override the critical intuitions of judges about missing information in the affidavit that are critical to assessing probable cause accurately. The counterintuitive result is that judicial failure to quantify probable cause is a strength, not a weakness. Knowing less about the standard improves how the standard is applied.

I. UNKNOWNS AND THE WARRANT PROCESS

Imagine the police believe a crime has been committed. They have a suspect, so they try a range of investigative techniques to show the suspect committed the offense. Some of the techniques come up empty and provide no helpful information. Other techniques work, however, and they point to the suspect as the likely criminal. The police figure that whoever committed the crime likely stored evidence of the crime in his home. So when the police have enough evidence, they apply for a warrant to search the suspect's home for evidence of the crime.

The warrant application requires two documents. First, the police must write up a proposed warrant for the judge to sign allowing the police to search the suspect's home for the evidence described. Second, the police must write up an affidavit making the case for probable cause that the evidence described will be found in the home. The affidavit will explain the reasons why the government thinks the suspect committed the crime. That is, it will list the investigative steps that the government took that collectively might establish probable cause. The judge will then read the affidavit and decide whether the facts described in the four corners of the affidavit establish probable cause that the evidence will be found in the place to be searched. If the magistrate concludes that probable cause exists and the rest of the warrant application is satisfactory, the magistrate will sign the warrant.

Notably, the affidavit ordinarily provides only a very limited picture of the investigation. A complete picture of the investigation would include three sets of information: (1) an understanding of all the possible techniques that the police could have tried to gather evidence; (2) an understanding of which techniques the police actually tried, together with why they tried them and why they did not try the untried alternatives; and (3) an understanding of what techniques the police tried that actually

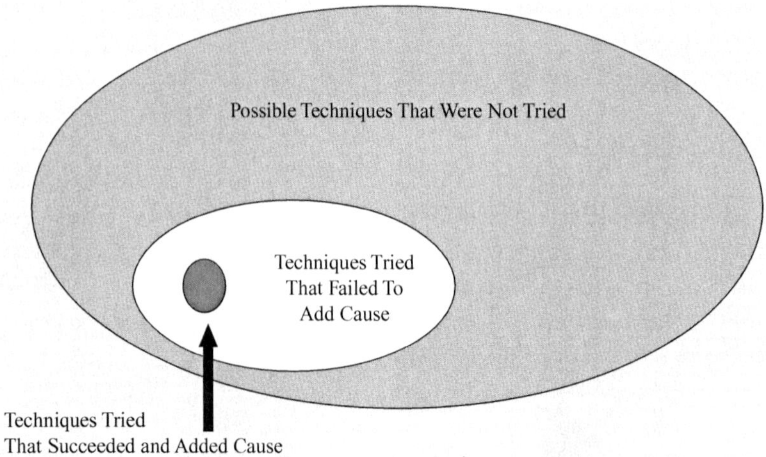

FIGURE 7.1. Visual conception of an affidavit.

worked. Importantly, however, the affidavit typically includes only the third item. The affidavit explains what steps the police took that helped show cause, but it does not say what techniques were never tried, why they weren't tried, or what techniques were tried but failed to yield any additional cause. We can see this visually in Figure 7.1.

To be sure, the law imposes some limits on excluding information from the affidavit. Under *Franks v. Delaware*,[7] the police cannot intentionally or recklessly misrepresent whether probable cause exists. Lower courts have held that this applies to withholding material facts from an affidavit: The police cannot intentionally or recklessly withhold exculpatory evidence from an affidavit that, if included, would establish that no probable cause existed.[8] But this standard is a high one that generally applies only to warrants obtained by fraud, as it applies only when the exculpatory evidence was so great that probable cause clearly would not have existed if it had been included. Further, this limitation arises only rarely because most victims of searches will not know when the police have exculpatory evidence: If they do not know the information, they cannot challenge the affidavit based on its absence. As a result, affidavits ordinarily will report only the limited subset of techniques that were tried and that helped establish cause to conduct the search.

[7] 438 U.S. 154 (1978).
[8] See, e.g., Whitlock v. Brown, 596 F.3d 406, 411 (7th Cir. 2010).

Why does this matter? It matters because the missing information can be critical to the probable-cause inquiry. Figure 7.1 hints at the reason why: The chances that evidence will be located in a particular place depend on more than what techniques were tried and worked. The limited nature of the facts in the affidavit allows the police to exclude facts that seem innocent in isolation but can lessen the likelihood of probable cause in context. If the police try other techniques that are potentially exculpatory, the judge probably won't know about that. And if the police decide not to try certain techniques that could be exculpatory, the judge will never know about that, either. Even worse, the judge won't know what he doesn't know: Just looking at the affidavit, the judge probably won't think about how small a picture of the facts appears within it.

The dynamic brings to mind the wisdom of the great legal mind Donald Rumsfeld:

> There are known knowns. These are things that we know we know. There are known unknowns. That is to say, there are things we know we don't know. But there are also unknown unknowns. These are things we do not know we don't know.[9]

In a warrant application, the fruits of techniques that were tried and provided cause are the "known knowns." The judge sees them and understands their scope in the four corners of the affidavit. The fact that some techniques were tried but failed to provide evidence will be the "known unknowns." Judges will know they might exist but not know exactly what they are. Finally, the techniques that were never tried are the "unknown unknowns." Judges won't know whether they exist, or why, or what choices the police made to try certain techniques and avoid others.

II. THE CASE OF THE HARVARD DORM SEARCH

We can see the importance of these unknowns by considering the following hypothetical. Imagine the police apply for a warrant to search a particular Harvard College dormitory room for marijuana. The case for probable cause consists solely of two pieces of information. First, the police offer a scientific study by top Harvard scientists showing that marijuana can be found in 60 percent of Harvard dormitory rooms. Second, the police provide proof that the room to be searched is a Harvard dormitory room. Assume, for the sake of argument, that the scientific

[9] Available at http://www.defense.gov/transcripts/transcript.aspx?transcriptid=2636.

study is widely acknowledged to be authoritative: The study conclusively establishes that 60 percent of Harvard dorm rooms contain marijuana. Now ask yourself, is there probable cause? Or more specifically, what are the chances that marijuana will be found in the dorm room?[10] Think carefully about it. Come up with your answer before continuing.

When you have your answer, let's next fill in some unknowns. The first unknown addresses the techniques that the police tried and that failed to provide evidence. Specifically, imagine that the local Cambridge police had conducted an undercover investigation into drug possession in Harvard dorms. The police investigation, which was independent of the study by Harvard scientists, involved a group of officers who posed as students and who mapped out the extensive network of drugs sales and use in the dorms. Exactly half of the dorm rooms were implicated in the investigation as rooms in which drugs were stored or sold. The dorm room to be searched in the warrant application was not one of them. Throughout the investigation, no evidence ever suggested that drugs would be found in that particular room.

Now let's add another unknown – the techniques that were never tried. Specifically, assume that the Cambridge police recently purchased a new high-tech surveillance device called the Potdetector 9000. The Potdetector 9000 detects trace amounts of marijuana in the air, and it can be used lawfully without a warrant to detect marijuana nearby. It is cheap and easy to use. If placed near the entrance of a dorm room, it can tell with 99 percent certainty if marijuana is inside the room. For reasons that remain unclear, however, the police decided not to use the Potdetector 9000 for this particular dorm room.

Ask yourself again: Does probable cause exist? What are the chances that marijuana will be found in the dorm room? Note how the picture has changed. Before I filled in the unknowns, you probably estimated the chance that drugs would be found in the dorm room at 60 percent. After all, that's what the scientific study showed. However, with the unknowns filled in, the odds drop considerably. First, you realize that there are really two sets of dorm rooms: The 50 percent of dorm rooms implicated by the investigation and the 50 percent of dorm rooms *not* implicated by the investigation. If 60 percent of the rooms have marijuana inside, and the rooms implicated by the investigation have a much higher

[10] This is a variation on the well-known "blue bus" hypothetical. See, e.g., Laurence H. Tribe, *Trial by Mathematics: Precision and Ritual in the Legal Process*, 84 Harv. L. Rev. 1329, 1372 (1971).

likelihood of having drugs inside, then the likelihood that drugs are in a room *not* implicated by the investigation is much lower than 60 percent.

Next consider the role of the Potdetector 9000. The police chose not to use it. But why? According to the hypothetical, the Potdetector 9000 provides a quick, easy, and extremely reliable way to determine if there are drugs in the room. If the Potdetector 9000 had been used, and it had signaled marijuana in the room, then that positive "hit" would have been featured prominently in the affidavit. The decision not to use the Potdetector 9000 suggests the significant possibility that the police had reason to think that the room did *not* contain drugs. That is, perhaps the police avoided using the Potdetector 9000 to maintain plausible deniability that they suspected the room was clean. If that is the case, the chance that drugs are in the room drops once more. Again, there are two sets of rooms, not one: The rooms for which the Potdetector 9000 was used, and the rooms for which it wasn't used. The room to be searched in our hypothetical was part of the latter group, for which there is a lesser chance than 60 percent that drugs will be found inside.

The affidavit in our hypothetical gave only generalized evidence: 60 percent of all Harvard dorm rooms contain marijuana. That means a Harvard dorm room picked at random would have a 60 percent chance of containing marijuana. But that doesn't mean the affidavit established a 60 percent chance that marijuana will be found in the specific room that the officers wanted to search. Places to be searched are not picked at random. To know the chances that marijuana would be found, a judge needs to know why the police submitted an affidavit consisting solely of statistical evidence to search that particular room. They need to know the back-story about how the investigation developed. Only a complete picture of the facts would allow a magistrate judge to accurately predict the likelihood that evidence will be found. But that won't happen, because such facts don't generally appear in the affidavit.

III. INTUITIONS OF PROBABLE CAUSE AND THE ROLE OF UNKNOWNS

Accurate determination of probable cause requires accurate assessments of unknowns. But how? The current definition of probable cause allows judges to assess unknowns intuitively. When the unknowns are likely to be significant, judges will get a feeling that something is amiss. They may not know exactly why something is wrong, but they will instinctively resist finding probable cause based only on the evidence in the affidavit.

In my view, these sorts of feelings are not only rational but necessary: The instinct that something is amiss reflects a "situation sense"[11] that we're not seeing the whole picture. They are intuitions of circumstances in which the unknowns are likely to bias the probable-cause determination. Because probable cause is a vague, unquantified concept, such instinctive judgments are permitted to influence determinations of probable cause.

Let's return to the affidavit to search a Harvard down room based only on a statistical study. When I first asked if probable cause existed, you probably felt instinctively uncomfortable about answering "yes." You probably wanted some sort of specific cause that linked the drugs to that particular apartment. You may have even felt that you were being irrational in your conclusion: After all, the statistics proved that the chances of drugs being in the room were 60 percent, and yet you fought that logical statistic because your brain wanted concrete evidence.[12] Surely this reflects your human irrationality, right? Not so, in my view. You were being quite rational. You were instinctively recognizing the unknowns, and you were instinctively factoring them into the probable cause determination.

Here's why: The instinct to want to see some sort of particularized evidence beyond the statistical study reflects the commonsense intuition that the officers must have picked that particular dorm room for a reason. If the officers are acting in good faith, we expect to see particularized evidence specifically tagging that room to the crime. Finding particularized evidence in the affidavit fulfills our expectation and calms any fears about the unknowns. It fills in the unknowns in a particular way. It suggests that this investigation was a typical investigation with no funny business that never made it into the affidavit.

However, if the affidavit does *not* link the statistical study to the room to be searched, we intuit that the government may be hiding something. The government isn't sharing why it picked that room. This triggers our concerns about the unknowns. What is the back-story, we wonder? The feeling that something is fishy reflects our sense that we're not getting the complete picture in the affidavit. We want to see particularized evidence in the affidavit because its absence suggests that there are unknowns that

[11] Karl Llewellyn referred to "situation sense" as a learned judicial intuition about accepted practices that allows judges to reach consistent results absent formal rules. See Karl Llewellyn, The Common Law Tradition: Deciding Appeals 268–285 (1960).

[12] See, e.g., Sherry F. Colb, *Probabilities in Probable Cause and Beyond: Statistical Versus Concrete Harms*, 73 Law & Contemp. Probs. 69 (2010).

render the evidence in the affidavit unreliable. In that setting, we intuit that probable cause is absent: The absence of expected information signals the likelihood of unknowns that alter whether probable cause exists.

Notably, all this proceeds by instinct. Indeed, because the instinct leads us to question statistical evidence, we may feel that we are being emotional and illogical. The opposite is true. We are using our situation sense to intuit that the facts in the affidavit are not telling us the whole story. We are filling in the unknowns needed to assess probable cause.

IV. QUANTIFICATION AND COGNITIVE BIAS

Let's return now to the problem of whether probable cause should be quantified. In my view, the problem with quantifying probable cause is that quantification blocks our essential intuitions about the unknowns. When we start thinking in terms of numbers, we focus on the numbers. Our intuitions take a backseat. This is no place for mere feelings, we think to ourselves. This is now a question of mathematics! The result is that we naturally downplay the significance of the unknowns. But ignoring unknowns introduces significant error: Downplaying the unknowns leads to less accurate probable cause determinations by effectively disabling the instincts that we rely on to determine probable cause accurately.

Two cognitive biases help explain the reason. The first is the representativeness heuristic.[13] The representativeness heuristic refers to the tendency to measure probability by reference to data that seem to resemble the probability to be estimated. Consider a well-known example introduced by Amos Tversky and Daniel Kahneman.[14] Imagine a taxi cab was involved in a hit-and-run traffic accident. There are two cab companies in the city. One company uses blue cabs and the other uses green cabs. An eyewitness saw the accident and agrees to testify. He takes the stand and testifies that the cab was blue. Let's further assume we know that the eyewitness's reliability is 80 percent. That is, the eyewitness can identify the color of a cab correctly 80 percent of the time. Now estimate the probability that the cab involved in the accident was actually blue. And let me add one more piece of information: 85 percent of the cabs in the city are green cabs and 15 percent are blue cabs.

[13] See generally Amos Tversky & Daniel Kahneman, *Judgment Under Uncertainty: Heuristics and Biases*, 185 Science 1124, 1128–1130 (1974).

[14] See generally Amos Tversky & Daniel Kahneman, *On Prediction and Judgment*, Oregon Research Institute Bulletin 12 (4) (1972).

Many people conclude that the chances the cab was blue are 80 percent.[15] They focus on the established 80 percent reliability of the eyewitness. The eyewitness's reliability seems a lot like the problem at hand: It is an estimate of probability of a fact. But relying so heavily on eyewitness reliability leads to significant error. The actual probability is nowhere near 80 percent. It is only about half of that. To see why, step back and think about the possibilities. The eyewitness testified that the cab was blue. There are two logical possibilities: Either he correctly identified a blue cab or he incorrectly identified a green one. Because green cabs are much more common than blue cabs, the chances that the eyewitness wrongly identified a green cab are actually *higher* than the probability the eyewitness correctly identified a blue cab.

Think about why. If you don't know anything about the accident except for the statistics about witness reliability and the relative number of cabs, then there was a 15 percent chance that the cab was blue and an 80 percent chance the eyewitness would testify correctly. The overall probability of correct testimony that the cab was blue is 80 percent of 15 percent, for a total of 12 percent. In contrast, there was an 85 percent chance the cab was green, and a 20 percent chance the eyewitness testified incorrectly about its color and wrongly said the cab was blue. The overall probability of incorrect testimony that the cab was blue is 20 percent of 85 percent, for a total of 17 percent. The chance that the eyewitness testimony of a blue cab was accurate is therefore the chance of accurate testimony divided by the total probability of that testimony. That is, 12 percent divided by the sum of 12 percent and 17 percent, which is a total probability of 41 percent. The common guess of 80 percent is not just a little off. It's *way* off. And remember how the error occurred: The natural instinct was to rely on the readily available probability – that is, the known reliability of the eyewitness. That instinct proved extremely misleading.

Anchoring effects would also weaken probable-cause determinations if probable cause were quantified. Anchoring refers to the mind's tendency to make estimates of unknowns by starting from some point and then adjusting upwards or downwards to it.[16] If you ask people to estimate the average temperature in San Francisco, they will guess one number. If you ask them whether the average temperature in San Francisco is higher

[15] Maya Bar-Hillel, *The Base Rate Fallacy in Probability Judgements*, 44 Acta Psychologica 211, 220 (1980).

[16] See supra note 13.

or lower than 558 degrees, and then ask them to estimate that average temperature, their answers will on average be significantly higher simply because their minds started from the (obviously absurd) starting point of 558 degrees.[17] The key lesson is that the introduction of a number has an anchoring effect: The mind is influenced by the starting point, and it tends to bias estimates of probabilities and uncertainties by using whatever anchor was introduced.

These cognitive biases ensure that quantification of probable cause would create predictable errors. If the Supreme Court quantified probable cause, magistrate judges would begin to think in terms of numbers. They would scan affidavits for any numerical or probabilistic evidence, and any numerical or probabilistic evidence would take on a far greater role than it should. The new focus on numbers would limit the role of intuition, limiting the ability of judges to recognize when the information in the affidavit is only a part of the picture and that critical information is missing. Owing to cognitive biases, judges would follow the numbers to their detriment. It is strange but true: Knowing more about probable cause would make it harder to for judges to apply the standard accurately.

V. WORKING WITH A QUANTIFIED PROBABLE-CAUSE STANDARD

The Harvard dorm hypothetical again provides a helpful example. This time, assume the Supreme Court has quantified probable cause. Let's say it has declared that probable cause means exactly a 47 percent likelihood. If the chances that evidence will be found are at or above 47 percent, then probable cause exists; if they are below 47 percent, then probable cause does not exist. Now imagine you are a magistrate judge presented with the affidavit based on the Harvard study. The only evidence you have is the study showing that 60 percent of Harvard dorm rooms contain marijuana, plus proof that the room to be searched is a Harvard dorm room. Is there probable cause?

In all likelihood, you would answer that question by focusing on the numbers. Probable cause means exactly 47 percent. Does the affidavit satisfy that likelihood? You would start with 60 percent as your anchor. The study seems quite impressive, and it starts the probability at 60 percent. That probability closely resembles the probability you're trying to calculate, so it has a strong influence on your assessment. Focusing

[17] Scott Plous, The Psychology of Judgment and Decision Making 146 (1993).

on the numbers, you see that 60 percent is considerably more than 47 percent. A significant gap of 13 percent separates them. So the issue is whether anything in the case might lower the probability from 60 percent to 59 percent to 58 percent to 57 percent, and so on, all the way down to below 47 percent.

You probably will conclude the answer is "no," and therefore that probable cause has been established. Nothing in the case jumps out at you as sharply altering the probability from that 60 percent mark. When faced with the contrast between hard and definite numbers on the one hand, and fuzzy instincts on the other, the numbers will play an outsized role. The numbers will seem like everything, even though they are not. The 60 percent figure seems the right probability, just like the 80 percent figure seemed so significant in the case of the eyewitness who testified about the blue cab.

But let's reintroduce one of the unknowns in the hypothetical, this time with numbers, to see how easily unknowns can make a major difference in the probability. Recall the first unknown in the dorm hypothetical: Exactly half of the dorm rooms were implicated by the local police undercover investigation as rooms in which drugs were stored or sold, but the dorm room to be searched in the warrant application was not one of them. Let's further assume that 90 percent of the dorm rooms implicated in the investigation as rooms in which drugs were stored or sold do actually contain drugs.

Under these assumptions, the role of the unknown has a dramatic impact on the probability. The probability has dropped in half. Because the overall probability is 60 percent, and the Harvard dorm rooms are divided equally between rooms implicated in the investigation and rooms not so implicated, the 90 percent likelihood for dorm rooms implicated in the investigation must be balanced out by only a 30 percent likelihood of drugs in rooms not implicated. If probable cause means a 47 percent likelihood, the addition of the unknown has quietly but firmly shifted the probability from well above probable cause to well below it.

Further, slight differences in the unknown can have a major impact on the probability. Imagine that instead of the Harvard rooms implicated in the undercover investigation being divided 50/50, they were instead divided 60/40. That is, the undercover investigation pointed to drugs being sold from or stored in 60 percent of Harvard rooms, but the room to be searched is not one of them. If 90 percent of the implicated rooms contain drugs, then 56 percent of Harvard dorm rooms will be dorm rooms implicated by the study in which drugs are found (60 percent of the rooms at a 90 percent probability). Because the Harvard study tells us that drugs will be found in 60 percent of Harvard dorm rooms overall, the 40 percent of dorm rooms not implicated in the undercover investigation should account for only 4 percent of the remaining Harvard dorm rooms containing drugs. The percentage likelihood of a typical room not implicated in the investigation containing drugs now drops to only 10 percent.

CONCLUSION

Understanding probable cause requires judgment and experience. Learning the standard requires reading the leading cases. Over time, experience teaches where the line should be drawn. Reducing probable cause to a number would bypass this time-consuming process. A quantified probable cause would take seconds, rather than many hours, to learn. For that reason, the instinct to quantify probable cause is understandable. It aims to simplify and explain a judgment that otherwise must be learned over time.

Although such a shortcut has obvious appeal, it is also unrealistic. Unknowns that do not appear in the affidavit play too critical a role in probable cause for the shortcut to work. Only an approach to probable cause steeped in learned judgment, based on intuition and situation sense, can accurately reflect the unknowns and ensure accurate probable cause determinations. By keeping probable cause vague, the Supreme Court has retained the role of intuition in assessing it. The fuzziness of the standard makes ample room for the learned intuition that is essential to incorporating unknowns. If probable cause were quantified, cognitive biases would make the numbers expressed in the affidavit seem far more important than they are. They would make the unknowns seem largely if not entirely irrelevant. The vagueness of probable cause is the key to applying it accurately. To ensure that courts continue to factor in unknowns, the courts should keep probable cause unquantified.

8

DNA and the Fifth Amendment

Erin Murphy

Bill Stuntz caused me trouble for as long as I can remember. He first caused me trouble as a young lawyer, because as a public defender I had grown pleasantly accustomed to throwing constitutional rights at all the perceived ills of the criminal justice system. You know that old saw, "when all you have is a hammer, everything looks like a nail"? Well, to a public defender, every problem looks like a potential motion. To thus be told that in fact it was my *motion* that was the problem – well, that was disconcerting. Reading Bill Stuntz's work may have convinced me to put down my hammer, but it left me wanting to reach for a match.

Fortunately, I managed to overcome such destructive impulses and joined academia in order to think constructively about the criminal justice system. Unfortunately, that just brought me to my second problem with Stuntz, which is the one that I encountered as a young scholar and continue to encounter even today. That problem is this: Every time I think I have some new idea or path-breaking original thought, I do a little research only to find that Bill Stuntz already had the same realization years earlier and, worse yet, published something about it. In fact, he usually wrote better, more clearly, and with more nuance and careful understanding than I ever could. But it was always hard to become too upset, since if I had to get scooped, I cannot think of a nicer or smarter person to claim as having preempted me.

In all fairness, though, I must also admit that, in true Stuntzian fashion, the trouble that he caused me as a public defender and as an academic

* This chapter commemorates and celebrates the life and work of Professor William J. Stuntz. It is dedicated to his memory and to the lasting impact that he had both on the field of criminal justice and on the many scholars, myself included, whose hearts and minds he touched.

also served to lift me up in both professions. As a young practicing lawyer interested in pursuing an academic career, reading his work helped to affirm for me that my two paths were not incompatible – that it was possible and even desirable to be a scholar deeply invested in questions related to how criminal justice actually works in the real world. And as an academic, I have countless times relied on his insight to guide me in the exploration and development of my own thoughts about the criminal justice system.

It is these two lessons – now legacies – of Bill Stuntz's that I keep in mind as I turn to an emerging issue particular to my own research: namely, the problem of genetic evidence in the criminal justice system, with specific emphasis on its relationship to the Fifth Amendment. This chapter begins with an overview of the relationship between DNA and Fifth Amendment doctrine today, which could really be summed up quite briefly in three words: There is none. But I will proceed by urging one way in which a link might be forged, which is through an analogy to the compelled documents cases. The chapter concludes by acknowledging that, yet again, Bill Stuntz is causing me trouble, because the two major arguments against such an approach – both of which I find entirely persuasive – come directly from him.

DNA AND THE FIFTH AMENDMENT

By now it surprises no one to hear that DNA is serving an increasingly important role in the investigation and prosecution of criminal cases. It rarely even surprises people to learn that as of September of 2011, the federal DNA database contained over 10 million known offender profiles, and almost 400,000 crime scene profiles.[1] Statutes mandating the collection of DNA from convicted offenders have been broadly enacted and approved, and several jurisdictions even authorize the mandatory sampling of arrested persons. DNA is now used not just to confirm the guilt of already identified suspects, a practice I call "confirmatory" testing here, but also to generate lists of suspects from cold-hit database searches, or "prospective" or "investigatory" usages. In this latter form, law enforcement officers troll DNA databases for matches between known offenders

[1] FBI, U.S. Department of Justice, National DNA Index System Statistics, available at http://www.fbi.gov/about-us/lab/codis/ndis-statistics.

and evidentiary samples in cases that are either long cold or in which there is little information with which to identify a suspect.

In the course of the past ten or fifteen years, countless challenges to mandatory DNA collection statutes have been brought under the Fourth Amendment's prohibition against warrantless, suspicionless searches.[2] Also popular have been challenges based on procedural and substantive due process, the ex post facto clause, the cruel and unusual punishment clause, equal protection, separation of powers, the commerce clause, the privileges and immunities clause, and even the prohibition on Bills of Attainder. What there have not been much of, however, are challenges based on the Fifth Amendment protection against self-incrimination.[3]

The reason that Fifth Amendment claims are unpopular vehicles for DNA challenges relates to the well-established distinction between so-called testimonial and nontestimonial evidence. The opinion most famous for elaborating this concept was of course *Schmerber v. California*, in which the defendant contested the forcible drawing of his blood to measure its alcohol content.[4] In rejecting Schmerber's claim that the blood draw violated his right against compelled self-incrimination, the Supreme Court observed that it had long been acknowledged that the Fifth Amendment does not protect against a "compulsion to submit to fingerprinting, photographing, or measurements, to write or speak for identification, to appear in court, to stand, to assume a stance, to walk, or to make a particular gesture."[5] Such acts, although "an incriminating product of compulsion," are neither "testimony nor evidence relating to some communicative act," nor are they, in another popular formulation of the standard, "expression[s] of the contents of an individual's mind."[6]

Consistent with this conclusion, we see that the one court willing to devote any particular attention to the question of the relationship between

[2] See, e.g., Erin Murphy, *Paradigms of Restraint*, 57 Duke L. J. 1321, 1331 & n. 40 (2009).

[3] To illustrate this point in an entirely cursory and nonscientific fashion, consider that a search in the allcases database of Westlaw for "DNA /p 'self-incrimination' 'fifth amendment'" yields 304 entries, whereas the same search with "fourth amendment" yields 1,011 entries. Reading a selection of the Fifth Amendment cases renders it painfully evident just how weak self-incrimination claims are, given that most courts dismiss them in less than one paragraph. See, e.g., United States v. Hook, 471 F.3d 766 (7th Cir. 2006); United States v. Reynard, 473 F.3d 1008 (9th Cir. 2007); United States v. Zimmerman, 514 F.3d 851, 853 (9th Cir. 2007); Wilson v. Collins, 517 F.3d 421, 431 (6th Cir. 2008).

[4] 384 U.S. 757 (1966).

[5] Id. at 764.

[6] Doe v. United States, 487 U.S. 201, 210 n. 9 (1988).

DNA collection and the Fifth Amendment perfunctorily concluded that the

> claim of unconstitutional self-incrimination . . . fails because the taking of blood samples . . . is not testimonial evidence and as such is not protected by the Fifth Amendment. . . . Accordingly, the DNA collection done here by means of a non-testimonial blood draw is not protected by the Fifth Amendment. Moreover, the information that is extracted from the blood, DNA, is another form of physical, genetic identification of an individual not unlike a photograph or fingerprint and is thus also not protected by the Fifth Amendment.[7]

With respect to DNA typing, then, it seems that everyone has gotten the memo: The Fifth Amendment will provide no aid for those seeking refuge against a governmental demand for potentially incriminating *physical* evidence. As an aside, however, I will note that at least two important people might volunteer to redraft that memo. Justice Thomas, joined by Justice Scalia, remarked in his concurrence in *United States v. Hubbell*[8] that "a substantial body of evidence suggests that the Fifth Amendment privilege protects against the compelled production not just of incriminating *testimony*, but of any incriminating evidence."[9]

However, even without tracking as far back on the testimonial–nontestimonial road as Justices Thomas and Scalia might, is there another way to argue that DNA merits Fifth Amendment protection? After all, physical evidence has come a long way since the *Schmerber* days, and it is increasingly heading in unanticipated directions. *Schmerber* itself, way back in 1966, acknowledged that "[s]ome tests seemingly directed to obtain 'physical evidence,' for example, lie detector tests measuring changes in bodily function during interrogation, may actually be directed to eliciting responses which are essentially testimonial."[10] In other words, physiological measurements used as a proxy for or as an emblem of mental cognition – say, those taken by a functional MRI imager – would arguably fall within the amendment's scope. Further, even while acknowledging that the submission and testing of a DNA sample does not involve the same kind of physiological *response*, is it really right for the Fifth Amendment to lump the multifaceted nature of forensic DNA together with one-dimensional methods such as hair, voice, and handwriting, just

[7] *Hook*, 471 F.3d at 774.

[8] *Hubbell*, 530 U.S. 27 (2000).

[9] Id. at 49. Concededly, Justice Thomas's opinion focuses almost exclusively on documentary physical evidence, rather than personal physical samples.

[10] See 384 U.S. at 764.

because they are all physical products of the body? Are there not in fact quite significant differences among blood, sweat, and tears?

DNA AND THE FIFTH AMENDMENT, RECONSIDERED

Admittedly, it is difficult to make any claim that there is something different or special about DNA typing, as compared to more routine forms of physical evidence such as hair or handwriting, or even to other forms of blood testing, such that it deserves regulation by the Fifth Amendment. No less an authority than the Supreme Court has squarely stated that "blood test evidence, although an incriminating product of compulsion, [is] neither... testimony nor evidence relating to some communicative act or writing," and therefore "not inadmissible on privilege grounds."[11] Nonetheless, I will endeavor to sketch out here an argument to the contrary. In honor of the logical reasoning section of the LSAT, I call this the "*Fisher*: *Hubbell*; *Schmerber*: DNA" argument, which may not be a catchy title but is a descriptively succinct one. It goes like this.

In *Fisher*, taxpayers under criminal investigation by the Internal Revenue Service had transferred documents from their accountants to their attorneys. The attorneys challenged government subpoenas for the documents on Fifth Amendment grounds. Finding in essence that the summons "did not compel oral testimony, nor [did it] compel the taxpayer to restate, repeat, or affirm the truth of the contents of the document sought,"[12] the Court held the privilege inapplicable. Even acknowledging that the act of *complying* with the subpoena "has communicative aspects of its own," because it effectively conceded the existence of the papers, the Court doubted that "implicitly admitting the existence and possession of the papers [rose] to the level of testimony within the protection of the Fifth Amendment."[13] After all, the Court observed, the government had already known of the existence and location of the papers, along with their probable contents. The trivial degree to which receiving them confirmed their existence was akin to a suspect who incidentally discloses her capacity to write while being compelled to give a writing exemplar – communicative, perhaps, but of "minimal testimonial significance."[14]

In the wake of *Fisher*, and in light of additional developments, many scholars rang the death knell for *Boyd v. United States*,[15] the late 1800s

[11] Fisher v. United States, 425 U.S. 391, 408 n. 10 (1976).
[12] Id. at 409.
[13] Id. at 411.
[14] Id. at 412.
[15] 116 U.S. 616 (1886).

case that recognized strong Fourth and Fifth Amendment protections around even commercial documents, not to mention personal ones. Many of those scholars speculated, or even lamented, that it seemed possible that the Court no longer believed that compelled disclosure of private papers raised Fifth Amendment issues. Writing over ten years later, Bill Stuntz himself described this shift as "[p]robably the most important development in Fifth Amendment doctrine in recent years."[16]

But then, in *United States v. Hubbell* in 2000, the Court distinguished *Fisher* and affirmed that "the act of producing documents in response to a subpoena" – there, 13,000 pages worth of information – "may have a compelled testimonial aspect," when the production "itself . . . implicitly communicate[d] 'statements of fact'" about the documents' "existence, custody, and authenticity."[17] And, it added, this remains true even when the contents of the documents themselves are not independently inculpatory.[18] "While in *Fisher*," the Court wrote, "the government already knew that the documents were in the attorneys' possession and could independently confirm their existence and authenticity," the government in *Hubbell* "has not shown that it had any prior knowledge of either the existence or the whereabouts of the . . . documents ultimately produced by respondent."[19] In essence, *Hubbell* viewed the Fifth Amendment as precluding the government from engaging in a documentary fishing expedition in the hopes (or even expectation) of uncovering something of use.

Bill Stuntz himself prefigured (if not outright predetermined) *Hubbell*'s logic in an article that, naturally, the Justices cited in the case. Stuntz argued that because the existence of the incriminating information was not a "foregone conclusion," the Fifth Amendment protected it from compelled disclosure.[20] By way of illustration, Stuntz observed that if the government had amassed probable cause to obtain a search warrant for the documents, then there would have been no need for testimonial compulsion. But where a warrant would have been impossible, because the requestors did not know what they would find, the act of disclosure

[16] William J. Stuntz, *Self-incrimination and Excuse*, 88 Colum. L. Rev. 1227, 1277 (1988).

[17] *Hubbell*, 530 U.S. at 36.

[18] Id. at 38. As the Court held, "compelled testimony that communicates information that may 'lead to incriminating evidence' is privileged even if the information itself is not inculpatory." Id.

[19] Id. at 44–45.

[20] Id. at 42 n.2 3 (citing Stuntz, *Self-Incrimination*, supra note 16).

(regardless of what was disclosed) revealed information that the amendment should justly protect.

What does this have to do with DNA collection? My analogy is this: Just as *Hubbell* elevated the testimonial significance of document production in cases in which the information sought is itself not already known to the government, so too might we elevate the testimonial significance of interrogating physical evidence like DNA when it is done as a means of developing, rather than merely confirming, government suspicions. It might be argued, in other words, that when investigators collect a DNA sample on the basis of a suspicion in a particular case, and check for a match against a crime scene sample, they are operating in a manner akin to that in *Fisher*. They obviously know the suspect has the relevant thing (DNA), but they also have a quantum of suspicion about the thing's specific characteristics (i.e., that it matches a particular crime scene sample). Indeed, that suspicion is why they seek the suspect's sample. In such a case, as in *Fisher*, we might consider the act of production (here, the "handing over" of the suspect's actual genetic code) to be trivial. Given the independent suspicion of investigators, it is in fact not giving up that much – kind of like the driver at the accident scene who by law must provide her name and address.[21]

Now, if we conceive of DNA as no more than a physical sample, then that would be the end of the inquiry. But if we consider it a vessel – a container of information known to be in the suspect's possession but about which the government can either have strong suspicions or know nothing – then perhaps further consideration is justified. Imagined this way, confirmatory DNA sampling would implicate no testimonial interest, but exploratory use might be different, because prospective and investigative collection or examination of samples would be akin to what happened in *Hubbell*. It is a form of a generalized demand made by law enforcement, in the hopes of stumbling upon information that may be

[21] Cf. California v. Byers, 402 U.S. 424, 432 (1971) (finding no infringement of Fifth Amendment in statute requiring motorists involved in accidents to stop and give name and address, calling it an "essentially neutral act"); see also Braswell v. United States, 484 U.S. 99 (1988) (holding that a corporate officer may not refuse to produce documents that incriminate him personally); United States v. Doe, 487 U.S. 201 (1988) (concluding that compelling an individual to sign a form to consent to disclose foreign bank records did not infringe Fifth amendment); Marron v. United States, 275 U.S. 192 (1927) (upholding the right to seize a "ledger and certain bills" used in commission of crime); Adams v. New York, 192 U.S. 585 (1904) (assuming applicability of Fifth Amendment and finding no violation in seizure of "policy slips and papers relating to his private affairs" used to show a writing sample and occupation of the searched office).

incriminating. In such a view, wide-scale sampling programs aimed at collecting and amassing millions of samples from persons, without suspicion, would violate the Fifth Amendment.

In other words: The problem in *Hubbell* was that the compelled documents gave the government something that it *did not already have* – that is, proof of the existence of powerful evidence that incriminated the defendant – and *could not get* any other lawful way. Similarly, we can imagine that the DNA profile of a convicted person – say someone who has served a sentence and been released from prison – is similarly otherwise unobtainable. Just as agents lacked the probable cause necessary to get Hubbell's papers with a warrant, so too would they lack the probable cause or reasonable suspicion required by the Fourth Amendment to compel a swabbing. Conversely, just as the agents in *Fisher* knew of the paper's existence and had justified expectations of their inculpatory contents, so too might agents in a confirmatory DNA case know that a suspect possesses genetic information likely to be inculpatory of a particular crime.

In this way, it might be argued that *Schmerber* places outside of Fifth Amendment concern the development of physical evidence to confirm or bolster some quantum of suspicion already held by the government, but does not speak to the question of Fifth Amendment protection related to the acquisition or development of physical evidence when untethered to such suspicions. It is like the difference between the government compelling a person to write out by hand a ransom note for comparison to an existing piece of evidence versus the government compelling a person to generate writing samples without regard to any particular case, but merely to keep on file in the event of future utility. Arguably, the contextual mimicry and directed suspicion that characterizes the first act strips it of its testimonial nature, whereas the naked originality and suspicionless probing of the second act brings it closer to the confines of the Fifth Amendment. In short, whereas in *Fisher* and *Schmerber* the incriminating information that the government compelled was retrospective and confirmatory by nature, in *Hubbell* and with investigatory DNA searches it is prospective and speculative.

Although radical, this idea also dovetails nicely into Fourth Amendment doctrine, which is the more common source of protection for government seizure of physical evidence. When it acts with suspicion, the government may overcome a suspect's Fourth Amendment right against physical intrusion by, say, drawing blood. Likewise, suspicion mitigates the incriminatory aspect of forced production with respect to the Fifth Amendment: if officers have independent reason to believe that the evidence exists and contains specific relevant information, then commanding its disclosure largely constitutes a procedural act, not a substantive one. Without suspicion, however, the law enforcement demand is wholly exploratory and thus limitless – and hence invalid under both Fourth and Fifth Amendment doctrine.

Reconceiving the examination of physical evidence as a subject of Fifth Amendment concern is a matter deserving serious consideration, because at present, new technologies like DNA typing enable the government to readily divorce the "questioning" from the case. Historically, physical evidence – hair, fingerprints, handwriting – was collected for confirmatory purposes alone. The government found a suspect, pulled some hair or took some prints, and then checked them against the crime scene material. But DNA profiles (and, these days, even fingerprints) are collected and retained in databases, where they can be (and are) digitally interrogated over and over again. It is as though the blood sample in *Schmerber* did not just reveal that the driver had been drinking on the night in question, but could also alert authorities to every drink he had taken in the past or might take in the coming future.

In this regard, it is easy to forget, but imperative to remember, that wide-scale, efficient databasing is a law enforcement tool that really has taken root in only the past ten or so years.[22] To the extent that many forms of physical evidence have long been collected, it is essential to recall that this collection has been primarily case-based and suspicion-based – in other words, one-hit wonders.[23] But the database enables the reversal of the traditional arc of investigation – one that starts with suspects and moves to suspicion as opposed to vice versa. And the Fourth Amendment, with its lamentable focus on acquisition rather than use, has proved not quite up to the task of regulating the retention and later reinterpretation of lawfully obtained personal information.

Furthermore, new technologies have the capacity to reveal far more sensitive information than their scientific predecessors, such as tests for blood type or current intoxication level. Although DNA typing at present tends to be used primarily to uncover genetic markers of identity, far more delicate areas may also be implicated. Already DNA is used to reveal

[22] Erin Murphy, *Databases, Doctrine, and Constitutional Criminal Procedure*, 37 Fordham Urb. L. J. 803 (2010).

[23] Even the few forms of information storage that might have had longer shelf lives – say, a photograph of a criminal suspect or the suspect's blood type – were of limited probative value because they expressed information that was to a large extent imprecise, temporally contained, and highly mutable.

intimate information like familial connections[24] or physical characteristics,[25] and it may one day disclose genetic predispositions like pedophilic tendencies or mental illness. And other methods, like fMRI imaging, purport to discern veracity with a flip of a switch in place of a "testimonial" inquiry. Quite clearly, new technologies can edge much closer to the firewall around the "contents of the mind" than a handwriting or fingerprint sample ever could.

Of course, it is not lost on me that what I am suggesting would require a radical reworking of Fifth Amendment doctrine. So please do not misunderstand me and assume that I think this will actually happen. Honestly, I'm not even myself convinced that I think it *should* happen. But at the very least, in the approaching era of technologically sophisticated forms of physical evidence, it might be worth revisiting an understanding of the Fourth and Fifth Amendments that views them as interrelated and conversant with one another – the idea the *Boyd* court so firmly embraced but that has all but disappeared from doctrine. As a range of powerful new techniques appears on the horizon, it might be time to revive the old question reserved in *Warden v. Hayden* of whether "there are items of evidential value whose very nature precludes them from being the object of a reasonable search and seizure."[26] Or, similarly, the suggestion in *Schmerber* that some physical evidence might warrant greater protection because it serves too closely as a proxy for the mind.[27] If so, then the Fifth Amendment might be a place to lodge some restrictions against what kinds of intimate information the government can force from an individual prospectively and disconnected from any individualized suspicion, with only a goal of future investigative utility.

REVENGE OF THE STUNTZ, PART I: DNA AND THE CRUEL TRILEMMA

But of course, before I get too carried away, I have to concede at least two big obstacles to my approach. Both, unsurprisingly, come courtesy of Bill Stuntz. First, a theoretical complaint: to the extent that there exists a "theory of the Fifth Amendment," it is Bill Stuntz's articulation of it that causes me the most trouble. Second, a practical problem: even if Fifth

[24] See, e.g., Erin Murphy, *Relative Doubt: Familial Searches of DNA Databases*, 109 Mich. L. Rev. 291, 297 (2010).
[25] Id. at 335 n. 171.
[26] 387 U.S. 294, 302–03 (1967), cited in *Fisher*, 425 U.S. at 408 n. 9.
[27] 384 U.S. at 764.

Amendment regulation were possible as a matter of doctrine, Stuntz's work on the dynamics of criminal justice institutions suggests it might not be desirable as a matter of policy.

Let us start with the theoretical concern. Fifth Amendment protection for investigatory searches of DNA evidence comports nicely with the theories that conceive of the amendment as a bulwark against government cruelty or abuse, or as a protector of privacy and autonomy, or as a means of forcing the government to develop its own proof, or even as a tool for minimizing false positives. What it *does* not fit so well with, however, is Bill Stuntz's conceptualization of the Fifth Amendment, specifically with his notion that the Fifth Amendment bears a relationship to the substantive criminal law principle of excuse.

That is, in an early article titled *Self-Incrimination and Excuse*,[28] Stuntz took on the thankless task of attempting to provide a coherent theory of the Fifth Amendment. The conundrum of Fifth Amendment doctrine can be stated succinctly, if simplistically, as follows. Pursuant to *Miranda*,[29] the amendment affords broad protections to prevent a defendant from self-incrimination in the context of custodial interrogation. However, it supplies only minimal protection against self-incrimination in the form of disclosure of documents, and virtually no protection against compelled incriminating conduct or physical evidence, nor for noncustodial or non-"interrogation"-based exchanges. To make matters more confusing, the "heightened" protection for interrogation is itself internally schizophrenic – on the one hand there is an absolute right on the part of a suspect to refuse to answer questions that will incriminate her, but on the other hand that absolute right is easily waived or relinquished.[30] Under what theory might the Fifth Amendment accord such indiscriminately expansive, even if arguably hollow, safeguards in one narrow context – custodial interrogation – while ignoring or stingily defining an individual's interest against self-incrimination and compulsion in numerous other situations?

Stuntz answered this question by reconciling the disparate strains of doctrine according to a descriptive account of the Fifth Amendment that is grounded in the familiar legal concept of excuse. Just as the concept

[28] William J. Stuntz, *Self-Incrimination*, supra note 16.

[29] Miranda v. Arizona, 384 U.S. 436 (1966).

[30] See, e.g., Charles D. Weisselberg, *Mourning Miranda*, 96 Calif. L. Rev. 1521 (2008); Berghuis v. Thompkins, 130 S. Ct. 2250 (2010); Maryland v. Shatzer, 130 S. Ct. 1213 (2010); Florida v. Powell, 130 S. Ct. 1195 (2010). I will ignore the legion of problems created by declaring *Miranda* a constitutional requirement.

of excuse in substantive criminal law is a concession to the imperfect and fallible nature of human beings, he argued, so might the seemingly incongruent threads of the Fifth Amendment privilege be woven together by a principle that both recognizes "society's moral preference for truth" and yet understands that few guilty people have the courage to fess up to crime. Protection under the Fifth Amendment thus hinges entirely upon whether the compelled production forces the individual into the "cruel trilemma" – the choice among incrimination, perjury, or contempt.

"The concept of 'testimony,'" Stuntz argued, "is really a stand-in for the presence or absence" of the cruel trilemma.[31] Physical evidence, then – like blood samples or handwriting and voice exemplars, are easy cases for exclusion under this theory of excuse. In Stuntz's words, "[s]ince one cannot falsify physical characteristics such as blood, there is no falsehood to excuse and therefore no need to immunize noncooperation."[32] Recognizing that there might be "fringes of the doctrine" where that assertion becomes problematic – say, the capacity to falsify by manipulating one's handwriting – the difficulty of such tasks attests to the core truth in the central assertion. Generally speaking, physical evidence cannot confront an individual with the cruel trilemma, because it cannot (easily) be made to lie. One's blood alcohol content, or hair, speaks – and speaks truthfully – for itself.

As though this were not persuasive enough, five years later Stuntz offered some further thoughts about the testimonial/nontestimonial distinction in his article *Lawyers, Deception, and Evidence Gathering*.[33] There he elaborated his notion that physical evidence cannot be made to lie by adding the argument that physical evidence also, therefore, is an excellent indicator of guilt. If so, then exclusion of physical evidence on Fifth Amendment grounds serves primarily, if not exclusively, to aid the guilty. In contrast, exclusion of compelled oral or testimonial evidence helps both the innocent and the guilty, because it protects suspects from excessive coercion and defendants from unfair judgment on the witness stand. Accordingly, the testimonial/nontestimonial distinction could be justified as one founded in part on a desire to minimize the negative externalities of unnecessarily excluding evidence, while maximizing

[31] Ronald J. Allen, Joseph L. Hoffman, Debra A. Livingston, & William J. Stuntz, Comprehensive Criminal Procedure 784 (2d ed. 2005).

[32] Stuntz, *Self-Incrimination*, supra note 16, at 1276.

[33] William J. Stuntz, *Lawyers, Deception, and Evidence Gathering*, 79 Va. L. Rev. 1903 (1993).

the protection afforded to innocent persons susceptible to government coercion.

Using either set of intuitions, it is pretty clear that DNA under the Fifth Amendment would be dead to rights. Like blood or hair evidence, DNA is hard to falsify. Moreover, as a legion of newspaper accounts tell us, it is a remarkably reliable form of proof. I could argue that investigatory uses of DNA raise reliability concerns because the genetic evidence is often the dominant evidence of guilt, and in some cases a person may have indeed left the sample but not actually be the perpetrator, but surely such instances are outliers. Generally speaking, if we accept that the Fifth Amendment is about nothing more than preserving the individual from the cruel trilemma, then exclusion of investigatory DNA searches seems outside the amendment's concern. And so in response, I would argue only that I think that autonomy and dignitary interests ought to be embedded in the amendment. After all, many persons would find it more offensive for the state to pry open a suspect's mind by means of an advanced technology than by the old rubber hose.

REVENGE OF THE STUNTZ, PART II: DNA AND THE CRIMINAL JUSTICE SYSTEM

But even if we discard Stuntz's analogies to excuse and seek refuge in one of the many theoretical alternatives as a means of arguing for Fifth Amendment regulation of investigatory DNA searches, his legendary work on the political economies of criminal justice would still pose a second, independent set of challenges.

When long ago I first read *Uneasy Relationship* and *Pathological Politics*,[34] I started mentally referring to them as the "whack a mole" theory of criminal justice – the idea that announcing a rule to regulate behavior *here* may not put an end to the behavior, but simply cause it to pop back up and surprise you *there*. At the farthest remove, Stuntz's work details the patterns of exchange among the three branches – the executive, legislative, and judicial actors responding and reacting to one another, locked in an eternal dance. He posits that the judicial branch raises the overall cost of criminal enforcement by bestowing broad constitutional entitlements that both hinder investigation and hamstring adjudication;

[34] William J. Stuntz, *The Uneasy Relationship Between Criminal Procedure and Criminal Justice*, 107 Yale L. J. 1 (1997); William J. Stuntz, *The Pathological Politics of Criminal Law*, 100 Mich. L. Rev. 505 (2001).

the legislative branch responds by widening substantive criminal law and enhancing criminal penalties; and that enables the executive branch to bring greater and more serious charges, which it then bargains away for pleas and sentences unencumbered by the burdens of too many procedural entitlements. Announce, adapt, evade. Repeat.[35]

Using the Stuntzian lens but zooming in a little further, let us examine just one sliver of the system: the evidentiary form of DNA. If the judicial branch threw the Fifth Amendment at compelled DNA collection and database profile retention, would law enforcement officials simply accept that the investigatory DNA road had come to an end? If a person could assert a Fifth Amendment interest not to disclose DNA when not suspected of a particular crime, or perhaps even to remove a profile from a database once his or her name was cleared, then would databases as we know them cease to exist?

Of course not. Investigators would probably just try to get their DNA elsewhere, rather than compel it directly from the individual. Such efforts would be inefficient, but they are also eminently possible. Think here of the countless quantities of "shed" DNA that can be picked up from discarded bottles or cigarettes, light switches or licked envelopes. Think also of the petty deceits already used to acquire samples, such as officers posing as fast food workers or sweepstakes officials in order to dupe a suspect into supplying some cells.[36] There are even scientific means of acquiring information about a person's likely genetic profile – namely, through inferences about relatives for whom DNA was lawfully obtained or even a man's particular surname.[37]

None of these necessarily even requires resorting to the Fourth and Fifth Amendments' favorite standby: waiver and consent.[38] There already

[35] Such relationships characterize not just the entire system but also its component parts. One need only look within a single branch to find the same pathologies reinscribing. Consider, for instance, Carol Steiker's observations that the opinions in the era after the Warren Court took a particularly sinister form. Rather than directly dial back the expansive doctrines that restricted police conduct, the Burger Court and the Rehnquist Court simply adjusted by tweaking the consequences that flowed from a breach of those rules. Carol Steiker, *Counter-Revolution in Constitutional Procedure*, 94 Mich. L. Rev. 2466 (1996).

[36] Murphy, *Relative Doubt*, supra note 24, at 346 nn. 213–14.

[37] See id. at 315 n. 108.

[38] Of course, if the Fifth Amendment were to apply to some forms of physical evidence collection, then it remains for us to wonder what the scope of such protection might be. Methods presently sanctioned under the Fourth Amendment might become impermissible under the Fifth Amendment. A detailed exploration of this question is outside the limits of this chapter, but suffice it to say that several alternatives obviously present

have been a number of mass DNA dragnets, in which individuals "voluntarily" submit information in order to aid in the solution of crime. Even assuming the Fifth Amendment applied to prohibit compelled collection, it is hard to imagine a constitutional rule that would bar retention of even voluntarily offered samples. And if the *Miranda* waiver rate is any indication, a large number of consensual samples are likely to be taken and stored.

Moreover, police investigators are not the only members of the executive branch who could arguably adjust to procedural restraints. Prosecutors could use their institutional power to bargain away the individual's interest – such as the practice in Orange County, California of offering "spit and acquit" deals to certain offenders.[39] If a suspect voluntarily gives a DNA sample for inclusion in the local database, the current charges could be lessened or dropped. Or correctional authorities could choose to offer early release to those who voluntarily waive their rights, just as shorter terms are now available to those who accede to some form of community supervision.

Finally, legislators can also aid in such circumventions by allocating resources toward forensic laboratories or equipment dedicated to DNA processing, and away from other forms of investigation or even scientific testing. In some senses, they already have. Between 2004 and 2008, the federal government designated 80.5 million dollars for the improvement of forensic science generally (including DNA techniques), but during the same period bequeathed nearly 600 million dollars to forensic DNA programs alone. That this attention is disproportionate is particularly evident when one considers that DNA constitutes only 5-8% of the backlog in forensic science testing in the nation, and only a small percentage – by one estimate, a mere 5% – of the overall forensic workload.[40] It stretches no imagination to speculate that when, in the very near future, an affordable,

themselves. It could be that the amendment would in essence bar collection of such evidence, should the Supreme Court return to the zero-sum approach of *Boyd*. Alternatively, we might imagine a *Miranda*-like regime, in which production of the evidence was considered not compelled as long as adequate warnings were provided and waived in advance – say, as a condition of a plea. Lastly, it is of course possible to imagine an altogether new approach to regulation, which might for instance model itself on a *Garrity*-style regime in which compulsion was not allowed, but failure to comply could carry noncriminal consequences. Cf. Garrity v. New Jersey, 385 U.S. 493 (1967).

39 Tracy Wood, "Supervisors Approve DA's 'Spit and Acquit' Program," *Voice of OC*, Dec. 14, 2010.

40 See Erin Murphy, *What 'Strengthening Forensic Science' Today Means for Tomorrow: DNA Exceptionalism and the 2009 NAS Report*, 9 Law, Probability & Risk 7, 10–12 (2010).

on-scene DNA typing technology becomes available, there will be many a legislator willing to fund its purchase. In such an event, prosecutors might even elect to delegate some "spit and acquit" power directly to the police rank and file. The "right not to share your genetic information" might then become as readily a foregone entitlement as the "right to remain silent." In short, with regard to just this one piece of the criminal justice system – one discrete evidentiary form – the larger patterns that Stuntz so effectively captured and described could easily play out on a smaller scale.

But I, myself, don't think that is an intolerable eventuality. It might be exhausting to engage in an endless game of cat-and-mouse with the scientists and law enforcement officers and industry developers and legislators invested in maximizing the utility of DNA as an evidentiary form, but I do not find it depressing, and I definitely do not find it pointless. Many scholars decry *Miranda*'s promise as hollow, but many others credit it as bringing an end to the routine use of physical violence. Criminal justice entitlements may not solve every problem, but that does not mean that they do not ever partially solve some of them. And when one considers the ramifications of current DNA policy when it comes to racial and socioeconomic distributional justice – issues that Stuntz turned to with great care and concern in his later years[41] – it is clear that thinking about the scope of constitutional entitlements is important. To anyone deeply committed to principles of equity in criminal justice, like Stuntz was himself, it is obviously a task well worth engaging.

CLOSING

Finally, it is in this kind of steadfast commitment to figuring it out, and figuring it out right, that Bill Stuntz manages again to have the last word. Perhaps because I grew up in an environment where religious commitments were woven seamlessly and unselfconsciously into public life, I have always found Stuntz's explicit embrace of Christian principles of justice and compassion appealing. To know an academic with unimpeachable intellectual credentials who also held such a deep and personal faith – a scholar *and* a believer – was for me a source of comfort and pride.

In the Catholic worker movement, which is committed to social justice and communitarian principles, much is made of the piece of scripture that

[41] See, e.g., William J. Stuntz, *Unequal Justice*, 121 Harv. L. Rev. 1969 (2008).

decrees "faith without works is dead."[42] It is an adage that applied well to Bill Stuntz the scholar. Ultimately, despite his often grim depictions of the politics of criminal justice, he always seemed to keep faith in the possibility of a system that justly and equitably resolves conflicts, and throughout his career he worked tirelessly to describe and therefore shape the doctrines and institutions that would bring about that vision. It also applied well to Bill Stuntz the person, who showed the same unwavering confidence in young scholars, including myself, and who also (again to my great advantage) manifested that generous spirit in his willingness to engage any earnest new idea. And that was true even of an idea as unconventional as discarding the testimonial distinctions for prospective, investigatory collection and use of intimate physical evidence under the Fifth Amendment.

[42] James 2:20 (New King James Version).

PART III

Emotion, Discretion, and the Judicial Role

9

Two Conceptions of Two Conceptions of Emotion in Criminal Law: An Essay Inspired by Bill Stuntz

Dan M. Kahan

I.

My goal in this essay is to reexamine a solution to an important puzzle about the significance of *emotions* in substantive criminal law. Indeed, the reexamination is in the nature of a qualification bordering on confession of error. The position I want to question was forged in the course of a sustained, multifaceted, and very satisfying scholarly conversation in which I myself played a part. But now, as a result of my participation in another set of scholarly conversations – ones that had until recently struck me as entirely collateral to emotions and criminal law – I find myself compelled to call attention to what I regard as the likely inadequacy of an account I had a significant hand in promoting.

I am not disheartened, though, to find myself in this position. There is, to be sure, discomfort in admitting doubt about arguments that had once struck me as both compelling and complete. Yet there is an even bigger reward: the discovery of continuing vitality in a problem that once filled me, and now does again, with intellectual energy. Other scholars, too, might find it awkward for me to express misgivings at this point about claims that built on and were extended by their work. But I feel confident that they, rather than resenting my second thoughts, are likely to welcome them for supplying an occasion to test whether conclusions they once formed continue to warrant their considered assent.

There is a reason, moreover, I discern opportunity, and not mere cause for embarrassment, in my deficiencies, and expect encouragement, not disparagement, from my colleagues for my equivocation. I and they have been shaped by the example of Bill Stuntz.

Bill possessed in abundance every one of the signal virtues of a scholar. He was irrepressibly curious, and took joy in surprise. His appetite for conversation was insatiable. He was brilliant, certainly, yet he famously *cultivated* humility, I think as a strategy (more likely instinctive than conscious; virtue works that way) to dispel any risk that pride might dull his apprehension of new insight. He treated the production of knowledge as a solemn moral enterprise. But at the same time, he was the epitome of open-mindedness and tolerance.

These qualities were at the root of the bountiful contributions Bill made to the inventory of ideas we enjoy today as students of criminal law. But they also furnish us with something just as indispensable to our realization of the highest ends of our calling: a vivid and inspiring model of what the emotional life of the good scholar consists in.

2.

To introduce (or reintroduce) the puzzle I am concerned with, I will start with a pair of old decisions, both by the Oklahoma Court of Criminal Appeals. The issue in each was the same: whether the trial court erred by foreclosing the effective presentation of an insanity defense by a man charged with murder for killing his wife's paramour.

In the first case, the court reversed the defendant's conviction.[1] "Two doctors," the court noted, "testified that the defendant . . . temporarily lost control of his mental processes" as a result of the "provocation" of his wife's seduction.[2] "[W]e can perceive," the court continued, that

> a man of good moral character such as that possessed by the defendant, highly respected in his community, having regard for his duties as a husband and the virtue of women, upon learning of the immorality of his wife, might be shocked, or such knowledge might prey upon his mind and cause temporary insanity. In fact it would appear that such would be the most likely consequence of obtaining such information.[3]

In the second case, however, the court *affirmed* the conviction.[4] In that case, the court noted, "the state, over the objections of the defendant," introduced evidence of "specific conduct tending to show . . . the defendant [to be] . . . a rounder and a libertine":[5]

> Facts were shown indicating that defendant's ideals of the sanctity of the home and the virtue of women were not so exalted, and that therefore the

[1] Hamilton v. State, 244 P.2d 328 (Okla. Crim. App. 1952).
[2] Id. at 335. [3] Id.
[4] Coffeen v. State, 210 P. 288 (Okla. Crim. App. 1922).
[5] Id. at 290.

> shock to his mind and finer sensibilities could not be so very great – at least not so great as to unbalance his mind....
>
> We think, in reason, that the shock would not be so great as it would to a man of refined sensibilities, having high conceptions of the sanctity of the home and the virtue of women.[6]

Thus, any trial rulings that prevented *him* from presenting a temporary insanity defense, the court held, were at most harmless error.

What's really going on here? That's the question that any thoughtful reader who sets these two opinions out next to each other will feel compelled to ask. The court's conclusion is straightforward: Discovery of a wife's infidelity is likely to deprive a sexually faithful man of his ability to comprehend or control his actions; such a discovery is not likely to have that effect, however, on an unfaithful man. But what's not so straightforward is how to integrate the mélange of psychological and moral concepts that inform the court's reasoning – "intensity of mental shock," "unbalan[cing of the] mind," "loss of control," on the one hand; "good moral character," "regard for... the virtue of women," "rounder and libertine," on the other – into a coherent whole. How exactly does the court conceive of the nature of the emotional state of the "mentally insane" offender? What is it, precisely, about that condition that entitles someone to a defense?

These questions try to make sense of the decisions in philosophical or jurisprudential terms, but we might also feel impelled to ask "what's going on here" from a psychological or even political point of view. Do the judges *really* believe their own explanation of the distinction between the two cases? Or are they deliberately concealing part of what they think from view? If concealing, are they trying to fool us, or are they just being coy? Do we imagine them straight-faced and earnest, or winking and slyly grinning, as they pronounce their judgments?

What's likely to strike thoughtful readers as puzzling about these two decisions, it turns out, is *the* puzzle of emotions in criminal law. The discordant pictures that the decisions paint – of "highly respected" men of "good moral character" who are "shocked" to the point of mindless "loss of control," on the one hand; of "rounders and libertines," whose own lack of virtue insulates them from "mind-unbalancing" assaults on their reason, on the other – pervade basic doctrines and their application.

[6] Id. at 290–291.

"Detached reflection cannot be demanded in the presence of an uplifted knife," we are told.[7] Hence we cannot blame the "true man" who refuses to flee "an assailant, who by violence or surprise maliciously seeks to" drive him from a public place "where [he] has the right to be."[8] But the woman who "'believed herself... doomed... to a life of the worst kind of torture and... degradation" cannot on that basis be excused for killing her abusive husband in his sleep: Because she had the option of leaving their home and striking out on her own, her will was not overcome by the "primal impulse" of "self-preservation."[9]

A man who "discovered his wife *in flagrante delicto* with a man who was a total stranger to him, and at a time when [he] was trying to save his marriage and was deeply concerned about both his wife and his young child," will necessarily experience the form of "ungovernable passion" that mitigates first-degree murder to manslaughter.[10] The same volitional impairment cannot be imputed to the man who kills the lover of his mistress, however, for he "has no such right to control the woman as a husband has to control his wife."[11]

The deep "shame" of being subjected to rape is one of the "physical and mental injuries, the natural and probable result of which would render the [an unmarried woman] mentally irresponsible," making her subsequent commission of suicide an act attributable to her rapist, who could therefore be convicted of murder.[12] But a man could not be deemed to have "caused" the death of his (eight-months' pregnant) wife – "a high tempered woman" who was "hard to get along with" and who on previous "occasions ran off and left her husband" alone with the couple's infant – because her decision to expose herself to the nighttime cold of winter in fleeing their farmhouse was her own choice following a fight.[13]

Again and again, we are confronted with a kaleidoscope of dissonant reports of virtuous offenders too mentally enfeebled to obey the law and impassioned ones too vicious not to be deemed to have "voluntarily" chosen to transgress. So what's *really* going on?

[7] Brown v. United States, 256 U.S. 335, 343 (1921) (Holmes, J.).
[8] State v. Bartlett, 71 S.W. 148, 152 (Mo. 1902).
[9] State v. Norman, 378 S.E.2d 8, 11, 12–13 (N.C. 1989).
[10] State v. Thornton, 730 S.W.2d 309, 312, 315 (Tenn. 1987).
[11] Rex v. Greening, 3 KB. 846, 849 (1913).
[12] Stephenson v. State, 179 N.E. 633, 635, 649 (Ind. 1932).
[13] Hendrickson v. Commonwealth, 3 S.W. 166, 167 (Ky. Ct. App. 1887).

3.

I will call the answer I am interested in questioning the *two conceptions thesis*, or TCT. This label derives from a framework that Martha Nussbaum and I developed in an article we wrote in 1996.[14] But the basic position – this particular solution to the puzzle of emotions in criminal law – was in line with ones that other scholars, including Sam Pillsbury[15] and Victoria Nourse,[16] were developing at roughly the same time, and that many others, including Cynthia Lee[17] and Carol Steiker,[18] have since refined and extended.

TCT posits that substantive criminal law features two competing views of what emotions are and why they matter. The first is the *mechanistic conception*, which sees emotions as thoughtless surges of affect or "impulses." Emotions excuse or mitigate, on this account, because – and to the extent – that they deprive an individual of the power to control his or her actions.

The second account is the *evaluative conception* of emotion. This view treats emotions and related sensibilities as a species of moral judgment that express an actor's evaluation of contingencies that threaten or promote ends the actor cares about. As such, emotions, on this view, can be *evaluated*, not just as strong or weak, but as good or bad, right or wrong, reasonable or unreasonable, depending on whether the values they express are ones we think are appropriate for someone in the actor's situation.

Each conception of emotion has an impressive pedigree in philosophy and psychology,[19] and both are on display in the Oklahoma Court of Criminal Appeals decisions I started with. The mechanistic figures in those portions of the opinions emphasizing the "intensity of mental shock," and resulting "loss of control," "unseating of reason," and "unbalancing of [the] mind" that attend the discovery of adultery; the evaluative in those

[14] See Dan M. Kahan & Martha C. Nussbaum, *Two Conceptions of Emotion in Criminal Law*, 96 Colum. L. Rev. 269 (1996).

[15] See Samuel H. Pillsbury, Judging Evil: Rethinking the Law of Murder and Manslaughter (1998).

[16] See Victoria Nourse, *Passion's Progress: Modern Law Reform and the Provocation Defense*, 106 Yale L. J. 1331 (1997).

[17] See Cynthia Lee, Murder and the Reasonable Man: Passion and Fear in the Criminal Courtroom (2003).

[18] See Carol S. Steiker, *Punishing Hateful Motives: Old Wine in a New Bottle Revives Calls for Prohibition*, 97 Mich. L. Rev. 1857 (1999).

[19] See generally Kahan & Nussbaum, supra note 14, at 275–301.

that distinguish the "man of good character" and "refined sensibilities," whose aggrievement warrants our solicitude, from the "rounder and libertine," whose resentment of a man whose disregard for "the sanctity of the home" and "the virtue of women" he himself shares, does not.

On their surface, the doctrines of criminal law are pervaded by mechanistic idioms and metaphors. But at their core, TCT asserts, they are evaluative. All of the doctrines contain one or another normative element that invites (or at least enables) decision makers to confine their liability-discharging or punishment-mitigating consequence to offenders whose emotional evaluations decision makers morally approve of. If they find that element to be satisfied, they needn't find that the offenders' passion embodied any particular quantum of volition-destroying force; if they find this particular quality to be absent, they needn't afford the slightest dispensation, no matter how overwhelming or irresistible the offender's passion (or victim's, in the case of "intervening causation") was.

The anger of the man who kills his wife or her paramour, for example, is *right* for someone in his situation, because adultery is "the gravest possible offence which a wife can commit against her husband"[20] and "the highest invasion of [a man's] property" by another man.[21] Having "no such right to control the woman as a husband has to control his wife,"[22] in contrast, the resentment of the man who kills the lover of his mistress reveals a morally incorrect overvaluation of his own prerogatives. Only the "heat of passion" of the former, then, will be deemed to have been "*adequately* provoked" for purposes of the involuntary manslaughter doctrine.

The woman who aids the armed robber to protect her child appropriately loves her children more than she loves strangers, whereas one who acquiesces in the abuse of her own child to avoid harm to herself excessively prefers her own well-being to her children's. The threat to the former, then, but not the latter is sufficient to "overcome the will of a person of *reasonable* firmness" – not because their wills were any more or less compromised but because reasonable women appropriately value their children's well-being over that of anyone else's, including their own.

What's "true" about the man who stands his ground and kills is his character: like a "true beam," it is straight, not warped.[23] Because

[20] See Greening, 3 KB at 849.

[21] Regina v. Mawgridge, 84 Eng. Rep. 1107, 1115 (1707).

[22] Compare People v. Romero, 13 Cal. Rptr. 2d 332,340 (Cal. Ct. App. 1992) with United States v. Webb 747 F.2d 278, 283 (5th Cir. 1984).

[23] See Dan M. Kahan, *The Secret Ambition of Deterrence*, 113 Harv. L. Rev. 413, 429–430 (1999).

he appropriately values his "rights," "liberty," and "sacredness of... person" more than the life of a "wrongful" aggressor who tries to drive him from a public place where he has a "right to be," he "reasonably" perceives flight to be as destructive of his "*self*-preservation" as death.[24] The true *woman*, quite evidently, does not make the mistake of thinking her right to stay put ahead of the life of her abusive husband, even if the alternative is to remain in "a life of the worst kind of torture and... degradation."[25]

The law refuses to accept any expert definition of "mental disease" for purposes of insanity. "[F]or all his insight into the dynamics of behavior, [the medical expert] has not solved the riddle of blame. The question remains an ethical one, the answer to which lies beyond scientific truth."[26] However implausible, then, it might be to think the explosive shock of infidelity invariably reverberates with greater intensity in the mind of a "man of refined sensibilities, having high conceptions of the sanctity of the home and the virtue of women," than in that of a "moral degenerate, in the habit of consorting with prostitutes and dissolute women,"[27] it is perfectly compatible with the law to characterize the former alone as sick.

The TCT solution to the puzzle of emotions in criminal law has three principal strengths. The first is its *explanatory power*. The evaluations that decision makers make of the values expressed in impassioned offenders' emotions are informed by social norms. It is thus no surprise to see decision makers who are using the evaluative conception of emotion selectively exonerating (in whole or in part) offenders whose emotional valuations conform to prevailing expectations of what goods and states of affairs individuals occupying particular social roles are *expected* to value.

These norms, of course, are not fixed. They shift over time, and at any given moment might well be in a state of flux and contestation. Two additional puzzles that TCT explains are why the law's appraisal of impassioned offenders shifts over time and why at any given moment it can be the focus of intense political conflict. As egalitarian gender norms have ascended, the stock of the cuckold has steadily declined[28] and that of the battered woman steadily risen. Precisely because citizens perceive the law's treatment of impassioned offenders to be a type of official

[24] Bartlett, 71 S.W. at 152. [25] Norman, 378 S.E.2d at 11.

[26] State v. Guido, 191 A.2d 45, 52 (N.J. 1963).

[27] *Coffeen*, 210 P. at 291.

[28] See Kahan & Nussbaum, supra note 14, at 346–50.

endorsement of certain visions of how we should live and a repudiation of others, the appropriate grading of particular offenses – ones motivated by animus, say, against homosexuals – generates controversy that is often immensely out of proportion to any impact their resolution might be expected to have on behavior.[29]

A second, related strength of TCT is its *critical power*. The same selectivity that those decisions show in their recognition of the excusing or mitigating consequence of passion is often mirrored in the writings of commentators. TCT proponents have often successfully exposed the conservative bias of these analysts, who piously denounce as "political" any shift or proposed reform in the law's treatment of impassioned offenders while displaying a comically blind eye to the necessarily political content of the evaluations that inform traditional doctrines and their applications. Nourse, for example, devastatingly exposed this flaw in the once-common "abuse excuse" critique of the battered woman syndrome.[30] Steiker did the same in responding to "hate crime" legislation critics, whose arguments, she showed, were shockingly imperceptive of the myriad facets of traditional substantive law that rank offender culpability on the basis of morally partisan evaluations of offenders' motivations.[31]

The third and final attraction of TCT is its *prescriptive power*. Critical commentary begs the question: What *should* the law be? Accounts that treat the mechanistic veneer of the doctrine seriously don't help; at best they produce muddle, and at worst they make us unwitting apologists for the norms that just below the surface inform traditional doctrine and doctrinal applications. If the core of the law is evaluative, then those who want to make the law as good as it can be should be self-consciously evaluative, TCT proponents (myself included!) argued.[32] We should face up to the necessity and appropriateness of making the law a reflection of the best moral and political understanding we can fashion of the values that good people ought to have.

4.

So what's wrong with TCT? Despite its considerable explanatory power, TCT still leaves one obvious mystery unresolved: Why is the mechanistic

[29] See Kahan, supra note 23, at 472–476.

[30] See Victoria Nourse, *The New Normativity: The Abuse Excuse and the Resurgence of Judgment in the Criminal Law*, 50 Stan. L. Rev. 1395 (1998).

[31] See Steiker, supra note 18.

[32] See, e.g., id.; Nourse, supra note 30; Dan M. Kahan, *Two Liberal Fallacies in the Hate Crimes Debate*, 20 L. & Phil. 175–193 (2001).

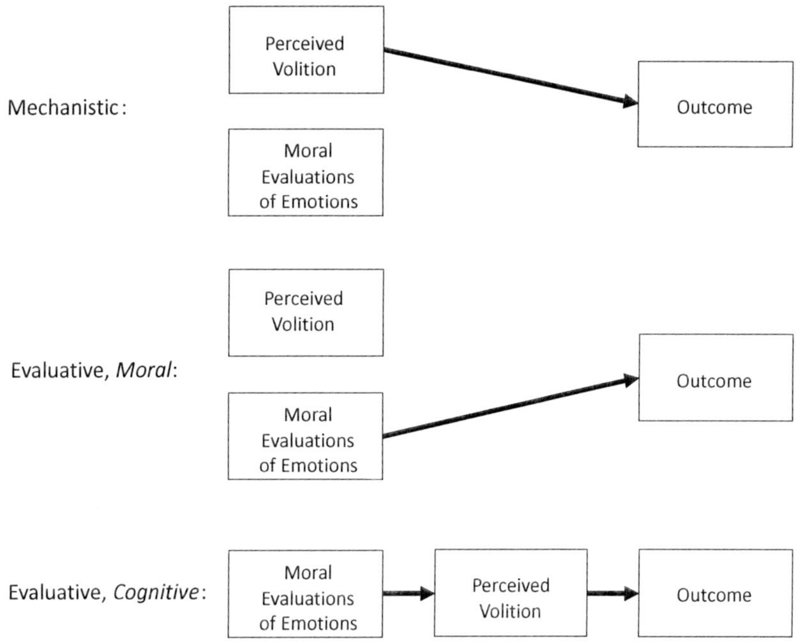

FIGURE 9.1. Three models of judging emotion.

conception so conspicuous in the law? If it is merely a veneer, why are the decision makers covering things up? Why don't they just say, in unmistakably clear terms, that they are evaluating the moral evaluations that that offender's (and sometimes victim's) emotions embody?

My answer is that they aren't covering up anything. I see this response as not so much an alternative to TCT, however, as an alternative to the version I have just described. I will call this alternative the *cognitive conception* of TCT (or C-TCT) and distinguish it from the standard one, which I will call the *moral evaluation conception* (ME-TCT).

To sharpen the relevant distinctions, consider three models of the role of emotions in criminal law (Figure 9.1). The first contemplates that decision makers' perceptions of the impact of offenders' emotions should (and does when decision makers aren't being dishonest) determine outcomes wholly independent of any moral evaluations of the quality of those emotions. This is the naïve mechanistic view that TCT seeks to discredit and that it aggressively critiques when articulated by conservative opponents of reforming traditional doctrines. In its place, ME-TCT asserts that outcomes in fact flow from decision makers' evaluations of the moral quality of emotions independently of their perceptions of the impact of emotions on offenders' volition. This is what I'm calling ME-TCT. C-TCT, in contrast, accepts that decision makers are *honestly* (at least in most cases) reaching outcomes based on their view of the volitional impact of emotions. However, in assessing the intensity of emotions, they are unconsciously conforming what they see – actually, their perception of something that they can't literally *see* – to outcomes that reflect culturally congenial social meanings.

One reason that I find C-TCT more compelling than ME-TCT is that I can't bring myself to take seriously any understanding of TCT that implies decision makers are being systematically disingenuous when they appeal to the mechanistic conception of emotion to explain their legal determinations. The idea that they might be secretly invoking it en masse in order to conceal their commitments to politically contestable evaluative norms is preposterous; there's no way the ever-expanding number of insiders could maintain – or even be expected uniformly to want to maintain – such a conspiracy![33] The idea that they are being openly disingenuous – that they are winking and grinning as they turn loose the cuckold, the homophobe, or the battered woman – also doesn't ring true. People just aren't that cynical; on the contrary, anyone who has taught substantive criminal law to thoughtful people will see that they are as intensely earnest as they are divided about the mental life of cuckolds, battered women, beleaguered subway car commuters, and all the others, a point that Mark Kelman has brilliantly explored.[34]

Even more important, though, I find myself compelled to accept C-TCT by what I've learned about the phenomenon of *motivated reasoning* during the years since I coauthored *Two Conceptions of Emotion in Criminal Law*. Motivated reasoning refers to a complex of unconscious cognitive processes that converge to promote formation of factual beliefs that suit some end or need extrinsic to the actual truth of those beliefs.[35] One such end is the stake individuals have in protecting their association

[33] This is not to say that particular decision makers who appreciate the false appearance of mechanism might not nevertheless decide for prudential reasons to resort to it for prudential or strategic ends. See Kahan, supra note 23, at 432–435, describing Holmes's admission that he didn't "say all [he] th[ough]t" about the honor of standing one's ground in *Brown v. United States*, 256 U.S. 335 (1921).

[34] See Mark Kelman, "Reasonable Evidence of Reasonableness," in Questions of Evidence: Proof, Practice, and Persuasion Across the Disciplines 169–188 (J. Chandler, A. I. Davidson, and H. Harootunian, ed. 1994).

[35] See generally Ziva Kunda, *The Case for Motivated Reasoning*, 108 Psychol. Bulletin 480 (1990).

with and status within groups united by their commitment to shared understandings of the best life and the ideal society.[36]

In the course of an ongoing research project that I have had the good fortune to be a part of, my collaborators and I have studied how this dynamic shapes perceptions of *risk*.[37] People unconsciously search out and selectively credit information that supports beliefs that predominate in their cultural affinity groups; they turn to those who share their values, and whom they therefore trust, to certify what sorts of empirical claims they should believe; they even construe their first-hand experiences, including what they *see* and *hear*, to fit expectations that cohere with their defining group commitments. As a result, even when they *agree* on ends – safe streets, a clean environment, a prosperous economy – they end up culturally divided on the *means* of how to secure them.[38]

Our research group has recently begun to use these methods to explain disagreement about legally consequential facts. We've found, for example, that people of diverse cultural outlooks form systematically different impressions when they view videotape evidence bearing on the degree of risk associated with a high-speed police car chase[39] or on the intent of political demonstrators to intimidate passersby.[40]

Much like the work I did earlier on emotions in criminal law, moreover, this work is part of a multifaceted and dynamic scholarly conversation. Our work on cultural cognition and law builds on that of social psychologists such as Mark Alicke.[41] More recently, too, other scholars, including Janice Nadler and Mary-Hunter McDonnell,[42] and John Darley and Avani Sood,[43] have completed important studies

[36] See David K. Sherman & Geoffrey L. Cohen, "The Psychology of Self-Defense: Self-Affirmation Theory," in 38 Advances in Experimental Social Psychology 183 (2006).

[37] Relevant information relating to the project, including published studies, can be found at www.culturalcognition.net.

[38] See Dan M. Kahan, *The Cognitively Illiberal State*, 60 Stan. L. Rev. 115 (2007).

[39] See Dan M. Kahan, David A. Hoffman, & Donald Braman, *Whose Eyes Are You Going to Believe? Scott v. Harris and the Perils of Cognitive Illiberalism*, 122 Harv. L. Rev. 837 (2009).

[40] See Dan M. Kahan, David H. Hoffman, Donald Braman, Danieli Evans, & Jeffrey J. Rachlinski, *"They Saw a Protest": Cognitive Illiberalism and the Speech-Conduct Distinction*, 64 Stan. L. Rev. (forthcoming 2012).

[41] See generally Mark D. Alicke, *Culpable Control and the Psychology of Blame*, 126 Psychol. Bulletin 556 (2000).

[42] See Janice Nadler & Mary-Hunter McDonnell, *The Psychology of Blame: Criminal Liability and the Role of Moral Character*, 97 Cornell L. Rev. (forthcoming 2012).

[43] See Avani M. Sood & John M. Darley, *The Plasticity of Harm in the Service of Punishment Goals: An Experimental Demonstration*, Calif. L. Rev. (forthcoming 2012).

supporting the likely impact of motivated reasoning on perceptions of legally consequential facts.

C-TCT flows naturally out of this work. The most plausible reason that the mechanistic conception is so conspicuous in the criminal law, on this view, is that ordinary people, including the ones who become judges, juries, and legislators, *believe* it. They believe (not without reason, including personal experience!) that volition-constraining affect is a signature element of emotion; they also accept that the intensity of such affective responses *should* have moral consequence akin to what doctrines informed by the mechanistic view seem to say they should. But in assessing one or another form of evidence that bears on offenders' emotions, culturally diverse individuals unconsciously gravitate toward perceptions that connect them to and otherwise are congenial to persons who share their defining commitments.

There are two studies, in particular, that are supportive of this conclusion. One is a study that Donald Braman and I did, in which we found that mock jurors of opposing cultural outlooks formed opposing pro-defendant or pro-prosecution fact perceptions in a self-defense case involving a battered woman who killed her sleeping husband – and then flipped positions in one involving a beleaguered subway commuter who killed an African-American panhandler.[44] Another study, by Nadler and McDonnell, found that extrinsic facts bearing on the moral quality of parties' characters influenced mock jurors' perceptions of various facts, including intent and causation.[45]

I certainly would not say that the verdict is in on the relative strength of C-TCT and ME-TCT. But I'm convinced the case *can* and *should* be decided by empirical proof, and that the weight of the evidence to date supports C-TCT.

5.

I've suggested the need to reconsider a solution to the puzzle of emotions in criminal law. I've proposed a substantial modification to the answer that that solution gives to the "what's *really* going on here" question posed in cases like the two Oklahoma Court of Criminal Appeals decisions with which I started. Now I want to consider the question "what

[44] See Dan M. Kahan & Donald Braman, *The Self-defensive Cognition of Self-defense*, 45 Am. Crim. L. Rev. 1 (2008).

[45] See Nadler & McDonnell, supra note 42.

difference does it make?" What's at stake in the choice between C-TCT and ME-TCT as a practical matter?

Nothing, I'd say, as far as the explanatory power of TCT is concerned. According to TCT, the distinctions drawn among impassioned offenders and shifts in those distinctions over time track social norms. C-TCT doesn't call this insight into question. It suggests only that such norms affect legal outcomes indirectly, through their unconscious impact on decision makers' perceptions of volition, rather than directly through decision makers' moral appraisals of the quality of offenders' emotional motivations. C-TCT can also explain political conflict over the law's treatment of different classes of impassioned offenders much as the theory of motivated reasoning explains political conflict over risk: Citizens of diverse commitments can be expected to form opposing sets of culturally congenial beliefs about the validity of competing empirical claims relating to which offenders lack volitional capacity; they can also be expected to suspect one another of advancing such claims disingenuously as a form of symbolic political action.[46]

Nor does C-TCT dull the *critical power* of TCT. Indeed, it sharpens it. The conservative critics who apprehend the responsiveness of the law to politically contested evaluations of offenders' emotional motivations only when those evaluations diverge from traditional ones can themselves be understood to be displaying a form of motivated reasoning. The indictment of their selective vision is freed of any implausible insinuation that the critics are part of a secret conspiracy to hide the law's cultural partiality.

Where C-TCT and ME-TCT are likely to diverge is on *prescription*. Proponents of TCT have embraced the evaluative conception of emotion as normative for law. That is, they haven't objected to conforming the law to moral (or political) evaluations of offenders' emotional motivations; they've argued only that the law should get it *right* in deciding between true men and battered women, the "homosexual panic defense" and hate-crime penalty enhancements for homophobic killings.[47]

C-TCT, in contrast, takes the moral theory behind the mechanistic view more seriously. If motivated reasoning is at work, then judges and juries, legislators, and ordinary citizens really *believe* that the law *should* handle impassioned offenders on the basis of volitional impairment, or at least that it *should*n't be drawing distinctions between them on the basis of culturally partisan visions of the good life.

46 See Kahan, supra note 38.

47 See supra p. 10 & n. 32.

For ME-TCT theorists, the norm-pervaded assessments that we make of impassioned offenders are reliable forms of moral perception. It should be appropriately conditioned and harnessed by the law, which should shed any pretense of neutrality in the contest between the opposing views of the good that animate political controversy over the treatment of impassioned offenders.

C-TCT envisions the correspondence appraisals of offenders' values and apprehension of their volition as a form of *bias*. It supports reforms aimed at muting decision makers' unconscious responsiveness to extrinsic cultural values as a means of securing effective liberal neutrality. In the years to come, I anticipate a resurgence of a style of liberal criminal law theorizing energized by the psychological realism of C-TCT.

6.

Or that at least is how I now understand the solution to the puzzle of emotions in criminal law. The moral status of culturally motivated perceptions of volition, like that of culturally motivated perceptions of risk and related facts, is a complicated one. I acknowledge that I might be wrong, and I hereby reserve the right to modify my view in light of what I learn from my engagement with others.

There was a time in my career as an academic when I think I would have viewed that sort of conclusion, as well as the admission with which I introduced this essay, to be embarrassing. But that was before I learned how much more one can learn, and hence how much better one's life as a scholar can be, if one is attentive to the fallibility of one's insights and to the pleasures of intellectual surprise when scholarly conversation helps one advance so much farther than one could possibly get on one's own. That was, in short, before I had the benefit of being exposed to the character of Bill Stuntz.

10

Patrolling the Fenceline: How the Court Only Sometimes Cares about Preserving Its Role in Criminal Cases

Andrew D. Leipold

INTRODUCTION

One of Bill Stuntz's many contributions to the legal academy is that he helped bring doctrinal scholarship back into fashion. Not doctrinal work in the narrow sense of describing the evolution of legal rules, but in a richer, more sweeping sense of identifying the larger themes that help explain the forces that shape the inputs and outflow of judicial decisions. Whether he was describing how societal forces such as race and poverty affect the criminal process or discussing the role of institutional actors like police or defense counsel,[1] Bill managed to offer penetrating theoretical insights without forgetting that cases matter, facts matter, and that sometimes, law is simply "what judges do."

In this spirit, if we look back over the past decade of Supreme Court case law on criminal procedure, some important themes emerge. This chapter discusses two of those themes and offers an argument that, regardless of the correctness of particular case outcomes, the Court has gone off course in two important areas.

I. PROMINENT CASES AND LURKING THEMES

If we asked fifty criminal procedure professors to name the most important legal developments of the past ten years, a few entries would make

* A disclaimer: I currently serve on the Advisory Committee for the Federal Rules of Criminal Procedure, and some matters that have come before the committee intersect with issues discussed in this chapter. The views expressed here are my own; they should not be read as reflecting the views of the committee or any of its other members.

[1] See, e.g., William J. Stuntz, *Race, Class, and Drugs*, 98 Columbia L. Rev. 1795 (1998); William J. Stuntz, *Local Policing After the Terror*, 111 Yale L. J. 2137 (2002).

almost everyone's list. Most people would point to the sentencing revolution cases, including the decisions in *Apprendi*,[2] *Booker*,[3] and *Gall*,[4] which radically reduced the impact of the Federal Sentencing Guidelines and restored a great deal of sentencing discretion to judges. The United States incarcerates so many people that any change in sentencing policy is big news, and these cases were the headline story of the decade. Collectively the decisions can be characterized as part of an ongoing struggle between Congress, the executive, and the judiciary over the hugely important topic of how best to balance the need for sentencing uniformity and the requirement of individualized justice.

Many professors would also point to the war-powers decisions,[5] even though they are not strictly criminal cases. Here the court has struggled to define judicial authority in the murky world of enemy combatants in an undeclared war against nonstate opponents. Issues such as civilian versus military tribunals, the role of habeas corpus, and the rights of American citizens who give aid and comfort to the enemy have required the judiciary, with some reluctance, to pull up a chair in the war room. The judicial branch of government is by design reactive, and its ability to accommodate the new forms of armed conflict with its duty both to protect the rights of citizens and to check the excesses of the elected branches is being sorely tested. The number of criminal and habeas cases that have emerged from the war on terror is small, but the effect on the justice system as a whole has been disproportionately large (consider the growth of Foreign Intelligence Surveillance Act [FISA] Court warrants[6]).

[2] Apprendi v. New Jersey, 530 U.S. 466 (2000) (other than the fact of a prior conviction, any fact that increases the penalty for a crime beyond the statutory maximum must be submitted to a jury and may not be evaluated as a sentencing factor by a judge).

[3] U.S. v. Booker, 543 U.S. 220 (2005) (Federal Sentencing Guidelines discretionary rather than mandatory).

[4] Gall v. United States, 552 U.S. 38 (2007) (the same abuse of discretion standard applies to review of sentences regardless of whether a sentence is inside or outside the Sentencing Guideline range).

[5] See Boumediene v. Bush, 553 U.S. 723 (2008) (Military Commissions Act, which denied federal court jurisdiction to consider habeas petitions from alien detainees at Guantanamo Bay that were pending at the time of the act's enactment unconstitutionally suspended writ of habeas corpus); Hamdan v. Rumsfeld, 548 U.S. 557 (2005) (procedures for proposed military commission trials of suspected alien terrorists violated both the Uniform Code of Military Justice and the Geneva Conventions); Hamdi v. Rumsfeld, 542 U.S. 507 (2004) (U.S. citizen being held as enemy combatant must be given meaningful opportunity to challenge factual basis for detention); Rasul v. Bush, 542 U.S. 466 (2004) (district court had jurisdiction to consider habeas petitions filed by alien detainees at Guantanamo Bay).

[6] See 50 U.S.C. § 1803. In 2009 the Foreign Intelligence Service Court approved 1,320 applications for authority to conduct electronic surveillance and physical searches, or

These two lines of cases are important in their own right, but they also share an important characteristic: The Supreme Court has insisted that, whatever the substantive merits of the Congressional scheme and the executive branch's plans, the judiciary retains an important voice in the process. The battle over sentencing has little to do with which sentences are imposed for which crimes, whether sentences should be longer or shorter, or whether retribution rather than deterrence should be the dominant rationale for punishment. Instead, the battle has been over the proper sphere of influence in sentencing decisions: What are the proper roles for the legislature, an independent agency, and the judiciary?

So too with the terrorism cases. Regardless of how the battle over the detainees is resolved, the outcome for individual prisoners might not change much. What makes those cases significant is the line drawn between the powers of the president to wage war and the power of the courts to protect the rights of those detained. The pushback by the Court against the sweeping claim of presidential authority is likely to have long-term effects that are out of proportion to the impact on the detainees who have asked for judicial review.

Stated differently, the Supreme Court's influence is at its peak when it is patrolling the fenceline between institutional actors and between branches of government, using its constitutional authority to allocate and limit power among actors. And whether we agree or disagree with the direction the Court has taken, few doubt the need for the court to watch these developments and, at times, intervene. Both as a matter of constitutional theory and as a matter of institutional competence, the Court has a critical if nonexclusive obligation to actively monitor the push and pull of power among the players.

A third line of cases that might make our professors' all-decade list is the Court's *Crawford v. Washington* opinion and its offspring,[7] which substantially altered the rules for admitting hearsay evidence in criminal

on average more than 3 per day. The court made substantive modifications in 14 of those applications, and denied 1 application in whole and 1 in part during that year. See Letter from Assistant Attorney General Ronald Weich to Senate President Joseph R. Biden, Jr., at 1–2 (April 30, 2010), http://www.fas.org/irp/agency/doj/fisa/2009rept.pdf.

[7] Crawford v. Washington, 541 U.S. 36 (2004). See also Melendez-Diaz v. Massachusetts, 129 S.Ct. 2527 (2009) (state crime lab analyst's conclusions were "testimony" that must be presented by the analyst in court, rather than through a certification of results); Giles v. California, 128 S.Ct. 2678 (2008) ("forfeiture by wrongdoing" not an exception to Confrontation Clause unless the defendant intended to bring about witness's unavailability); Davis v. Washington, 547 U.S. 813, 830 (2006) (domestic battery victim's statements to a 911 operator were not "testimony" covered by Crawford, but the victim's written statements to police officer were covered testimony).

trials. Overruling a quarter century of precedent,[8] the Court held that out-of-court testimony that was not subject to cross examination is inadmissible on Confrontation Clause grounds, no matter how reliable the information otherwise appears to be.

As with the sentencing and war-powers cases, *Crawford* was decided in the face of loud cries that the Court was following a path of ruin – that the Justices were acting without a full appreciation of the impact its decision would have on the existing system. Critics predicted that the Congressionally blessed Sentencing Guidelines would be undermined, the President's war powers would be compromised, and law enforcement would lose lots of valuable evidence, all in the name of abstract fidelity to the Constitution. But the Court – or at least a majority of the Justices – was undeterred.

Crawford was similar to other watershed cases in its impact, but it also presents an additional theme, one reflected in a seemingly unrelated case. In *U.S v. Gonzalez-Lopez*[9] (a case no law professor would put on the greatest-hits list), the court quietly ruled that criminal defendants who can afford to hire their own lawyer normally cannot be deprived of the lawyer of their choice. The court affirmed the reversal of the resulting conviction, despite the government's argument that the lawyer the defendant ended up with was fully capable, and the defendant suffered no harm as a result of the deprivation.

The link between *Crawford* and the right to counsel requirement is not obvious, but the Supreme Court connected the dots. In *Crawford*, all sides agreed that the Constitution requires that evidence used at trial be reliable, but the majority found that the Constitution requires more. The Sixth Amendment demands not just reliable testimony but testimony that has been proven reliable in a certain way – by cross examination. In fact, said the court, it was affirmative error to look beyond the procedure itself in an attempt to satisfy the goals the procedure was designed to advance:

> Admitting statements deemed reliable by a judge is fundamentally at odds with the right of confrontation. To be sure, the Clause's ultimate goal is to ensure reliability of evidence, but it is a procedural rather than a substantive guarantee. It commands, not that evidence be reliable, but that reliability be assessed in a particular manner: by testing in the crucible of cross-examination. The Clause thus reflects a judgment, not only about

[8] Crawford overruled Ohio v. Roberts, 448 U.S. 56 (1980).
[9] 548 U.S. 140 (2006).

the desirability of reliable evidence (a point on which there could be little dissent), but about how reliability can best be determined.[10]

Similarly, said *Gonzalez-Lopez*, the Constitution requires not just a fair trial, but a fair trial conducted in a certain way – with the assistance of the specific counsel that the defendant has retained. Even if the ultimate ends of a fair and accurate trial can be ensured through other means, these other means are not substitutes for the procedures specified in the Sixth Amendment.

The value of identifying these various themes is that it allows us to evaluate other cases – other data points – to see if the court is acting comparably in other areas. The argument of this chapter is that there are at least two significant occasions in the past decade in which the Supreme Court has acted inconsistently, and has done so in decisions that are surprisingly and woefully undertheorized.

The first occasion was *United States v. Ruiz*,[11] which involved the scope of a prosecutor's Brady obligation to disclose evidence prior to a guilty plea.[12] In finding that the prosecutor had no duty to disclose a subset of Brady material prior to a plea, the court abandoned its chance to play a meaningful role in the plea-bargaining process, which, as Bob Scott and Bill Stuntz have pointed out, "is not some adjunct to the criminal justice system; it *is* the criminal justice system."[13] By failing to protect its own role in this central feature of the criminal process, the court gave up considerable ground to the executive branch, without an explanation that is worthy of such a big move.

A second decision also came in 2002, in *United States v. Cotton*,[14] where the court was asked to consider whether the failure to properly allege a crime in the indictment deprived a federal court of jurisdiction over a case. Here the court, without meaningful explanation, failed to follow the approach it would later follow in *Crawford* and *Gonzalez-Lopez*,

[10] Crawford, 541 U.S. at 61. See also *Giles*, 554 U.S. at 375: "It is not the role of courts to extrapolate from the words of the Sixth Amendment to the values behind it, and then to enforce its guarantees only to the extent they serve (in the courts' views) those underlying values" (opinion of Scalia, J.).

[11] 536 U.S. 622 (2002).

[12] Under Brady v. Maryland, 373 U.S. 83, 87 (1963), the due-process clause requires a prosecutor to turn over to the defendant information that is favorable to the accused and material to the issue of guilt or punishment.

[13] Robert E. Scott & William J. Stuntz, *Plea Bargaining as Contract*, 101 Yale L. J. 1909, 1912 (1992).

[14] 535 U.S. 625 (2002).

by refusing to give effect to procedures that are at least suggested in the constitution for invoking jurisdiction.

Section II discusses *Brady* and *Ruiz*; Section III discusses *Cotton* and federal jurisdiction. Section IV tries to tie the pieces together.

II. *BRADY*, BARGAINING, AND NONDISCLOSURE

Angela Ruiz was caught with thirty kilograms of marijuana in her luggage, and the government offered her a fast-track plea agreement. In return for a favorable sentencing recommendation, Ruiz was asked to waive her right to trial and appeal, plus waive her right to receive from the prosecution any impeachment evidence or other information that would support an affirmative defense. The defendant balked at giving up access to any potential Brady material (it's not clear that there was any) and rejected the proposed deal. Negotiations broke down, and Ruiz eventually got the worst of both worlds – a guilty plea with no Brady disclosure and no benefit of any bargain. She argued in the Supreme Court that her plea was invalid, because she claimed to have a nonwaivable right to receive Brady material before she pled guilty.

The Court rejected the argument, and predictably so – to do otherwise would have dramatically changed the manner in which guilty pleas are processed. But its reasoning was superficial, even dismissive, which is curious treatment for an issue that can potentially arise in tens of thousands of federal criminal cases every year. More fundamentally, the opinion represented a large step back (or perhaps, failed to take a large step forward) in maintaining for the judiciary a meaningful role in the process by which most criminal cases are resolved.

The reasoning in *Ruiz* can be criticized on many grounds. First, the court apparently found it significant that, as part of the proposed plea deal, the prosecution stated that it already had turned over "any [known] information establishing the factual innocence of the defendant" and acknowledged its "continuing duty to provide such information."[15] It is hard to know what to make of this. Presumably there was no such information to disclose, and in all likelihood, there *never* will be – if the government really "knows" of information that establishes the defendant's "factual innocence," a voluntary dismissal of the indictment should be the next step, not a disclosure followed by a resumption of plea bargaining. To offer this seemingly comforting provision in a plea agreement

[15] 536 U.S. at 625 (internal quotation marks omitted).

is like promising the accused that the government manufactured no evidence and suborned no perjury in building its case. The government is either saying nothing, or it is suggesting something that should make us nervous.

Second, the proffered deal in *Ruiz* said that the accused was waiving her right to receive "impeachment information relating to any informants or other witnesses[,] as well as the right to receive information supporting any affirmative defense the defendant raises if the case goes to trial."[16] This provision is also puzzling because, had she agreed to the term, Ms. Ruiz would have been waiving a subset, but *only* a subset, of the Brady material she would receive if the case were tried. For reasons that are unclear, the prosecutor in *Ruiz* drew distinctions between three categories of Brady material: (a) impeachment evidence and evidence related to affirmative defenses, which now clearly do not have to be disclosed before a guilty plea; (b) information that is "known" to establish factual innocence, which, although the court didn't say so, presumably has to be disclosed; and (c) everything else that constitutes Brady material, about which the court said nothing.

The recognition of this third category is only implicit in the opinion, but the inference is inescapable. There is a sizable amount of Brady material in the world that will not fall into the two categories identified in *Ruiz*, but would obviously have to be disclosed if the defendant went to trial. This would include favorable, material information that was not "known" to the prosecution but should have been known, as well as nonimpeachment evidence that does not "establish factual innocence" but puts a sizable dent in the prosecutor's case. Examples of this might include a witness's misidentification of the perpetrator, the presence of an alternative suspect, or the presence of inconsistent physical evidence.

This recognition of three categories of Brady material is surprising. For several years after *Brady*, courts struggled with whether there was a constitutionally significant difference between "exculpatory" and "impeachment" evidence, finally deciding in *Giglio v. United States*[17] that it was a distinction without a difference – it was all Brady material and was to be treated the same regardless of the label. (The court would reaffirm this melding of exculpatory and impeachment information both before and after *Ruiz*.[18]) To reopen this divide without explanation potentially

[16] Id. (internal quotation marks omitted). [17] 405 U.S. 150, 154 (1972).

[18] More than a decade after Giglio, the Court would reverse an appellate court that tried to reintroduce the distinction. The Ninth Circuit ruled that withholding impeachment

leaves the law worse off than when the court found it. Even if *Ruiz* itself reached the right result, it leaves unresolved whether a defendant who pleads guilty can raise a Brady claim for nonimpeachment evidence that is both favorable and material to the accused, a distinct category that had previously disappeared from this area of the law. Not surprisingly, lower courts have not been uniform in answering this question.[19]

Ruiz might well be defensible as a matter of policy. One reason for the prosecutor to strike a plea bargain is to avoid the burdens of preparing for trial, a burden that includes uncovering and disclosing Brady information. A contrary rule in *Ruiz* would remove that time saver, and it might in the long run simply slow down the process without much change in the overall case results. *Ruiz* might also be normatively defensible because, by definition, the defendant is about to plead guilty and admit to the charge (or at least, admit to some charge). If the defendant is going to confess his guilt, how unfair can it be that he was kept in the dark about evidence that might have helped him beat the rap at trial?

An easy but unsatisfying answer comes from our knowledge that people sometimes confess to crimes they did not commit, simply because the prosecutor offered a benefit for pleading guilty and the defendant does

evidence was subject to a different standard than withholding exculpatory material, but the Supreme Court reminded lower courts that "This Court has rejected any such distinction between impeachment evidence and exculpatory evidence." U.S. v. Bagley, 473 U.S. 667, 676 (1985). Also, two years after Ruiz, the court would return to the description of Brady material as covering without distinction both impeachment and exculpatory information. See Banks v. Dretke, 540 U.S. 668, 691 (2004).

19 In reaffirming circuit precedent that a guilty plea waives the right to claim a Brady violation, the Fifth Circuit rejected the argument that Ruiz was limited to impeachment material: "Ruiz never makes such a distinction nor can this proposition be implied from its discussion." United States v. Conroy, 567 F.3d 174, 179 (5th Cir.2009), cert. denied, 130 S.Ct. 1502 (2010). In addition, the Fourth Circuit has said that Ruiz foreclosed a claim that a guilty plea was invalid because the prosecutor failed to turn over potentially mitigating evidence in a death penalty case. Jones v. Cooper, 311 F.3d 306, 315 n. 5 (4th Cir. 2002). The Fourth Circuit later found that the question whether Ruiz precluded any Brady claim when defendant pled guilty was "a close one," but found it unnecessary to reach the question on the facts presented. U.S. v. Moussaoui, 591 F.3d 263, 286 (4th Cir. 2010).

Other courts have read Ruiz differently. In McCann v. Mangialardi, 337 F.3d 782, 787–788 (7th Cir.2003), the Seventh Circuit concluded that Ruiz drew a distinction between impeachment information and exculpatory evidence of actual innocence, although it did not address exculpatory evidence that did not show actual innocence. Furthermore, in U.S. v. Danzi, 726 F. Supp. 2d 120, 128 (D. Conn.), opinion clarified, 2010 WL 3463272 (2010), the district court acknowledged the uncertainty in the law but found that the pre-Ruiz circuit precedent "require[d] the pre-plea disclosure of exculpatory material to criminal defendants."

not trust the system to vindicate his or her innocence. Although this scenario undoubtedly occurs (a visit to the Cardozo Innocence Project web site confirms the point[20]), the explanation won't take us far. Not only do we lack a reliable way to measure the frequency of the occurrence, but also the criminal system as structured simply cannot accommodate a widespread possibility of innocent defendants falsely admitting to crimes. The ability to process large numbers of criminal cases would be crippled if a robust concept of finality did not attach to a guilty plea.

But even granting that in-court confessions establish factual guilt, they may not tell us much about whether the prosecutor would have been able to prove *legal* guilt beyond a reasonable doubt had the case gone to trial. It is entirely possible that a defendant is guilty in fact (he or she intentionally committed fraud), but had the defendant known of the Brady material, he would have gone to trial and won, because the prosecution's witness had an undisclosed perjury conviction, because the forensic results were inconclusive, because the main witness originally gave inconsistent grand jury testimony, and so on.

This, then, is the real concern with *Ruiz*: It sends a worrisome signal that the court is indifferent to a defendant's *legal* guilt.[21] We can with clear conscience feel no sympathy for the factually guilty defendant who is induced to admit guilt, while still being concerned about a process that treats factual guilt as the only relevant issue. Plea bargaining is built on a model of two equal parties who know the case better than anyone, negotiating a settlement that is in the best interest for defendant and society alike. Stephanos Bibas has persuasively described how the pressures and incentives of the plea-bargaining process pull us away from this ideal – a guilty plea is made in the shadow of lots of things, not just trial[22] – and *Ruiz* takes us a long step beyond this. Each time a defendant pleads to a crime that the prosecutor could not prove, the values captured by the trial process itself are at risk. The challenges that a defendant would have brought had he or she not waived them to induce a more favorable

[20] See www.innocenceproject.org/understand/False-Confessions.php ("In about 25% of DNA exoneration cases, innocent defendants made incriminating statements, delivered outright confessions or pled guilty").

[21] The concern about factual, as opposed to legal, guilt may explain why the government included in the plea agreement a commitment that it knew of no evidence that would exonerate the accused, and why the court seemed to find this provision significant. See supra the text accompanying note 15.

[22] Stephanos Bibas, *Plea Bargaining Outside the Shadow of Trial*, 117 Harv. L. Rev. 2463 (2004). See also William J. Stuntz, *Plea Bargaining and Criminal Law's Disappearing Shadow*, 117 Harv. L. Rev. 2548 (2004).

deal, the government overreaching that might have been exposed had the prosecutor been forced to prove its charges to a jury, even the confidence in the factual guilt that comes from the adversarial process and a jury verdict, are all potential benefits lost.

By refusing to hear claims that the prosecutor had not disclosed favorable information in its possession at the time of the plea, the court has largely quit the field in ways that it could have, but did not, in the sentencing and terrorism cases. Whether the defendant made a truly informed choice to admit guilt,[23] whether the defendant might have had a valid defense had he or she gone to trial, and whether a different bargain might have been struck if the defendant were fully informed are issues that remain vested almost entirely in the hands of the executive branch, to be determined as a matter of grace rather than as a matter of right. This is not to say that courts are irrelevant to the plea process, but as discussed below in Section IV, the court's remaining role is hardly sufficient to make it a major player until after the conviction has been entered.

The judicial step-back from the plea-bargaining process creates a vacuum, because there are few other mechanisms available to monitor the prosecutor's charging decisions. Preliminary hearings, bills of particulars, and pretrial discovery, even if they occur before the plea, are hardly designed to ensure that the defense is working with adequate information. The grand jury is also supposed to shield the accused from improper charges, but nobody outside of the Supreme Court believes that it does.[24]

There is nothing that compels courts to take such a hands-off approach to plea bargaining. At its core, *Brady* is a constitutional conclusion that the outcomes of criminal *cases* are not truly fair if the government is permitted to withhold information that might change the result. And while parts of *Ruiz* suggest that *Brady* is only about making sure that *trials* are fair,[25] there is no developed rationale offered by the court to explain why a jury verdict based on withheld information is unfair, but a guilty plea based on the same inadequate information becomes fair.

The best argument against *Ruiz* is that a contrary rule would be too burdensome, but this is not a reason to avoid *any* governmental obligation at the plea-bargain stage. A full-blooded requirement to ensure that

[23] As used here, an "informed" choice is meant in the colloquial, not legal, sense of the word. See Section IV of the text.

[24] See infra note 43.

[25] Justice Thomas, concurring in the judgment, says "The principle supporting *Brady* was 'avoidance of an unfair trial to the accused.' That concern is not implicated at the plea stage regardless." 536 U.S. at 634 (citation omitted).

there is no favorable material information anywhere in the government's control surely could throw sand in the gears, but a sensible rule would not necessarily impose such a duty. In the context of a plea negotiation, it may be enough to require the government to disclose any information that it already knows about by the time the plea agreement is reached. In other words, a Brady rule for guilty pleas might not require the government to go scour the files, but it would at least obligate a prosecutor to reveal what is already sitting on her desk. And while perhaps the defendant could still waive the right to receive this information, the principles that underlie *Brady* would be better served by allowing a defendant to trade a protection he or she is entitled to, rather than making the defendant buy something in the plea-bargaining process (which may or may not exist) that is required for an informed plea.

A commitment to plead guilty is the seminal event in criminal cases, and for the court to disclaim any role in ensuring that the government is not trading on the defendant's ignorance of the case against him strikes a surprisingly passive pose. More broadly, the court seems unconcerned about a decision to step back from the plea-bargaining process, leaving virtually all of the important work to be done by the executive branch. This reticence seems out of place in a court that is so willing to take an assertive approach in other parts of its docket.

III. FEDERAL CRIMINAL JURISDICTION

Those of us intimidated by the subject of federal courts nonetheless remember a few things about jurisdiction. We know that, despite the steady expansion of the federal sphere, federal courts remain ones of limited jurisdiction. We know that jurisdiction cannot be conferred by the consent of the parties, and that challenges to subject-matter jurisdiction cannot be waived. We know that courts have an independent obligation to satisfy themselves of their own jurisdiction before ruling, and that any action taken in the absence of jurisdiction is void.[26] In short, we know

[26] See, e.g., Steel Co. v. Citizens for a Better Environment, 523 U.S. 83, 101–102 (1998): ("For a court to pronounce upon the meaning or the constitutionality of a state or federal law when it has no jurisdiction to do so is, by very definition, for a court to act ultra vires"). See also Ex parte McCardle, 7 Wall. 506, 514, 19 L.Ed. 264 (1868): "Without jurisdiction the court cannot proceed at all in any cause. Jurisdiction is power to declare the law, and when it ceases to exist, the only function remaining to the court is that of announcing the fact and dismissing the cause." See generally Ruhrgas AG v. Marathon Oil Co., 526 U.S. 574, 583–584 (1999): "Subject-matter limitations

that jurisdiction is a weighty matter, one that is central to the vitality of a federal–state system.

On the civil side, jurisdiction is taken very seriously. There is subject-matter jurisdiction (the capo of the jurisdiction family), supplemental jurisdiction, and personal jurisdiction, each of which demands the careful attention of sophisticated litigators and anxious law students. But the same scrutiny hardly seems to attach to federal criminal cases. Here the powers given by Congress to the federal courts are sweeping and deceptively simple: District courts have original and exclusive jurisdiction over all federal offenses.[27] There is no diversity requirement, and no amount in controversy or similar complexities to worry about. Sometimes the relationship between federal courts and Native American tribal courts can get complicated, as can the relationship between civilian and military tribunals. In general, though, federal subject-matter jurisdiction for criminal cases gets relatively little attention in the cases, literature, or casebooks.[28]

Perhaps it should. If we take seriously the idea that jurisdictional requirements are appropriate restraints on federal power, then we should at least have a clear sense of what these restraints are, and whether current notions of what federal courts can and cannot do are defensible. At a minimum, we should be able to articulate the basic requirements of what it takes to invoke, establish, and challenge a federal court's exercise of authority over a criminal case.

A. *Invoking Jurisdiction*

Federal jurisdiction in this context means the power given by Congress to the courts to hear criminal cases. As scholars have noted and observation confirms, Congress has been generous, even promiscuous, in granting this authority. The number and breadth of federal crimes are large and increasing, as real or imagined failures of the states to prosecute antisocial

on federal jurisdiction serve institutional interests. They keep the federal courts within the bounds the Constitution and Congress have prescribed. Accordingly, subject-matter delineations must be policed by the courts on their own initiative even at the highest level."

[27] 18 U.S.C. § 3231 ("The district courts of the United States shall have original jurisdiction, exclusive of the courts of the States, of all offenses against the laws of the United States").

[28] But see Roger A. Fairfax, Jr., *The Jurisdictional Heritage of the Grand Jury Clause*, 91 Minn. L. Rev. 398 (2006); Norman Abrams et al., Federal Criminal Law and Its Enforcement (5th ed. 2010).

behavior results in a predictable call to federalize the offense, a call that is often answered.[29]

Because states are the primary enforcers of the criminal law, the creation of a federal offense requires Congress to identify some federal interest that is implicated by the crime; that is, there must be some federal jurisdictional "hook." The crime must have been against a federal official, for example, or have made use of the facilities of interstate transportation or communication. Other federal crimes are legitimized by the commerce power, which, with the occasional exception,[30] gives Congress enough room to reach large chunks of undesirable conduct. And of course, for many federal offenses, the physical location of the offense moves it from the state to the federal column. If the crime moved between states, or if it occurred on one of the 650 million acres (about 30 percent of the country[31]) of federal land, and if the behavior would have been a crime had it occurred in the state encompassing the area, the behavior becomes a federal offense.[32] (One result of this is that about 4 percent of the federal criminal docket involves defendants charged with traffic offenses.[33])

In short, except for purely local crimes, there are not many jurisdictional barriers to federal prosecution. The primary restraints on the exercise of federal criminal authority are instead limits imposed by the executive branch on itself. U.S. Attorneys, facing more federal crime than they can handle, will typically limit their prosecution efforts to a relatively small pool of offenses in which they and the Justice Department have determined that there is a substantial federal interest at stake.[34]

[29] For an insightful discussion of this issue, see Sara Sun Beale, *Too Many and Yet Too Few: New Principles to Define the Proper Limits for Federal Criminal Jurisdiction*, 46 Hastings L. J. 979 (1994–1995).

[30] See U.S. v. Lopez, 514 U.S. 549 (1995) (holding the Gun-Free School Zones Act unconstitutional as beyond the scope of Congress's commerce clause power).

[31] The U.S. Geological Survey estimates that the federal government owns nearly 650 million acres of federally owned and managed lands. See http://www.nationalatlas.gov/printable/fedlands.html.

[32] 18 U.S.C. § 13.

[33] In fiscal year 2009, 4 percent of the 96,277 federal defendants who had their cases resolved were charged with traffic crimes as the most serious offense filed. Virtually all of these cases were misdemeanors (3,900 out of 3,922 defendants). The numbers are comparable for fiscal year 2008 (3,745 traffic defendants out of 92,149 total defendants, or 4 percent). These figures are compiled from the data sets kept by the Administrative Office of the U.S. Courts and found at http://fjsrc.urban.org/download.cfm, data set files AOUSCt 09out and AOUSCt 08out, variable FLOFFLV1, codes 7210 and 7220.

[34] U.S. Attorneys Manual § 9-27.220, § 9-27.230.

Given all this, we might think that invoking federal court jurisdiction in a criminal case would be simple. Nearly all federal felonies are prosecuted by indictment, and it should be easy enough for the prosecutor, as the drafter of the charges, to properly allege in the indictment a federal criminal offense. This allows the court to ensure its own jurisdiction at an early stage in the case, plus it ensures proper notice for the accused and avoids wasted resources if the case is somehow misfiled. Indeed, for many years this was the understanding of how to invoke jurisdiction. As the Supreme Court said in the late-nineteenth-century case *Ex parte Bain*,[35] if the indictment were defective, "the jurisdiction of the offense is gone, and the court has no right to proceed any further in the progress of the case for want of an indictment."[36]

What complicated this rule was the difficulty of correcting indictment errors. If the charge failed to properly allege a federal crime, the prosecutor couldn't just take out a red pencil and fix it. As Roger Fairfax has superbly argued, the original understanding was that a federal court had jurisdiction only if the grand jury approved a proper charge, and thus if the indictment were defective, the prosecutor had to return to the grand jury to get approval for a proper charge. Until that happened the case could not proceed, because grand jury approval was a constitutional prerequisite to a federal court's consideration of the case.[37]

The theoretical foundations of *Bain* eroded during the twentieth century. The most significant move came in the 1940s, when the new Federal Rules of Criminal Procedure permitted a defendant to waive the right to a grand jury indictment. There were sound practical reasons for the new rule, but the effects on the jurisdiction question were profound. If the defendant could waive indictment, then obviously grand jury approval could not be a jurisdiction prerequisite; it was a bedrock principle, then and now, that jurisdiction cannot be conferred by the consent of the parties. Still, for the next half-century, the relationship between the court's jurisdiction and the existence of a proper federal indictment remained

[35] 121 U.S. 1(1887).

[36] Id. at 13. The defect in the *Bain* indictment was that the trial court had stricken language that was not surplusage, which constituted an impermissible amendment of the pleading without grand jury approval. The resulting invalidity of the indictment meant that "[t]he power of the court to proceed to try the prisoner is as much arrested as if the indictment had been dismissed or a nolle prosequi had been entered. There was nothing before the court on which it could hear evidence or pronounce sentence." Id. at 13–14.

[37] See Fairfax, *The Jurisdictional Heritage of the Grand Jury Clause*, supra note 28.

unresolved, as some courts and even the Federal Rules continued to treat the failure to allege a federal crime as something more significant than a run-of-the-mill error.[38]

B. Cotton

In *United States v. Cotton*,[39] the Supreme Court resolved the issue – sort of. The indictment in *Cotton* failed to specify the drug amount attributable to the defendant, but the district court sentenced him based on evidence presented at trial that the crime involved more than fifty grams of cocaine base. On appeal there was no dispute that this was an error: If the prosecution wanted the defendant sentenced based on the fifty grams, it should have alleged the weight in the indictment. As a result, the Fourth Circuit concluded that "a court is without jurisdiction to . . . impose a sentence for an offense not charged in the indictment."[40]

The Supreme Court unanimously reversed, overruling *Ex Parte Bain* on the ground that its jurisdictional holding was outdated.[41] It reaffirmed that jurisdiction in this setting means "the courts' statutory or constitutional power to adjudicate the case," and it concluded that a failure to properly allege a crime is not part of the definition. Defects in the indictment, said the court, go to the merits of the case, not the court's authority to resolve it.

[38] For example, the court in Stirone v. U.S., 361 U.S. 212 (1960) did not quite say that a proper indictment by the grand jury was a jurisdictional requirement, but it came close: "The Bain case, which has never been disapproved, stands for the rule that a court cannot permit a defendant to be tried on charges that are not made in the indictment against him." The court went on to say that the Stirone indictment was defective because it did not properly allege an interference with interstate commerce, and that the omission "[was] critical since the Federal Government's jurisdiction of this crime rests only on that interference." Id. at 217, 218.

In addition, from 1946 to the present the Federal Rules have treated a claim that the indictment failed to allege a federal offense as one that can be considered by the court at any time, even if it is beyond the period set by the trial court for pretrial motions. See Rule 12(b)(3). In a sense, such a claim is treated the same as a motion challenging the court's jurisdiction (although notice that Rule 12 lists the failure to state an offense and lack of jurisdiction as distinct claims). This treatment, however, was premised on the idea that failure to allege an offense was a jurisdictional defect, a view that *Cotton* rejected.

[39] 535 U.S. 625 (2002). Chief Justice Rehnquist wrote for a unanimous court.

[40] U.S. v. Cotton, 261 F.3d 397, 404-405 (4th Cir. 2001).

[41] 535 U.S. at 630–631.

Cotton's analysis is terse – it takes only a couple of pages to reject *Bain* – and its reliance on authority is hardly compelling,[42] but no matter. For current purposes *Cotton* raises at least two unresolved issues, one theoretical and one practical. First, the case presents a puzzle: Why did the court care so little about constitutional procedures here when it cared so much about them just two years earlier (*Apprendi*), and two years later (*Crawford*)? Second, if a proper allegation of a federal crime is unnecessary to invoke the court's jurisdiction, it is unclear what steps are required; more pointedly, we might ask whether there is now *any* requirement that jurisdiction as such be invoked or ensured in a federal criminal case.

On the first point, *Crawford* said that regardless of precedent and regardless of the inconvenience, there was a certain constitutional process that had to be followed to ensure the right of confrontation; the *Apprendi* line of cases said similar things with respect to sentencing factors and the role of the jury. It is unclear why a similar reasoning did not prevail in *Cotton*, although the argument was clearly made. The U.S. Constitution is explicit that a felony defendant is entitled to be charged by a (presumably valid) indictment. To paraphrase *Crawford*, the U.S. Constitution demands not just that the accused be "informed of the nature and cause of the accusation" (one function of the formal pleading), but that he or she be charged in a certain way, by a certain process, one that includes a grand jury indictment. But if an indictment fails to properly allege a crime the required process has been aborted, and later claims

[42] *Cotton* relies on two cases to support its view that Bain's interpretation of jurisdiction was out of date. The first is Lamar v. U.S., 240 U.S. 60 (1916), a Holmes opinion. *Lamar*, however, involved a case where it appears that a federal crime was properly alleged in the indictment – Mr. Lamar was charged with impersonating an officer of the United States government. His claim was simply that the person he impersonated (a member of Congress) was not an "officer" within the meaning of the statute. So when *Lamar* rejected the jurisdictional claim and concluded that "The objection that the indictment does not charge a crime against the United States goes only to the merits of the case," it was not at all clear that the opinion was concluding that, as *Cotton* suggests, *any* defect in the indictment goes to the merits rather than to jurisdiction. A flawed indictment of the type presented in *Cotton* simply was not presented in *Lamar*.

The second case, U.S. v. Williams, 341 U.S. 58 (1951), is more persuasive, because there the Court directly concluded that an indictment that later proves to be defective does not deprive the court of jurisdiction (although it admits that "[t]he line is narrow and often wavering between errors in the proceedings and lack of jurisdiction." Id. at 68). But the claim in *Cotton* that these two decisions show that "this Court some time ago departed from Bain's view that indictment defects are 'jurisdictional'" still seems bold. In neither case was *Bain* discussed or even cited, making the court's shift in its thinking on jurisdiction quite subtle.

that the jury was properly charged with the correct elements of the crime, that the defendant was not surprised by the evidence, that the evidence showed the presence of the jurisdictional element, and so on, might easily have been found to be beside the point.

On the other hand, maybe this is not much of a puzzle. One way to view *Cotton* is that it is just another of many examples of the Supreme Court's indifference to the health and usefulness of the grand jury.[43] A prosecutor still has to prove that the defendant committed all the elements of a federal crime, but perhaps the need for this pretrial screening device is not as important as the U.S. Constitution makes it out to be. Calling a valid indictment "jurisdictional" would be to say that a defendant could not waive the right, and the court is simply disinclined to upset existing practices without something more important at stake than the theoretical protections that the grand jury provides. The court may also be thinking that the failure to allege a federal crime is very likely to be the product of oversight rather than the true absence of chargeable conduct – if the prosecutor cannot allege *some* federal crime she must not be trying very hard – and the court may be especially loath to insist on preliminary proof of something that it believes will almost always be true.

The larger question after *Cotton* is what it means to say that a court "has no power to hear a case." If the failure to properly allege a federal crime is not a bar to a court trying a defendant, it is not clear when we can say that jurisdiction is absent. To be sure, a defendant can still challenge the indictment for failure to state an offense, but unless and until that happens, it appears to be enough for the prosecutor simply to represent that a federal crime has occurred, with no obligation to provide a proper allegation that would allow the court to see for itself.

Perhaps the court only loses power to adjudicate a matter when there is no *proof* that the defendant violated federal law. But this would be an odd outcome, because now there is no difference between saying that the

[43] Grand juries were included in the Bill of Rights to ensure that charges were legitimate and supportable, but the institution has for decades suffered from Supreme Court apathy. At least since Costello v. United States, 350 U.S. 359 (1956), the court has refused to allow judges to play a meaningful role in overseeing grand jury affairs; whenever a party seeks to have the courts consider claims involving grand jury evidence, procedures, or practices that would make the screening process more meaningful, they routinely fail, usually in the name of deference to grand jury autonomy. See, e.g., U.S. v. Williams, 504 U.S. 36 (1992) (prosecutor not obligated to disclose exculpatory evidence to grand jury); Bank of Nova Scotia v. U.S., 487 U.S. 250 (1988) (grand jury errors do not result in dismissal of indictment absent a showing of prejudice); U.S. v. Mechanik, 475 U.S. 66 (1986) (most grand jury errors rendered harmless per se after conviction).

court lacks jurisdiction and saying that the prosecutor cannot prove the substantive charge because the evidence for some element of the crime is missing. By the time the lack of jurisdiction is actionable, the case is presumably over.

To extend the reasoning of *Cotton* to its end point, suppose the defendant's felony case never goes before the grand jury at all, and instead he or she is charged by information. (Perhaps the prosecutor mistakenly thought the charge was a misdemeanor rather than a felony, or perhaps the defendant waived grand jury but the waiver was invalid.) Would a court still have jurisdiction over the case? *Cotton* suggests that it would, because the return of a proper indictment is now a merits claim, not a prerequisite to the exercise of authority. Interestingly, this question – what if there were no grand jury at all? – was raised by the Supreme Court at oral argument, but it was never fully answered by the government.[44]

IV. IMPLICATIONS

There are two points we might extract from *Ruiz* and *Cotton*. First, and less importantly, we can be disappointed that in two significant areas of criminal procedure the Supreme Court made major decisions with unsatisfying rationales. Regardless of whether prosecutors should or should not disclose Brady material prior to a plea, and regardless of whether the procedures specified in the U.S. Constitution are a prerequisite to the exercise of federal jurisdiction, the outcomes deserve a better explanation than was given. Modesty in opinion writing is a virtue, but economy at the expense of clarity is not.

The second and more important point is the Supreme Court's apparent decision to sound a judicial retreat from the subject areas. This is especially worrisome in the case of plea bargaining. Prosecutors have unfettered discretion to decide whom to investigate and whom to charge, and they can easily avoid preliminary hearings that would impose some judicial review on charging practices.[45] Judges play no role in the grand jury's review (a process dominated by the prosecutor), and they are barred from participating in plea negotiations.[46] Given that more than 85 percent of all federal cases end with a guilty plea, it becomes apparent that

44 The transcript of the oral argument is on Westlaw at 2002 WL 753356; see id. at 21–23.

45 Federal Rule 5.1 provides that a preliminary hearing need not be held if the prosecutor obtains an indictment first. See Fed. R. Cr. P. 5.1(a)(2).

46 See Fed. R. Crim. P. 11(c)(1).

if there is to be *any* judicial involvement in the overwhelming majority of criminal cases – that is, if the judicial branch is going to play a meaningful role prior to sentencing – it needs to come from judicial monitoring of guilty pleas.

Currently there are two ways that judges participate in the plea process. First, courts use the Rule 11 colloquy to ensure that a defendant is not clueless about what it means to plead guilty. The judge makes sure the defendant understands the charges, the rights he is giving up, and the possible punishment he faces. We might wonder, in a world where nearly all defendants are represented by counsel, how often a defendant is truly unaware of some of these basic points. But the fact that the information will often be duplicative is no grounds for criticizing the process – better too much information about the effect of a plea than too little.

In fact, though, there are strong arguments that defendants do have too little information. The Rule 11 requirements are designed to ensure that a decision to plead guilty is voluntary and *knowing*, but the latter term has a particular and narrow meaning. There are lots of things a defendant does not need to "know" before confessing guilt: What sentence will I get?[47] Will I be deported?[48] Most importantly: If I go to trial, what are the chances that I will be convicted? This lack of knowledge will often flow from the undeveloped nature of the facts, but it also may flow from a defendant's ignorance that the prosecutor has a weak case, information that might be revealed if Brady material in the government's possession were disclosed. In other words, courts now must ensure that defendants know some things, but potentially not the single most significant piece of information that will affect the plea decision.

Second, judges make a substantive review of the parties' agreement that induces the plea, at least in some cases. The current level of merits-based scrutiny of plea bargains is important but minimal. The judge must accept some plea agreements ("Type A" and "Type C" deals), but not all of them (not "Type B").[49] When the court reviews the deals, it is

[47] Before accepting a plea the court must ensure that the defendant is aware of the maximum possible penalty, any mandatory minimum penalty, and the obligation to consider the effect of the Federal Sentencing Guidelines; the defendant does not need to know the sentence he or she will actually receive. See Fed. R. Crim. P. 11(b)(1)(H)–(M).

[48] But cf. Padilla v. Kentucky, 130 S.Ct. 1473 (2010) (recognizing that a defendant may have an ineffective assistance of counsel claim if he or she pled guilty without being advised that the plea carried the risk of deportation).

[49] See Fed. R. Crim. P. 11(c)(1)(A), (B), (C). Type A agreements provide that in return for a guilty plea, the prosecution agrees to drop or not pursue other charges. Type B deals obligate the prosecutor to make a nonbinding sentencing recommendation, but if the

hard to know what the judge is looking for; there is little case law on the standards for evaluating a plea, and no adversarial process that would highlight potential problems with the agreement. Indeed, at least with Type A agreements, it is hard to even know what it means to say the judge must "accept" the deal, because a prosecutorial agreement to "not bring, or [ ] move to dismiss, other charges" cannot be countermanded by the court even if it rejects the bargain. At best then, the judge's substantive role is limited to a decision that the court will not be bound to the sentence agreed to by the parties in a Type C case. But even this fails to provide a serious look at the propriety of the charge or the fairness of the resolution.

Judges also are required to ensure that there is a factual basis for the guilty plea,[50] and although this too is significant, it still leaves the court as a bit player on a big stage. The factual basis inquiry can be searching, but need not be, and may be based in whole or in part on what the prosecutor tells the court.[51] Most importantly, the court does not need to be convinced of the defendant's legal guilt, or even entirely sure of his factual guilt. The judge just needs to be satisfied that there is enough information indicative of factual guilt to permit the plea.

Rather than require judicial oversight, we instead delegate the task of policing the plea bargain process to defense counsel, who have both the expertise and the incentive to monitor the prosecutor. Turfing this responsibility to the defense makes sense in a system in which judges are already overburdened, but making the defense the primary guarantor of fair plea bargaining is different than saying that the defense should carry

judge does not follow the recommendation, the defendant is not relieved of his or her commitment to plead guilty. As a result, there is nothing about the plea bargain that requires court approval. Type C deals require the defendant to plead guilty, but only if the court agrees not to impose a sentence that is longer than the one the parties agreed to. Here the court is required to decide whether to accept the plea deal, because once it does, it may not impose a longer sentence than what the parties contemplated. If the court rejects the deal, the defendant is not obligated to plead guilty.

50 See Fed. R. Crim. P. 11(b)(3).

51 In determining whether there is a factual basis for a guilty plea, the test "is not whether a jury would, or even would be likely, to convict: it is whether there is enough evidence so that the plea has a rational basis in facts that the defendant concedes or that the government proffers as supported by credible evidence." U.S. v. Serrano-Beauvaix, 400 F.3d 50, 53 (1st Cir.), cert. denied, 546 U.S. 854 (2005) (internal quotation marks and citation omitted). See generally 1A Charles Alan Wright & Andrew D. Leipold, Federal Practice and Procedure: Criminal § 179 (2d ed. 2008), discussing the factual basis requirement. Of course, if the defendant is allowed to plead nolo contendere to the charge, there is no need for the court to find any factual basis.

the entire load alone. If courts are going to trust the defense when it says that the plea deal is in the best interest of the accused, perhaps they should be similarly interested when defense counsel say that the deal was based on a misinformation, or when material information that would have changed the decision was not disclosed.

Courts do this to some degree already. Even after a deal is made and a guilty plea entered, courts will still entertain motions to undo the plea if the prosecutor failed to abide by the agreement, if the defendant misunderstood the nature of the charge he or she pled guilty to, or if defense counsel's advice to plead fell below the standards for the effective assistance of counsel.[52] There is no obvious reason why courts should not also be receptive to a claim that, at the time the defendant pled guilty, the prosecutor was in possession of information that would have materially affected the defendant's decision to plead guilty. Simply being open to these claims would allow courts to play a larger role in ensuring that the most important part of most criminal cases is not left entirely in the hands of the executive branch.

Similar concerns follow the Supreme Court's stepping back from policing its own jurisdiction, although here the consequences are less pronounced. It is easy to argue that the practical effect of *Cotton* is trivial – if prosecutors file indictments that fail to allege a federal crime, defendants will simply file a motion to dismiss, which will lead to a new, proper indictment, or perhaps the end of the case if there really was no federal offense. Even if defense counsel fails to notice the defect until trial has begun, the prosecutor can correct the error with proof of the missing element at trial, and the court can properly instruct the jury on the elements it needs to find. And if the defendant does not notice the defect until after trial, either the error will be harmless because there was proof of the unalleged element, or the conviction should be reversed because the prosecutor failed to prove each element required by the statute. In any of these situations, there is little chance that a court will enter a judgment of conviction and have that conviction affirmed where there was in fact no authority to hear the case.

[52] See, e.g., Santobello v. New York, 404 U.S. 257 (1971) (guilty plea will be overturned where prosecutor fails to abide by terms of the plea agreements); Henderson v. Morgan, 426 U.S. 637 (1976) (guilty plea overturned where defendant did not understand the nature of the charge against him); Hill v. Lockhart, 474 U.S. 52, 56 (1985) (recognizing that defendant may overturn guilty plea by showing that counsel's advice to plead fell below Sixth Amendment standards).

For people who care about the niceties of jurisdiction, these arguments are little comfort. *Cotton* shifts the burden of detection and the risk of harm arising from an error onto the defendant, the party who is the least responsible for the mess. The obligation in the first instance to invoke the federal court's jurisdiction belongs with the prosecutor, who crafts the indictment alleging a federal crime. Responsibility next devolves to the courts; as the Supreme Court has frequently reminded, "The requirement that jurisdiction be established as a threshold matter 'spring[s] from the nature and limits of the judicial power of the United States'" and is "'inflexible and without exception.'"[53] And while the framers of the grand jury clause may not have had this precise situation in mind, the requirement of an indictment that informs the defendant of the charges has the happy benefit of providing the court with everything it needs to make this threshold determination – it need only decide on the face of the pleading that a federal crime has been properly alleged. Instead, *Cotton* steps back from this relatively easy chore, assuming instead that jurisdiction is proper unless someone tells the court otherwise.

CONCLUSION

There is no obvious, unifying variable that explains why the Supreme Court sometimes cares deeply about preserving a role for itself in important governmental functions and sometimes does not. Sentencing and the treatment of enemy combatants found the court doggedly preserving a constitutional voice when the executive and congressional branches thought it should have less of one. Likewise in the *Crawford* cases, the court found that the Constitution demands a certain process for carrying out a core judicial function and, at great cost to the existing infrastructure, insisted that the process be followed. These decisions were not easy, or inevitable, or even the most sensible resolution for a system already hard pressed to manage its business.

Perhaps the decisions are simply subject-matter driven. Many judges disliked the Sentencing Guidelines, and anything that moved the sentencing power from an independent agency back toward the courtroom looked to the court like a better construction of the Constitution, even if it took an upheaval such as *Apprendi* and *Booker* to do it. The war powers were and still are the domain of the elected branches, but perhaps cases

[53] Steel Co. v. Citizens for a Better Environment, 523 U.S. 83, 94–95 (1998), quoting Mansfield, C. & L.M.R. Co. v. Swan, 111 U.S. 379, 382 (1884).

such as *Korematsu*[54] taught the court the risks of deferring too quickly to presidential judgments about the trade-offs between security and civil liberty. On the other hand, the Court's view of plea bargaining over the past half-century has moved from tolerance to acceptance to enthusiastic encouragement, and any arguments that the plea process should slow down and become more complex were probably doomed from the start. Similarly, the Court's warm embrace of the harmless error and waiver doctrines may explain its lack of interest in criminal subject-matter jurisdiction; as long as there is only a small risk that courts will operate outside their authority, it is enough to leave the chore of identifying cases where there is no federal crime presented to the defense.

Or perhaps the Supreme Court recognizes that the law can tolerate only a few legal revolutions each generation. Even if the court believed that the plea-bargaining process had big problems that needed fixing (and there is no indication that it does), it might think the excessive use of hearsay evidence was worse, and that too many disruptive decisions are bad for the law and bad for the court. Indeed, it is this very feature of landmark cases that makes it so hard to explain their genesis. There are few sea changes in the law, which makes data points few and scattered.

All of this makes it hard to predict where the next set of big cases will arise, and what the animating themes will be. In the meantime, though, it seems worthwhile to identify some current themes; it also seems worthwhile to note the inconsistent application of those themes when the Supreme Court charts such an irregular course through its criminal procedure jurisprudence.

[54] Korematsu v. U.S., 323 U.S. 214 (1944).

11

Three Puzzles in the Work of Bill Stuntz

Louis Michael Seidman

In this essay, I explore three puzzles in the work of Bill Stuntz. I do not have complete solutions for any of them. Still, my hope is that my effort to think them through will provide some insights into the writings of this remarkable scholar and human being.

The first puzzle is this: Stuntz argued passionately and effectively that Christians should "come out of the closet" and bring their Christian perspective to bear on legal problems. It is true that in his writings making this argument, he sometimes drew on examples from the field of criminal justice, his primary academic interest. However, at least to my knowledge, his work focusing on criminal justice nowhere explicitly invoked his Christian commitments. Why did Stuntz decline to take his own advice?

The second puzzle: One of the most attractive conclusions that Stuntz drew from his religious beliefs was about the importance of humility. We are all sinners, he told us, and we all see through the glass darkly. A true Christian must be deeply humble. Nevertheless, this epistemic and moral humility was linked to remarkably audacious and confident (and, by my lights, implausible) claims about the historical truth of the resurrection and the ontological truth of eternal salvation. How could Stuntz have it both ways?

The third puzzle is deeply personal but, for me at least, the most important. Stuntz was a theologically conservative Christian and an unapologetic formalist with libertarian leanings. I am an atheist–agnostic Jew and an unreconstructed adherent of critical legal studies with communitarian leanings. Why do I feel a profound connection to this man and to his work?

I. THE FIRST PUZZLE

In his writings on Christian legal theory, Stuntz endorsed the view that Christian law professors should more openly express their faith commitments in their academic scholarship. Stuntz was characteristically balanced and ambivalent in making this claim. He recognized that "[r]eligion, law, and politics are a frightening mix," and that "[w]oven together they sometimes cause oppression, warfare, and murder." He understood that there was also a problem when citizens speak about public issues based on premises that are not universally shared. Still, Stuntz insisted, a norm that prohibits reference to religious beliefs

> requires people whose faith bears on public issues either to quit the conversation or to deny a piece of their identity. To see how alienating that formula is, imagine telling women that they must pretend they are men, or African Americans that they must think and talk white when entering into conversations about politics or law.

I believe that Stuntz was correct about this basic point. To be sure, when putting together a diverse coalition, there may be prudential reasons for using the rhetoric of "overlapping consensus." Nevertheless, this prudential concern is far removed from the Rawlsian principle of having political morality limit at least a certain class of speakers to "public reason." Stuntz was exactly right when he argued that requiring citizens to translate their deepest commitments into public reason's bland language entails a self-distancing that is ultimately in tension with serious and honest political commitment.

And yet Stuntz's own scholarly work about criminal justice used nothing but the rhetoric of public reason. Stuntz's dense and carefully argued forays into the doctrine and political economy of the criminal justice system were entirely secular in orientation. A reader unfamiliar with his writings about Christian legal theory would have no clue that Stuntz had a particular religious perspective, much less that he thought this religious perspective should influence his legal judgments. How can we explain this reticence about his religious faith in some settings when he was so open about it in others?

Before offering an explanation, I want to reject two fairly obvious possibilities. First, perhaps Stuntz had prudential reasons such as those I have already mentioned for eschewing religious rhetoric. Stuntz must have known that most of the members of the audience for the law review articles he wrote were at best indifferent about and more likely hostile toward theologically conservative Christianity. A scholar with Stuntz's religious views who wants to be taken seriously by such an audience would do well to hide those views. Not only will theologically based arguments be unconvincing; in certain circles the very embrace of these arguments serves to discredit their proponents.

One can imagine some Christian academics motivated by prudential concerns along these lines, but one cannot imagine Bill Stuntz motivated by them. There is no one in legal academia whose work was more honest and forthcoming than Stuntz's. He was unfailingly careful about what he claimed and attentive to arguments on the other side. His work is powerful precisely because he left so much of himself on the page. It is impossible to imagine him deliberately obscuring his beliefs and motivations. Moreover, much of his career was devoted to dispelling by the force of his example unfair stereotypes about theologically conservative Christians. In more forums than he or I could count, his very presence and openness about his religious views served to disprove the slander that conservative Christians are necessarily stupid, closed-minded, or intolerant. Anyone who thinks that Stuntz would deliberately suppress his religious views to gain rhetorical advantage misunderstands the man and the nature of his lifelong project.

A second possibility is that there is no overlap between Stuntz's version of Christianity and his area of scholarly concern. In his work on Christian legal theory, Stuntz flirted with this possibility. He was careful to make clear that Jesus belonged to no political party, had no commitment to a particular form of government, and endorsed no political platform. In Stuntz's view, the teachings of Christianity are overwhelmingly about the heart rather than about politics or law. In particular, Stuntz rejected the legal moralism of the religious right. It is simply a mistake to suppose that Jesus' teachings entail a legal regime that outlaws things such as gay sex, abortion, and gambling.

Nonetheless, if Jesus was not a conservative Republican, neither was he a Generation X-er who could not care less about law and politics. Ultimately, Stuntz believed, Christianity does entail some conclusions about the political and legal order, albeit tentative conclusions, and not the conclusions that many other theologically conservative Christians have reached. These conclusions fall into two categories.

First, there are Jesus' teachings about the poor and downtrodden. In Stuntz's account, Christianity is an "upside down" religion in which the last shall be first. Jesus asked us to empathize with, rather than condemn, society's losers. Christianity therefore pushes us toward economic redistribution. In a Christian republic, the rich and powerful should be made deeply uncomfortable.

These commands have special salience for the criminal justice system. On Christian premises, it is simply unacceptable for the system to focus so heavily on the economically disadvantaged. While rich defendants assemble "dream teams" of lawyers, the poor are asked to make do with underpaid and hugely overworked public defenders. While the rich enjoy their high-end intoxicants undisturbed in the privacy of their homes, poor drug addicts are regularly rounded up off the streets and sentenced to long prison terms.

More generally, even if it does not follow from Jesus' teachings that all punishment of criminals is wrong, it is at least true that Christians should be ambivalent about such punishment. Because we are all sinners and live in a fallen world, there is always an element of hypocrisy in the punishment of others. Instead of the smug self-righteousness that dominates public discourse about crime and punishment, we should be deeply ashamed of our massive, overcrowded, brutal, and barbaric prison system.

The second set of legal conclusions Stuntz drew from Christianity relates to the scope and ambition of law. Here, Stuntz turned the usual arguments for legal moralism on their head. Precisely because we are all sinners and we live in a fallen world, it is a huge mistake for government to attempt to legislate morality. Secular government can never produce God's kingdom on earth. Instead, even well-intentioned government programs will inevitably misfire. For example, the effort to ban widely tolerated practices such as abortion and gambling serve only to discredit the law. More fundamentally, if one takes Jesus' teachings seriously, it follows that each of us is in some sense a criminal, and no government can lock up all its citizens. The government must therefore limit criminal punishment to egregious wrongs, and then only when government intervention is likely to be effective rather than counterproductive.

Stuntz's Christianity leads to a second, overlapping argument for limited government: The "all" of us who are sinners emphatically includes government officials. Madison, as well as Jesus, taught us that angels are not and never will be in control, and that government power often turns into government oppression. These observations drove Stuntz toward formalism. Government agents must be controlled by rules that limit their discretion because they are bound to use their discretion in foolish, discriminatory, or self-serving ways. However, we can only get the discretion out of the system if we forsake the goal of correcting every wrong and punishing every evil act. Hence, government's jurisdiction must be limited.

As a secular leftist, I wish that Stuntz had explored more thoroughly the tension between his belief in redistribution on the one hand and his belief in limited government on the other. What, after all, will drive the redistribution he sought if not the government programs he distrusted? By my lights, Stuntz paid insufficient attention to the fact that limits on government power create reserves of private power. To be sure, government bureaucrats are not angels, but neither are private plutocrats. Precisely because government officials are not angels, they might do too little, as well as too much, to control private violence and oppression. Why was Stuntz so often worried about government, and so often unworried about the people whose excesses government might control?

As a follower of critical legal studies, I also wish that Stuntz had been more skeptical about the power of rules. The rule of law, like the discretion of law enforcers, is a human institution, so, on Stuntz's own premises, it too is bound to fail. A central teaching of critical legal studies, as well as of American Legal Realism before it, is that rules are highly malleable and that purported rule following too often masks partiality and the exercise of power. Moreover, even when rules do work, the abstraction and impersonality that they force upon us can blind us to individual human suffering.

For present purposes, though, it hardly matters whether Stuntz had all this precisely right. My quarrels with some aspects of Stuntz's positions should not distract us from the fact that these positions are firmly rooted in his Christianity. His work therefore leaves no doubt that there is indeed a substantial overlap between his version of Christianity and his analysis of legal issues.

For example, although Stuntz's tone was usually calm and scholarly, one detects the white heat of barely suppressed rage when he wrote about the way the war on drugs has amounted to a war on the poor, or about how the Miranda rule protects rich but not poor defendants. Similarly, a central theme in Stuntz's work was the way in which government programs miscarry. The Stuntzian world of criminal procedure is crammed full of unintended consequences, misaligned incentives, and foolish or perverse decisions. The political economy of the criminal justice system, taken together with ordinary human frailty, produces an endless tragedy of errors. Everything that could possibly go wrong has gone wrong, and there is little hope that things will get better any time soon.

To summarize, then, Stuntz certainly thought that there are limits to the relevance of Christianity to criminal justice, and the implications it does have are not what they are frequently imagined to be. Still, Stuntz was clear that Christianity *is* relevant, and much of his criminal justice work can be seen as an effort to spell out and elaborate upon that relevance, both with respect to concern for the poor and with respect to limited government. Why, then was the work written in solely secular language?

II. A PROPOSED SOLUTION TO THE FIRST PUZZLE THAT PRESENTS A SECOND ONE

Although I am not certain, I believe that, ironically enough, Stuntz's reticence about his Christianity may have derived from his Christian commitments. I have already suggested that his religiously based beliefs in concern for the poor and limited government may be in tension with each other. Here, I want to suggest a way in which they are mutually reinforcing, and together support a reluctance to utilize religious rhetoric.

Recall that Stuntz's commitment to limited government stemmed from his belief that, in a fallen world, even well-intentioned government policies are bound to go awry. Government officials know too little to get it right much of the time. Worse yet, they know too little about how little they know. Even when they know quite a bit, they, like the rest of us, are likely to be led astray by selfishness or slothfulness.

There is an important sense in which Stuntz's argument for redistribution stems from a similar fear. Just as government policy often fails, so too our society's pattern of rewards and punishments is bound to be askew. A fallen, sinful world will not select winners and losers based on desert. Through ignorance, prejudice, and shortsightedness, we are much more likely to punish the innocent, to reward the guilty, to ignore excellence, and to celebrate mediocrity.

What unites these two worries is a commitment to humility, and Stuntz was at his best when he celebrated this commitment. A Stuntzian Christian is deeply humble. This person understands how little she or he understands and worries deeply about pride and self-display. Importantly, these concerns are not limited to government policy makers. They apply as well – indeed apply especially – to legal academics. Stuntz was acutely aware of how often law professors strut and preen, how seldom they acknowledge doubt and complexity, and how consistently the profession rewards the wrong sort of scholarship and teaching.

Someone with different sensibilities might suppose that these are merely faults to be overcome. In contrast, Stuntz was deeply pessimistic. We should, of course, try to deal with these faults when we recognize them in ourselves, but the notion that we could ever succeed in completely escaping self-involvement and pride is, itself, deeply arrogant. Bill Stuntz was one of the most humble people I have known. Still, he was characteristically honest (and humble) in acknowledging that he himself had not escaped.

Although Stuntz did not fully explore the point, his stance leads to deep problems about how exactly a Christian lawyer or legal academic ought to proceed. It is important to understand just how radical Stuntz's claim was. Because we are human and limited, everything that we do is inevitably infected by sin. It follows, I think, that there is no way to write scholarship that is not prideful. The very essay that I am writing now, as hard as I try to make it about (or, I'm afraid, as hard as I try to make it *appear* to be about) Bill Stuntz, is inevitably instead all about me. Ultimately, I am writing these pages not to honor Stuntz or so that others will better understand Stuntz's scholarship, but to demonstrate to those not already fully convinced just how smart and virtuous I am. And, of course, my very recognition of this pridefulness is, itself, designed to pridefully demonstrate my self-awareness and honesty. There is a kind of recursive self-display even in the unflinching condemnation of self-display. (And need I add how proud I am of the cleverness of this point about recursive self-display?)

The same point can be made with regard to epistemic modesty. A good Christian, Stuntz told us, understands how little she or he understands. A good Christian scholar therefore proceeds with caution and acknowledges doubt. However, should one proceed with caution and acknowledge doubt about proceeding with caution and acknowledging doubt? There are, after all, circumstances that do not call for caution and doubt. As Walker Percy, the great Christian novelist and essayist, argued years ago, one who smells smoke in a crowded theater costs lives if he acts modestly and doubtfully. Stuntz might therefore be accused of immodestly advancing his plea for modesty. Why wasn't he more careful about recognizing the limits of the argument for carefulness?

To make these dilemmas concrete, consider the problem posed by the Supreme Court's decision in *District Attorney's Office v. Osborne*. Mr. Osborne was convicted by an Alaska court of a brutal sexual assault and attempted murder. The evidence against him was quite strong, and, based on the Supreme Court's summary of that evidence, I am prepared to believe that he was probably guilty. Still, our recent experience with DNA technology has demonstrated that many people who were "probably" guilty are in fact innocent. In Mr. Osborne's case, the state had, and has to this day, a DNA sample that would have conclusively demonstrated guilt or innocence if only someone would test it. Nevertheless, for reasons that it has never explained, Alaska has refused to test the evidence itself or to provide it to Osborne so that he could test it at his own expense. Osborne claimed that this refusal violated his right to due process of law, but Chief Justice Roberts, writing for a 5–4 majority of the court, disagreed.

Chief Justice Roberts's opinion embraces the rhetoric of humility. Roberts points out that the problems of when and how to make DNA testing available are complicated and involve difficult policy questions. Forty-six states (although, importantly, not Alaska) have enacted statutes dealing with access to DNA evidence. Roberts tells us that there is no reason to believe that Supreme Court Justices, acting as a matter of constitutional law and for the whole country, will do a better job of sorting through these problems than individual political officials at the state level.

Presumably, Stuntz would have applauded this sort of judicial modesty. As a Stuntzian Christian would hope, the Supreme Court doubts its own omniscience and its ability to correct all wrongs. In Stuntz's account, restraint and care in the exercise of power are central virtues.

But what, then, are we to say of Alaska's lack of humility? In its righteous certainty of Mr. Osborne's guilt, it has deliberately shielded itself from evidence that might demonstrate that it had made a mistake. Anyone who believes that government officials often get it wrong, that the innocent are too often punished and the guilty too often freed, and that we can never know the truth with certainty, is bound to be deeply troubled by this sort of state arrogance. The arrogance is compounded by Alaska's refusal to explain or justify its decision. Surely, this amounts to no more than a willful display of power directed against someone with no power at all. A Stuntzian Christian could no more accept this arrogance than the arrogance of Supreme Court Justices.

The problem, of course, is that control of Alaska's arrogance requires Supreme Court arrogance. It is true that judicial intervention might reflect a prideful belief in the Justices' own superior knowledge, but the failure to intervene lets stand Alaska's pridefulness. Worse yet, might not the Supreme Court's failure to act reflect the Justices' own overconfidence in the accuracy of the criminal justice system and failure to empathize with its victims?

The upshot is that whether the Supreme Court does something or nothing, government officials will have acted in the overconfident fashion that Stuntz deplored. There is a sense in which this fact merely confirms Stuntz's underlying point: There is simply no way that humans can escape evil. If that fact is true of judges and politicians, then surely it is true of legal academics as well. If scholars want to say anything at all, they must inevitably take a chance. They must throw caution to the wind, swallow their doubts, and speak. As soon as they do so, they are enveloped in the web of sin and arrogance that is simply our fate. Nor can the problem be solved by remaining silent. There is also a kind of self-involvement in remaining mum for fear of error or professional embarrassment.

So what is a humble Christian to do? It would be surprising if I had a solution to this problem, and in fact, I do not have one. It does seem to me, though, that the intractability of the problem might explain Stuntz's reluctance to inject Christian rhetoric into his legal scholarship. Stuntz might have understandably believed that if he could manage to insulate anything at all from the sin that infects everything else, it ought to be his religious faith. If academic and judicial writing is always and inevitably about pride and self-display, then religious rhetoric ought to be kept out of it.

There are two ways in which religious faith might be polluted in such a setting. First, the very public parading of religious beliefs in support of legal arguments might be prideful. Recall that all legal scholarship is inevitably about self-promotion. Consciously or unconsciously, then, an author of legal scholarship who uses religious rhetoric to persuade is making religion serve selfish goals such as prestige and acclaim. Moreover, reference to religion tends to suggest that the author has a higher moral status than others. Instead of merely doing quotidian scholarship, he or she is in some sense doing God's work. No one who truly understands Christian humility would want to make this claim.

Second, invoking religion implies a certainty about the merits of the argument that a Stuntzian Christian might want to avoid. Religious rhetoric suggests that a particular policy proposal is not just sensible or wise, but is actually God's command. It is easy to see why Stuntz would not have wanted to associate himself with a confident claim of this sort.

These worries, in turn, suggest the wisdom of Stuntz's initial intuition that Christianity should be more about the heart than about the law. It is, after all, public *display* that risks arrogance and pride. Someone who anonymously and quietly lives a daily life of service and love is less prone to these vices. But what, then, are we to make of Stuntz's writings urging Christians to apply their religious commitments to legal issues? I cannot be sure, but perhaps they might be interpreted as a plea for a change of heart rather than a change of rhetoric. A Christian perspective does make a difference with respect to some legal issues, Stuntz told us, so Christians who write about the law should be mindful of its teachings. Nonetheless, it is one thing to say that they should have those teachings in their heart, and another to say that they should publicly proclaim them as reasons for action. To do the former is to strive for the good life. To do the latter is to risk degradation of the values that matter most.

This is the best I can do to resolve the first puzzle. Unfortunately, though, it gives rise to a second one: Why doesn't Christian humility defeat the claims of Christianity itself? As a religious doubter, I find this puzzle especially vexing. Theologically conservative Christians must commit themselves to certain historical facts and certain cosmic truths. At best, the evidence for these facts and truths is contested. As even many believers acknowledge, the claims that Christianity makes are deeply mysterious and improbable. That is, after all, what makes the events recounted in the New Testament miraculous. No one can know for sure what happened in a remote corner of the world 2,000 years ago or what implications whatever did happen hold for the fate of mankind. At least no one can know for sure by utilizing the standard empirical techniques that we generally use to know things.

Perhaps Christian knowledge comes from sources other than the standard ones, and perhaps we should open ourselves to other ways of knowing. Still, if we are indeed imperfect humans with very limited understanding and vast abilities at self-deception, shouldn't we be skeptical about our ability to know, by any means, the great secrets of existence? Isn't the claim to know these secrets deeply prideful? Shouldn't a humble Christian not *be* a Christian?

III. A PROPOSED SOLUTION TO THE SECOND PUZZLE THAT ALSO SOLVES THE THIRD ONE

Of course, as a religious skeptic, my initial impulse is to answer all these questions with an emphatic "yes." My aim in the paragraphs that follow is to get beyond this initial impulse. To be clear, I make no claims that Stuntz himself would have embraced the argument I make here; I doubt that he would have. What I provide instead is unquestionably quite strange: a skeptical non-Christian's defense of Christian faith. This is not the place for an extended theological argument, and I am certainly not the person to provide it even if it were. What follows, then, is an amateur's sketch of an argument. It is the way that I understand Bill Stuntz even if it is not the way that he understood himself.

The first step in the argument is to see that doubters as well as believers have a serious problem with justifications for action. If the universe is indeed empty and meaningless – if there is no God or (worse yet) if there is a God who has no plans for us, how am I to make sense of my choices? The standard response among doubters is to point to the inevitability of choice and action. If the universe is indeed empty and meaningless, then it falls upon me to decide how to respond to this fact. I might respond by murdering and torturing others, or even by getting back into bed, but these are not the only possible responses and, by hypothesis, they are not responses that the universe requires. I might also respond by trying to be a good person. In a meaningless universe, I can choose whatever I want, but there is one crucial exception to the frightening truth that anything is possible: I cannot choose not to make a choice.

Once one sees that choice is inevitable, it becomes clear that some sort of commitment is inevitable as well. There is no refuge from deciding what sort of life I want to lead. Choosing to lead a meaningless or random life is to commit oneself to meaninglessness or randomness, and such a commitment is, itself, a way of giving a kind of point to the world. When one gets down to foundations, then, it is inevitable that even people who believe that the universe has no direction must provide their own direction.

The second stage of the argument is to see that if this is true for religious skeptics, then it must be true for religious believers as well. Those of us who suspect that the universe is empty and pointless should be the last to scoff at the religiously committed who use their religion to give it a point. For them, too, there is no escape from embrace of some sort of foundation. Christians, like everyone else, must live their lives either *as if* Christianity were true or *as if* it were not. In an empty universe, the embrace of Christianity is just a choice, no different and certainly no more disreputable in a cosmic sense from the embrace of anything else. Something, after all, must be embraced, so why not Jesus Christ? That is obviously not my choice, but it stands on no weaker foundations than the choice that I have made.

This inevitability of meaning creation puts a different light on the problem of humility. Being humble is a way of living, and so it too must be premised on some sort of commitment. However, the commitment that gives rise to it cannot itself be doubted, for to doubt the commitment is to doubt the virtue of humility, and so to no longer be humble. At the bottom of the chain of justification must be some sort of unambiguous choice. Although I can be certain of nothing else, I can be absolutely certain of this much: This is what I have chosen because this is the way I have decided to lead my life.

With this as background, I think it is possible to resolve the third puzzle. Bill Stuntz chose to live a life of Christian humility. That is not my choice, but my choice does entail valuing and admiring the choice that he made. He led the kind of life that I would like to lead. Although we start from radically different premises, we come out in much the same place. His Christianity and my agnosticism leave both of us not quite at home in the world. Things are not right, and we have an obligation to try to put them right, even as we know that we are forever fighting for a lost cause. For him, the cause is lost because of original sin. For me, it is lost because the universe is cold and unforgiving. Still, we agree on the crucial point that humans can achieve some dignity and some point to their lives by fighting the good fight.

The trick, which I must say I have not mastered, is to go about this work with energy, good humor, generosity of spirit, and kindness. It is to strike just the right balance between open-mindedness and skepticism on the one hand and persistence and commitment on the other. It is to avoid wasting time on the trivial and to throw oneself into what is important. Above all, it is to care for other people and to demonstrate that care in how one lives every day.

Bill Stuntz embodied all of those virtues. He was a deeply humble person, but he had less to be humble about than anyone I have known.

12

The Mercy Seat: Discretion, Justice, and Mercy in the American Criminal Justice System

Carol Steiker

It is a signal honor to succeed Bill Stuntz as the Henry J. Friendly Professor of Law at Harvard. To hold a Chair named for such a respected judge and held by such a respected scholar and beloved colleague and friend is not only an honor but also an inspiration – to hone my own craft, to think harder, and to reach farther, both professionally and personally.

Stuntz and Friendly were both brilliant and principled in their respective legal domains, but I'm sure I was not the only one to joke with Bill that he was more "friendly" than his Chair's namesake, who was known to be rather intimidating. My topics for this chapter – mercy and justice, in Bill Stuntz's work and my own – may lead some to a similarly amused bemusement, in that my approach to this topic is more explicitly religious in inspiration than Bill's own, despite the fact that he was a devout Christian and I am an (at most) agnostic Jew. Perhaps it was Bill's unconscious influence, or perhaps it was my very agnosticism that liberated me to explore theology as a source of public values, but it was I (and not Bill) who gave a keynote address at a Chicago Divinity School conference, on "Doing Justice to Mercy," and who later co-taught a course with a Harvard Divinity School professor on "Justice and Mercy in the Jewish and Christian Traditions and American Criminal Justice." In what follows, I hope to show that the theological origin of the concept of mercy offers both a contrast to and a path toward a human-scaled practice of mercy – a practice informed by and sympathetic to Bill's own criminal justice scholarship and Christian commitments.

[*] This chapter was presented as a Chair Lecture on November 9, 2011, at Harvard Law School to mark the assumption of the Henry J. Friendly Professorship of Law by Carol Steiker.

Let me start with an explicitly religious image – the most beautiful depiction I know of the reconciliation of the demands of justice and mercy. For those conversant with the Book of Exodus – or the movie *Raiders of the Lost Ark* – the image will be familiar: It is the Ark of the Covenant, the gold-covered wooden chest, carried by two gold-covered poles, that God commanded the Israelites to make to house the tablets of the Ten Commandments.[1] The lid of the Ark was formed, once again at God's command, by a slab of solid gold called the mercy seat – from the Hebrew *kapporeth*, translated sometimes as cover or lid, but more accurately in context as the covering or expiation of sins through sacrifice.[2] It was here that God commanded that the propitiatory blood of animal sacrifice be sprinkled on Yom Kippur, the Jewish Day of Atonement (*kapporeth* and *kippur* derive from the same Hebrew root). God also commanded the construction of two golden cherubim or angels at either end of the mercy seat, facing one another with their wings spread upward, covering the mercy seat in an arc, and with their faces turned toward the mercy seat itself. A common interpretation is that the two cherubim on the Ark represent the two faces of God – the face of Justice and the face of Mercy, looking toward each other over the physical embodiment of God's law in the stone tablets of the Ten Commandments.

The mercy seat represents both a puzzle and a promise. The puzzle is how God could possibly embody both perfect justice and perfect mercy. St. Anselm of Canterbury in the eleventh century noted the paradox of judgment and salvation emanating from the same source. If God is perfectly just, how can he also show compassion and grant mercy to the wicked? In St. Anselm's words, "What justice is it that gives him who merits eternal death everlasting life? How then, gracious Lord, good to the wicked, can you save the wicked if this is not just, and you do nothing that is not just?"[3] The promise is that justice and mercy *are* reconcilable; wrongdoing and forbearance from punishment are not necessarily in conflict; sin and salvation, law and love can coexist. The reconciliation occurs in Jewish tradition through God's covenant with the Jewish people and in Christian tradition through the sacrifice of Jesus Christ (thus the mercy

[1] Exodus 25: 17–22.

[2] T. K. Cheyne and J. Sutherland Black, eds., *Encyclopaedia Biblica: A Critical Dictionary of the Literary, Political and Religious History, the Archeology, Geography and Natural History of the Bible* Vol. III, 3027–3029 (London: Adam and Charles Black, 1902).

[3] "*Proslogium* IX," in Brian Davies and Gillian Evans, eds., *Anselm of Canterbury: The Major Works* (New York: Oxford University Press, 1998).

seat in Christian theology is thought to represent Jesus' atonement for the sins of humanity). However, the puzzle can be solved and the promise fulfilled only through God's mysterious perfection.

The problem of justice and mercy has an obvious human analogue. Our societies have their own laws, some not that different from the Ten Commandments, the most important of which we enforce by authorizing the imposition of criminal punishment. We vest in public officials the duty to enforce these laws, but we also frequently vest in them discretion as well – to decline enforcement altogether or to substitute a lesser charge or punishment than the law authorizes. We celebrate justice, often representing it in the image of a blindfolded woman holding scales and a sword. Nevertheless, we celebrate mercy, too, as a virtue, saying that it "tempers" or moderates justice and thereby improves it, in the same way that the tempering of steel makes it stronger. But how can the sword of justice be made stronger by sheathing it? How can justice and mercy, duty and discretion, be reconciled within our own legal tradition? When should our public officials "play God" and exercise merciful discretion to forbear from authorized punishment?

The answer, especially throughout most of the past century, has been that official discretion in criminal law enforcement is essentially problematic. Indeed, many of the most important innovations in the American criminal justice system during the twentieth century concerned controlling discretion in that system. The abuses of the criminal justice system toward blacks in the South, especially in the early decades of the century – the so-called legal lynchings that my colleagues Randy Kennedy and Mike Klarman have documented so well – led to the earliest forms of federal constitutional intervention in state criminal justice processes, such as the right to counsel in capital cases and protection from mob-dominated trials.[4] Concerns about abuses of discretionary police power, not only in the South but all over the country and especially in large urban areas, led to many formal investigations, starting with the Wickersham Commission in the 1930s (prompted by abuses rampant during the enforcement of Prohibition). Such concerns eventually led to the Warren Court's criminal procedure revolution of the 1960s, much of which consisted of new judicial oversight of police investigative practices.[5] Concern

[4] See Randall Kennedy, *Race, Crime, and the Law* (New York: Pantheon, 1997); Michael J. Klarman, *From Jim Crow to Civil Rights: The Supreme Court and the Struggle for Racial Equality* (Oxford: Oxford University Press, 2004).

[5] See David Alan Sklansky, *Democracy and the Police* (Stanford: Stanford University Press, 2007).

about prosecutorial discretion naturally followed from consideration of police discretion; former Harvard Law School Dean James Vorenberg, who served on President Johnson's Commission on Law Enforcement and the Administration of Justice in the 1960s, published an article in the *Harvard Law Review* in the early 1980s calling for "Decent Restraint of Prosecutorial Power."[6]

Judges came under the same sort of scrutiny as well. The disparities and lack of transparency that characterized the exercise of judicial sentencing discretion in the era of predominantly discretionary, indeterminate criminal sentencing led to the movement for sentencing guidelines and other forms of mandatory sentences.[7] The vaunted but highly unpredictable discretionary powers of juries, too, became the target of greater control, whether through greater regulation of juries' special capital sentencing powers in the post-*Furman v. Georgia* era,[8] or simply through the triumph of plea bargaining, which has expanded to cover the vast majority of criminal cases, now accounting for upward of 95 percent of all criminal dispositions.[9] Even the discretionary power of executive clemency and pardon, which remains essentially untouched by law, has fallen out of favor; the past several decades have seen a radical decline in the uses of such powers at both the state and federal level.[10]

All of these developments tended to start from the premise that discretion is at best a necessary evil in need of constant restraint, if not wholesale elimination – an enemy of the rule of law, an invitation to discrimination, a creature of backrooms and shadows that avoids transparency and sunlight, and a jealous master that leads discretionary actors to hoard rather than share power. The goal of systemic reforms, however, has only rarely been the elimination of discretion altogether. Rather, reformers have expressed the faith that discretion can be "cabined,"

6 James Vorenberg, *Decent Restraint of Prosecutorial Power*, 94 Harv. L. Rev. 1521 (1981).

7 See Stephen Breyer, *The Federal Sentencing Guidelines and the Key Compromises on Which They Rest*, 17 Hofstra L. Rev. 1 (1988).

8 See Furman v. Georgia, 408 U.S. 238 (1972) (constitutionally invalidating all extant capital sentencing statutes because of the standardless discretion they vested in sentencing juries).

9 See George Fisher, *Plea Bargaining's Triumph: A History of Plea Bargaining in America* (Stanford: Stanford University Press, 2003).

10 See, e.g., Elizabeth Rapaport, *Straight is the Gate: Capital Clemency in the United States from* Gregg *to* Atkins, 33 N. M. L. Rev. 349 (2003) (documenting decline in executive clemency in capital cases); Margaret Colgate Love, *The Twilight of the Pardon Power*, 100 J. Crim. L. & Criminology 1169 (2010) (documenting decline in presidential pardons).

"controlled," "restrained," "structured," "channeled," "standardized," or "rationalized" – or made more "transparent" or "accountable" or subject to "review" by another entity. The hope has always been that such restraint of discretion exercised by the various institutional actors of the criminal justice system would both manage the overall amount and kind of criminal punishment so as to promote its ultimate goals (deterrence, incapacitation, rehabilitation, and retributive justice) and prevent discrimination and arbitrariness in the distribution of criminal punishment.

A major theme of Bill's work is that, surprisingly and perversely, all of this regulation of discretion has done nothing of the sort. Like the boy who questioned the Emperor's sartorial choices, Bill has pointed out the naked truth that despite these many innovations, American criminal justice in our new millennium is in many ways *more* arbitrary, discriminatory, and unbalanced in terms of power than before the advent of all these discretion-cabining developments. Decades after the criminal procedure revolution and the sentencing guidelines movement, we have today both vastly more criminal punishment and vastly more unequal punishment. Bill's voice has been one of the most powerful in decrying the advent of what many now call "mass incarceration" – the exponential rise in America's prison population over the past forty years, and its huge disparate impact on the basis of race. Bill has described "the unprecedented punishment wave"[11] that caused the nation's imprisonment rate to more than quintuple[12] and has turned the United States into "a society where criminal punishment is a massive industry, of a size and severity unknown anywhere else in the democratic world"[13] – "the harshest in the history of democratic government."[14] Our criminal justice system, Bill lamented, is not only harsh but also "rife with inequality"[15] – one in which "for black males, a term in the nearest penitentiary has become an ordinary life experience, a horrifying truth that wasn't true a mere generation ago."[16]

[11] William J. Stuntz, *Unequal Justice*, 121 Harv. L. Rev. 1969, 1973 (2008) (italics omitted).

[12] William J. Stuntz, *The Collapse of American Criminal Justice* 5 (Cambridge: Harvard University Press, 2011).

[13] William J. Stuntz, "*Bordenkircher v. Hayes*: Plea Bargaining and the Decline of the Rule of Law," in Carol S. Steiker, ed., *Criminal Procedure Stories* 351, 379 (New York: Foundation Press, 2006).

[14] Stuntz, *The Collapse of American Criminal Justice*, at 3.

[15] Stuntz, *Unequal Justice*, at 1970.

[16] Stuntz, *The Collapse of American Criminal Justice*, at 1.

These pernicious developments, argued Bill, were in significant part the product of police and prosecutorial discretion run amok. Bill suggested – relishing, as he always did, the unintended perversity of good intentions – that the discretion-cabining reforms of the 1960s, championed by liberal reformers, actually helped to create the very conditions that led to the vast expansion of police and prosecutorial power that these same reformers, or their heirs, now decry. Regarding police power, Bill argued that the focus of Fourth Amendment jurisprudence on protecting the right of privacy helped contribute to the enormous race- and class-based disparities in law enforcement whose consequences are now so evident. Because the rich can buy so much more privacy than the poor – in terms of homes, offices, and cars – the Fourth Amendment's protection of privacy operates, in the public-choice terminology that appealed to Bill, as a kind of "tax" on the policing of the spaces in which the rich commit their crimes. In contrast, the policing of the streets is much cheaper in relative terms; thus, the more robust Fourth Amendment protection promoted by liberals to cabin police discretion may actually steer the police to overpolice the urban poor, particularly urban drug markets.[17] The consequences of such relative overpolicing are stunning: Out of every 100,000 black Americans, 359 are imprisoned on drug charges, whereas the analogous figure for whites is only 28, despite the fact that rates of drug use among the two groups are roughly equal.[18]

Regarding prosecutorial power, Bill developed a more encompassing version of his public-choice account of criminal procedural protections as taxes that affect not only the police, but prosecutors as well. Bill argued that the Warren Court's criminal procedural revolution in general operated as a kind of tax on criminal prosecutions, making them more expensive.[19] Legislatures thus were incentivized to expand the scope of the criminal law and to make sentences more severe in order to empower prosecutors to resolve cases more cheaply, chiefly by using the new crimes and punishments as leverage in plea bargaining. Bill also offered a political account of the backfiring of the Warren Court's criminal procedure revolution: By generating a political backlash against "soft on crime" judges, the Warren Court helped to make crime a highly salient political issue

[17] See William J. Stuntz, *The Distribution of Fourth Amendment Privacy*, 67 Geo. Wash. L. Rev. 1265, 1274–1277 (1999).

[18] Stuntz, *Unequal Justice*, at 1971.

[19] Id. at 2017.

and thus to shift control over it from disempowered minority urban communities to more powerful white suburbs. Once the control of police and prosecutors was wrested from the communities who bore the brunt of the human costs of law enforcement, moderating influences on the harshness of criminal justice faded. This dynamic was part of a larger and more timeless dynamic that Bill called, in an enormously influential article, "The Pathological Politics of Criminal Law."[20] Bill offered an account of how criminal justice has become a one-way ratchet by exploring its political economy – the incentives that both legislators and prosecutors have to expand criminal law and the inability or unwillingness of courts to limit that expansion.

What is to be done to address the tragic results of a criminal justice system that, in Bill's words, "has run off the rails?" Sometimes Bill's answers to this pressing question placed him in the traditional, discretion-limiting camp. On the one hand, Bill concluded that it would be impossible to "abolish" law enforcement discretion in criminal justice, or even to severely limit it, because of the inevitably discretionary tasks of investigating and screening cases.[21] He was also pessimistic about the efficacy of directly authorizing courts to constrain prosecutorial charging discretion.[22] However, Bill recognized that courts could be empowered to regulate prosecutorial discretion indirectly, by giving them constitutional power to share legislators' control over substantive criminal law. Bill argued that developing constitutional doctrines of notice, desuetude, and proportionality and equal-protection review of sentencing would give courts the tools to limit some of the worst abuses of prosecutorial power.

For example, if the Due Process clause's requirement of notice were interpreted to offer a defense to defendants who were reasonably ignorant of the law, prosecutors would no longer be able to induce guilty pleas by charging defendants under broad statutes that prohibit relatively innocuous behavior; rather, they would have to charge more serious crimes of which defendants could not plausibly claim ignorance, and thus they would have to test their proof at trial more often or offer more lenient plea deals.[23] Similarly, if due process were interpreted to prevent prosecutors from enforcing laws that had fallen into desuetude – that is, laws

[20] William J. Stuntz, *The Pathological Politics of Criminal Law*, 100 Mich. L. Rev. 505 (2001).
[21] Id. at 580–581.
[22] Id. at 581 ("[J]udicial review of charging decisions is probably unworkable . . . ").
[23] Id. at 587–591.

that had not been enforced for a substantial period of time – then prosecutors' currently unreviewable discretion to use fallow laws arbitrarily or pretextually would be eliminated.[24] In a different vein, if sentences were subject to review for comparative proportionality (i.e., have similarly harsh sentences been imposed in the past for similar conduct?) and for equal protection (i.e., are different racial, ethnic, and geographic groups sentenced similarly for similar conduct?), both the amount and the distribution of criminal punishment would likely change for the better.[25] All of these proposed reforms are in our system's most common mode of constraining discretion: judicial review. Despite Bill's skepticism about the efficacy of constitutional criminal procedure, he still held out some hope for constitutional criminal regulation of a more substantive kind.

However, Bill's most radical and intriguing contribution to addressing our bloated and skewed criminal justice system is his suggestion that the answer to discretion run amok might lie in *more* rather than less discretion. Perhaps discretion is not something that needs to be eliminated or even regulated; perhaps it needs instead to be placed in the right hands, so that it will produce outcomes that are more just. Take judges, for example. Instead of empowering them to conduct more searching review of prosecutorial discretion, perhaps the answer lies in simply giving them similar unreviewable discretion of their own, in the form of the power to reduce sentences according to their own lights. In some ways, Bill thought, creating constitutional doctrines of notice and desuetude would empower judges in this way, because such review is likely "not susceptible to detailed legal analysis" but instead "will likely be little more than an accumulation of seat-of-the-pants judgments by particular trial judges and appellate panels."[26] However, an even more direct way to empower judges would be to create a "constitutional right to mercy"[27] through which judges could simply refuse to impose sentences authorized or required by verdicts for any reason or no reason. Judges already have the power to acquit defendants for any reason or no reason when they sit as triers of fact; why, asked Bill, should they not have the lesser power of sentence reduction? "Logically, the greater mercy ought to include within it the lesser."[28]

[24] Id. at 591–594.
[25] See William J. Stuntz, *The Political Constitution of Criminal Justice*, 119 Harv. L. Rev. 779, 839–843 (2006).
[26] Stuntz, *Pathological Politics*, at 597.
[27] Id.
[28] Id. at 596.

Bill argued in a similar vein that reviving jury discretion to decline to convict according to jurors' own lights would also help to counteract overly punitive prosecutorial discretion. He suggested that it might have been the very vagueness of the substantive criminal law in earlier, less harshly punitive times that contributed to the relative lenity of those eras; hazier standards of mens rea and conduct invited jurors to refuse to convict when they believed that the conduct at issue was not sufficiently wrongful to merit criminal punishment.[29] Bill believed that the twentieth century's project of codifying criminal codes to make them more precise had the unintended consequence of promoting harshness in criminal punishment by limiting jury discretion to grant mercy.[30] Bill recognized that reviving jury discretion would require changing not only the substantive criminal law but also the composition of juries and the relative frequency of jury verdicts in relation to plea bargains. Hence, he advocated neighborhood-based selection of juries, with fewer peremptory challenges, as well as stringent appellate review of the factual basis and fairness of plea bargains.[31]

Bill did not seek merely to fight fire with fire – that is, to counterbalance prosecutorial discretion with beefed-up discretion by judges and juries. Rather, Bill sought to transform the underlying conditions in which discretion is exercised. Bill thought, for example, that police discretion might not be as much of a problem as liberals from the Warren Court era thought it was. They focused on abuses of on-the-street policing, but Bill argued that our concern should focus more on the back end of criminal justice, on the overflowing prison cells. From a wider-angled policy perspective, police and prisons appear to operate as substitutes in the war on crime. More police reduce crime without producing more prisoners, and the prisoners that get produced by more intensive policing are more evenly distributed racially – as the experiment with increased policing inaugurated during the Clinton era demonstrated.[32] Moreover, Bill believed that the movement begun during the 1990s toward so-called community policing has transformed the nature of police discretion by making "urban police forces more attentive to local needs and preferences."[33]

[29] See Stuntz, *Unequal Justice*, at 1993–1905 (discussing the open texture of the substantive criminal law and the high rate of acquittals at trial during the Gilded Age).

[30] See Stuntz, *The Collapse of American Criminal Justice*, at 194–195.

[31] See Stuntz, *Unequal Justice*, at 2034–2036.

[32] Id. at 2032–2033.

[33] Id. at 2033.

Even prosecutorial discretion, which Bill found most problematic and most responsible for what he deemed the "collapse" of criminal justice, could be made more palatable by transforming its politics. Bill recounted how, historically, control over both police and prosecutors shifted from the minority urban communities most directly affected by law enforcement to richer, whiter suburbs, whose attitude toward urban crime vacillated "between wholesale indifference and unmitigated rage."[34] Returning political control over police and prosecutors to the urban neighborhoods that stand to benefit and suffer most from aggressive law enforcement would transform those underlying attitudes and produce a balance of "moderate levels of mercy and retribution."[35]

Bill's work thus rejects the restraint of discretion as key to moving away from overpunishment and racial disparities but rather looks to the promotion of certain kinds of discretion by police, prosecutors, judges, and juries. Bill was interested in the *quality* of discretionary decision making rather than the amount of it; he focused our attention on the identity and judgment of the decision maker rather than on the discretionary quality of the decision. The "good" discretion that Bill sought to reclaim is one that is community based and more sensitive to contextual determinations of wrongdoing and the need for harsh punishment than the discretion we see exercised today by remoter institutions, such as state legislatures or even police chiefs and prosecutors for sprawling, heterogeneous, and highly segregated communities.

Bill's work on discretion has deeply resonated with and informed my own interest in the relationship between mercy and justice. In our own ways, we each have worked on building a vocabulary that permits normative evaluation of exercises of discretion in criminal justice. While Bill was exploring the "pathological politics" in the political economy of criminal law, I was drawn to the debate initiated by moral philosophers about whether mercy can be a public value at all and whether it has any place in a properly functioning criminal justice system.[36] Some moral philosophers take a skeptical view of mercy and argue that the duty of public officials to do justice – that is, to enforce duly enacted laws – is fundamentally incompatible with mercy. Forbearing from exacting just punishment may be a virtue when done by private individuals toward

[34] Id. at 1982.

[35] Id.

[36] See Carol S. Steiker, "Tempering or Tampering? Mercy and the Administration of Criminal Justice," in Austin Sarat and Nasser Hussain, eds., *Forgiveness, Mercy, and Clemency* (Stanford: Stanford University Press, 2007).

wrongs against themselves, these skeptics argue, but it is a vice in the public sphere.[37] Other moral philosophers seek to reconcile the virtues of justice and mercy by depicting mercy as the individuation or deeply contextual consideration that formal justice cannot achieve on its own.[38] A different response to the mercy skeptics acknowledges the incompatibility of justice and mercy but argues that they both are virtues, incommensurable goods that we have a duty to try to achieve, if only by imperfectly trading them off one against the other.[39] Still others respond to the competing demands of justice and mercy by rejecting both in favor of some other rubric, such as restorative justice, or subsuming both into some other overarching good, such as social welfare.[40]

My own view is that there is indeed an important role for mercy in our criminal justice system – not as an independent virtue that can be reconciled with or weighed against justice, but rather as a recognition of the myriad ways in which intractable aspects of our criminal justice institutions are skewed toward overpunishment. I call this a "prudential" theory of mercy[41] – a theory that is both more modest and more ambitious than the others I have canvassed. My account is more modest in that it is rooted in the predictable failures of our practices rather than on some new normative terrain. However, my account is simultaneously more ambitious in that it argues for a place for the exercise of mercy in institutions of criminal justice regardless of which normative theory or theories of punishment that criminal justice is thought to promote.

The development of my argument for the need for prudential mercy in criminal justice owes a debt both to Bill's pathological politics work and to some of his proposals for how we might resist or escape these pathological tendencies. Like Bill, I start with our country's unprecedented movement over the past forty years toward mass incarceration and address the urgent question of how we might reverse this course. Also like Bill, I see our criminal justice system operating as a "one-way ratchet" toward ever more severe criminal punishment,[42] and I worry about what I have called the "'stickiness' of the punitive turn."[43] I locate the source of that

37 Id. at 22.
38 Id. at 25–26.
39 Id. at 27–28.
40 Id. at 28–30.
41 See Carol S. Steiker, "Criminalization and the Criminal Process: Prudential Mercy as a Limit on Penal Sanctions in an Era of Mass Incarceration," in R. A. Duff et al., eds., *The Boundaries of the Criminal Law* (Oxford: Oxford University Press, 2010).
42 Stuntz, *Pathological Politics*, at 509.
43 Steiker, *Prudential Mercy*, at 37.

ratchet in the combination of certain stable or even immutable social facts and institutional arrangements that stand in the way of any large-scale, near-term retreat from punitiveness. First and most immutable are recently recognized facts about human cognition and behavior – most importantly, research into the neurological correlates of what psychologists call "altruistic punishment" and into the stubborn cognitive bias called the "fundamental attribution error."[44] In nonscientific terms, it turns out that we are hardwired to punish wrongdoers – in experimental settings, people will spend resources to punish those who they believe have acted wrongly, even when such punishment is costly and yields no gain to the punisher. Moreover, studies of people's brain activity during the act of punishing perceived wrongdoers suggest that punishment produces neurological rewards. In addition, people's attributions of wrongdoing are predictably biased; people tend to overascribe the behavior of other people to dispositional factors (such as moral character) and to undervalue the influence of situational facts (such as social and environmental influences). Although this bias has been widely observed across different cultures, it tends to be especially strong in so-called individualistic as opposed to collectivist societies.

Second, in addition to these relatively stable features of human cognition and behavior, I address the more contingent contributions of our current social, economic, and political arrangements to overpunishment. The combination of rising social and economic inequality, its disparate racial and ethnic effects, and widespread segregation in housing has produced an entrenched minority urban underclass that has proven to be a target for relatively cheap and high-impact "hot spot" policing.[45] The impetus to contain the crumbling disorder of the inner city through harsh criminal sanctions will correspond to strongly punitive policies to the extent that criminal justice policy is strongly responsive to broad-based popular will. Here I draw both on Bill's work and the work of political scientists and sociologists to explore how the American political system in general and the political economy of criminal justice in particular empower populist influences in criminal justice and shape the incentives of political actors to produce overpunishment.

I argue that these behavioral tendencies, social conditions, and institutional structures suggest a critique of the dominant justifications for

[44] Id. at 40–41 (citing social scientific research).

[45] Id. at 38; *see also* Carol S. Steiker, *Death, Taxes, and – Punishment? A Response to Braithwaite and Tonry*, 46 UCLA L. Rev. 1793 (1999).

criminal punishment that offers a rationale for the exercise of a robust veto power over legislatively authorized (or even required) punishment – that is, for robust mercy. Current penal policy is dominated by two major modes of justification – retributivism and social welfare theory (or what the media might call "just deserts" and "cost–benefit" arguments). Whatever can be said – and much has been – about the relative merits of these theories as guides for punishment practices, I contend that these theories are abstractions that are predictably distorted when applied through the prevailing conditions that I canvassed earlier. Retributivism's chief distortion is its inability to take account of the effects of widespread social and economic inequality on its central determination of "desert."[46] Social welfare's chief distortion is its inability to see how so-called bounded rationality limits the makers (as opposed to the targets) of criminal justice policy, leading them to undervalue both the costs of harsh penal policies and the benefits of rehabilitative policies.[47] I do not take issue with either theory in the abstract; rather, I seek in my account of mercy to remain deliberately agnostic about the moral foundations of the criminal law. I mean to suggest that both retributivism and social welfare theory, as discourses deployed in our current world, will tend toward overpunishment, even when policy makers and discretionary institutional actors self-consciously and in all good faith see themselves as merely trying to promote their appropriate ends.

My prudential case for discretionary mercy in criminal justice leads me to argue that discretionary actors throughout the criminal justice system, such as prosecutors, judges, juries, and chief executives wielding the powers of clemency and pardon, should see themselves as appropriately wielding a punishment veto. Moreover, my account suggests answers to both the central question of how the exercise of such vetoes should be normatively evaluated and the subsidiary question of how we should structure the discretionary powers of the various institutional players so as to promote normatively desirable vetoes. The short answer to the first question about normative evaluation is that vetoes are normatively desirable to the extent that they are responsive to the features that skew our current practices. For example, consideration of social and economic disadvantage is responsive to the role that such disadvantage plays in skewing the application of both retributive and social welfare theories.[48]

[46] Steiker, *Prudential Mercy*, at 44–45.
[47] Id. at 47.
[48] Id. at 54.

The short answer to the second question about power allocation is that discretionary powers should likewise be allocated in ways that respond to structural biases toward punishment. For example, if the politics of crime are indeed pathological, then greater discretionary authority should be located in actors more removed from those politics (such as appointed judges). Alternatively, reallocation of discretionary powers may undo some pathologies, such as by empowering local communities vis-à-vis distant ones in the control of local crime policies.[49]

My account of prudential mercy starts in a different place from Bill's approach to the problem of mass incarceration, but my vision of discretionary mercy in action shows how we eventually converge on similar policy prescriptions. Bill and I end up in roughly the same place by somewhat different paths. Interestingly, each of our accounts of the origins of the problem of mass incarceration and its possible solutions could be told without any reference to the concept of mercy. Bill, in particular, generally wrote most comfortably in the language of public-choice theory, analyzing the interplay of the private incentives of public actors. He could have spoken about adjusting incentives to produce optimal levels of punishment without venturing into the moral or quasi-religious connotations of mercy. Similarly, his concern about so-called pathological politics might more naturally have led to metaphors about "healthy" political orders rather than merciful ones. As for me, it is clear that I, like Bill, see our current criminal justice policies as profoundly unjust; hence, "mercy talk" presents a danger, because we tend to think of mercy as an undeserved gift, something that people beg or plead for, but to which they have no right. Why would a scholar of criminal *justice* want to invoke such an idea?

There are three reasons that the language of mercy is appealing and appropriate here, both for a secular criminal justice theorist like me and for someone with a richer and more personal appreciation of its religious connotations like Bill. First, mercy carries the connotation that rejecting authorized and apparently deserved punishment is a normative good. For lawyers steeped in the virtues of the rule of law, the language of mercy helps to evoke the countervailing moral intuition that there can be virtue, too, in declining to do what justice seems to demand. This is why, I think, Bill begins the Epilogue of his book, *The Collapse of American Criminal Justice*, by quoting Portia's famous speech from *The Merchant of Venice*:

49 Id. at 53.

> The quality of mercy is not strain'd,
> It droppeth as the gentle rain from heaven
> Upon the place beneath. It is twice blest;
> It blesseth him that gives and him that takes.[50]

This beautiful invocation of the blessings of mercy for both its givers and receivers – in a courtroom drama, no less! – disarms or softens the lawyer's natural resistance to the claims of mercy.

Second, returning to the more explicitly religious image of God's mercy with which I began, appealing for mercy in criminal justice highlights the one possible parallel that human mercy can have with God's mysteriously perfect mercy. God can be the source of both judgment and mercy because of God's perfect love for his children. Humans are far from perfect, but perhaps it is our capacity for love – and in particular our love for our own flawed children – that brings us closest to the attributes that allow divine judgment to coexist with mercy. For someone of deep religious faith like Bill, God's love is not an abstraction but a felt reality. Bill wrote movingly of his faith in and experience of God's love: "Our faith is a love song so achingly beautiful that you weep each time you hear it. At the center of that . . . song stands a God who does vastly more than remember his image in us. He pursues us as lovers pursue one another."[51] It makes sense that faith in God's perfect love might lead to faith in the capacities of human beings to show mercy – if they could be made to see themselves or their children in those who offend. Bill's faith that local communities would show more mercy to their own offenders than the more removed political communities that have driven mass incarceration was partially based in history, but it was also based in his faith in our human capacity for empathy with our fellows, which competes with our desire for protection from them: "Residents of *all* neighborhoods . . . have two warring incentives. On the one hand, they want safe streets on which to go about their business. . . . On the other hand, they are loath to incarcerate their sons and brothers, neighbors and friends. . . . [A]ll of those who have seen neighbors' sons behind bars, or their own, know the agony incarceration imposes on local communities."[52]

The third reason for the appeal of mercy talk lies not in the similarity between God's mercy and our own but in the sharp contrast between divine perfection and human failing. God's mercy is the great gift that the

[50] William Shakespeare, *The Merchant of Venice*, Act IV, Scene 1.
[51] William J. Stuntz, *Three Gifts for Hard Times*, Christianity Today (June 16, 2011).
[52] Stuntz, *The Collapse of American Criminal Justice* at 36.

Judeo-Christian tradition celebrates precisely because of human imperfection. We require and rejoice in God's mercy because our flaws call it forth every day. Those very flaws, however, should make us not merely grateful offenders against God's law but wary enforcers of man's law. As Bill wrote in one of his few works explicitly addressing the relationship of his Christian faith to law, "[L]aw must play must play a double game: restraining the worst wrongs by the citizenry without empowering judges and prosecutors to do wrong themselves."[53] The way in which the criminal law and the institutions of criminal justice skew toward overpunishment is precisely the kind of wrong that Bill is referencing here. Moreover, human imperfection contributes not only to the disproportionality of our punishments but also to the wrongdoing that calls punishment forth in the first place. Musing again on the relationship between Christianity and law, Bill addressed our collective responsibility for the incarceration of our prisoners, remarking that "those of us who live outside those awful warehouses have good reason to be penitent for what we have done to, and failed to do for, those inside."[54]

Bill never explicitly worked out the connections between his writing on Christian legal theory and his much more extensive work on discretion and mercy in the criminal justice system. This may well be, as Mike Seidman suggests in this volume, because of Bill's emphasis on the proper humility of Christians with regard to their faith's implications for law: "[I]nvoking religion implies a certainty about the merits of the argument that a Stuntzian Christian might want to avoid."[55] Nonetheless, I want to let Bill have the last word here. Something he wrote about the appropriate humility of legal scholars seems to me the most apt call for mercy of the prudential kind I advocate: "[W]e know less than we claim to know, and we are not as smart as we claim to be. Our theories may be beautiful things to behold . . . but they tend to ignore a great deal of messy reality especially the reality of our own limits."[56]

[53] David A. Skeel and William J. Stuntz, *Christianity and the (Modest) Rule of Law*, 8 U. Pa. J. Const. L. 809, 817 (2006).

[54] William J. Stuntz, *Christian Legal Theory*, 116 Harv. L. Rev. 1707, 1733 (2003).

[55] Louis Michael Seidman, "Three Puzzles in the Work of Bill Stuntz," at 208.

[56] Stuntz, *Christian Legal Theory*, at 1741.

13

Epilogue: Three Underrated Explanations for the Punitive Turn

Bill Stuntz

Scholarship about American criminal justice today focuses on two questions: How did Americans come to have a 2-million-plus inmate population, nearly half of it African American? How might that swollen inmate population be reduced without triggering a rise in crime? The second question is related to the first: If we can understand how our circumstances arose, we will be better able to change those circumstances in productive ways. Scholars have identified a host of answers to that first question, but three possible, partial answers have largely been ignored – I have certainly ignored them in my work, and I'm pretty sure the same is true more generally in the field as a whole. All are about the allocation of power over criminal punishment: precisely what has to change if the future of criminal punishment is to look different than its past. The first two partial answers concern institutional dynamics; the third stems from legal doctrine.

The first institutional dynamic concerns federalism, sort of. A rich vein of scholarship explores the lines between federal and state power, but those lines have only modest effects on the justice system, because the overwhelming majority of those inmates reside in local jails and state penitentiaries, not in federal prisons. The more important lines are between state and local power. Though a few perceptive scholars – Rachel Barkow's work on state sentencing commissions comes to mind – have begun to explore those lines, the exploration has not gone nearly far enough. As to local prosecutors, prison time is something close to a free good, paid for by the state. And local prosecutors, not state legislators or governors, have been the key actors in the explosion of America's prison populations. Changing that state of affairs is key to bringing those populations under control.

The second dynamic deals with the relationship between two sets of local officials: police officers and prosecutors. Both in the 1960s and again in the 1990s, trends in the number of police arrests and trends in the number of felony prosecutions diverged sharply. In the late 1960s and early 1970s, the rate of arrests by urban police forces grew by more than 20 percent while the number of prosecutions and prison sentences fell by nearly the same amount – all in a time of steeply rising crime. In the late 1990s and the early 2000s, the urban arrest rate fell significantly while prosecutions and prison sentences continued to rise. Why did these trend lines diverge the way they did? Why, both times, was it prosecutors rather than police officers who determined the size of the prison population: remarkably small forty years ago, astronomical today? The answers are unclear. However, if urban police officers had exercised more power and urban district attorneys less, the story of criminal justice over the past fifty years would look very different, and vastly better.

The relevant legal doctrine is substantive criminal law: the law that defines crimes. A great deal of writing has focused on the expansion of criminal liability; I have done some work in that vein myself. But those of us who have focused on overcriminalization have missed the real story: Criminal law has not just expanded its scope; it has changed its character. A half-century ago, criminal law was still a common-law field – crimes were defined by statute but courts exercised enormous power over their scope and definition. That was especially true of intent terms, but not only those. Furthermore – again especially with respect to intent, but not only there – the boundaries of criminal liability were usually fuzzy, leaving lots of room for judges and juries to exercise judgment when applying those boundaries to individual cases.

Today, the picture is radically different. Criminal law is statutory not just in name but in practice, and the relevant statutes are far more detailed and precise. The law of criminal intent has become almost wholly mechanical: The idea that the government must prove that the defendant acted with a "vicious will," to use Blackstone's words, has gone by the boards. Today, most criminal prohibitions require only that the government prove the defendant intended his or her physical actions – which nearly everyone does, so intent is essentially automatic. American criminal law has become a field of doctrinal detail and technicality; it has also become, very nearly, a strict liability field.

That has a lot to do with today's massive prison population. Technical and mechanical criminal law makes for easy convictions, which in turn makes for easily induced guilty pleas. What is more, without the sharp rise in the guilty plea rate during the 1970s, 1980s, and 1990s, America's prison population could not be what it is today. In effect, the generation-long change in criminal law helped make our justice system an efficient punishment machine, able to dole out punishment on a massive scale at minimal cost.

These three underrated explanations for America's punitive turn have a common theme: None of them stems from any clear decision or ideological stance. No one gave local prosecutors the power they exercise and the incentives that push them toward too much punishment in order to promote more populous prisons. Criminal law's character did not change because those doing the changing wanted to make the system more punitive – in part, the change came from those who wanted to make the system more *lenient*. (That was one of the goals of the Model Penal Code's authors, and that code contributed to the rise of textualist technicality in substantive criminal law.) As often happens in legal systems, things happened as they did without much reason. Large forces were set loose on the justice system without large causes driving them. That is part of the tragedy of criminal punishment's rise: In large measure, it happened more by accident than by design. Perhaps that is also cause for optimism. If we can find the right mechanisms, the justice system might be made fairer and less harsh without having to battle deeply held convictions by those who make the system what it is. Criminal justice did not become so unjust primarily because of ideology. Maybe it can grow more just without deep-seated ideological change – change of the sort that is hard to bring about generally, and impossible for mere academics.

Index